T0196853

THE ROAD TO RESCUE

THE ROAD TO RESCUE

The Untold Story of Schindler's List

MIETEK PEMPER

• • •

in collaboration with

VIKTORIA HERTLING

and

MARIE ELISABETH MÜLLER

• • •

translated by

DAVID DOLLENMAYER

OTHER PRESS

New York

The translation of this work was supported by a grant from the Goethe-Institute that is funded by the Ministry of Foreign Affairs of the Federal Republic of Germany.

Originally published in German as *Der rettende Weg: Schindlers Liste. Die wahre Geschichte* by Mietek Pemper.

First softcover edition 2011
ISBN 978-1-59051-494-8

Production Editor: Yvonne E. Cárdenas
Text design: Simon M. Sullivan

This book was set in 10 pt Sabon by Alpha Design & Composition of Pittsfield, New Hampshire.

10 9 8 7 6 5 4 3 2 1

 Printed in the United States of America on acid-free paper. For information write to Other Press LLC, 2 Park Avenue, 24th Floor, New York, NY 10016. Or visit our Web site: www.otherpress.com

LIBRARY OF CONGRESS CATALOGING-IN-PUBLICATION DATA
Pemper, Mieczyslaw, 1920–
[Rettende Weg. English.]
The road to rescue : the untold story of Schindler's list / Mietek Pemper ; in collaboration with Viktoria Hertling, assisted by Marie Elisabeth Müller ; translated by David Dollenmayer.
p. cm.
Includes bibliographical references and index.
ISBN 978-1-59051-286-9
1. Schindler, Oskar, 1908–1974. 2. Righteous Gentiles in the Holocaust—Biography. 3. World War, 1939–1945—Jews—Rescue. 4. Pemper, Mieczyslaw, 1920— 5. Jews—Poland—Kraków—Biography. 6. Concentration camp inmates— Poland—Plaszów—Biography. 7. Plaszów (Concentration camp) 8. Holocaust, Jewish (1939–1945)—Poland—Personal narratives. I. Hertling, Viktoria. II. Müller, Marie Elisabeth. III. Title.
D804.66.S38P4613 2008
940.53'183—dc22 2008007193

In memory of the millions of Holocaust
victims and in honor of Oskar Schindler,
whose courage allowed more than
a thousand Jews to survive.

CONTENTS

PREFACE

The occupation of Poland by Hitler's troops on September 1, 1939, was the beginning of a six-year martyrdom for large sections of the Polish population, especially for the Polish Jews. I feel a special obligation to report on those years of German occupation and the horrors of the camps. Although it seemed almost hopeless, some of us managed to survive. Against the deadly backdrop of war, persecution, and mass murder, I met honorable people on both sides of the conflict.

Jewish victims are often accused of not having engaged in resistance against the Nazis. But what could we have achieved, without weapons, against a brutal power equipped with the latest military technology? To be sure, there were some who attempted armed resistance against the National Socialist occupiers. In Kraków, as in other cities, their fury erupted in a series of assassinations. Unfortunately, with few exceptions, such actions were doomed to failure. These idealistic young people were almost always tracked down and ruthlessly murdered by the *Sicherheitspolizei*, the German security police. My God, I thought to myself, how can these brave individuals with a couple of homemade bombs expect to compel a powerful country that has conquered almost all of Europe to change its policies? Of course, these were important symbolic acts. They proved that Jews did not simply stand idly by while being systematically stripped of all their rights. However, such acts also provoked horrific reprisals from the Nazi occupiers, to which many Jews fell victim. Was it justified,

I asked myself, to take such risks? Or was there perhaps another road, an alternative? At the time, I did not know what this alternate path might look like. But one thing was always certain: I wanted to preserve human life without having to resort to violence.

Kraków-Płaszów—first a forced labor camp and then, from January 1944, a concentration camp—was a special case among the approximately twenty concentration camps. It was the only major concentration camp under German control that had begun as a Jewish ghetto. I know this because I spent almost all of my time in Płaszów as the involuntarily recruited personal stenographer and secretary of the camp commandant, Amon Göth. Just how unusual—and even contrary to the Germans' own rules—my job in the main office of a concentration camp was, I learned only later, when testifying in the 1951 war crimes trial of the SS-*Standartenführer*[i] Gerhard Maurer in Warsaw. Until 1945, Maurer was the supervisor of all camp commandants, in charge of work assignments for all camp inmates. More than a half-million people were under his command. At first, Maurer refused to believe my testimony that I had worked as the personal secretary of a camp commander and, as such, had had access to classified documents. During his trial, Maurer was almost speechless with astonishment that Amon Göth had gotten away with flouting strict regulations to such an extent. By the time Maurer's trial took place, I had already testified as the main witness for the prosecution in the 1946 trial of Amon Göth. But in that earlier trial, the extraordinary nature of my job had not even come up. Only Maurer's consternation in 1951 made me realize how unique my position in the Płaszów camp had been during the Holocaust. This was later confirmed by Holocaust scholars.

As a consequence of more than 540 days spent in the "epicenter of evil," my life is inextricably connected to the history of the Kraków-Płaszów camp. I worked in the camp headquarters—at first as the sole clerical worker—from March 18, 1943, until Sep-

i See Appendix 3 for a list of SS ranks and their US Army equivalents.

tember 13, 1944. But it was also there that my life became just as inextricably connected to Oskar Schindler, with whom I worked closely during much of that time and until May 8, 1945. I think it is fair to say that a higher percentage of Jews survived the Płaszów camp than other camps. That was the result of Schindler's rescue efforts, for one thousand survivors on Schindler's list were from our camp. My parents, my brother, and I owe our lives to Oskar Schindler.

The history of the Holocaust is closely intertwined with developments on the eastern front. At first, the German Wehrmacht and its allies had a clear advantage. That changed only after the enormous losses they suffered in their invasion of the Soviet Union, especially after the German defeat at Stalingrad. From February 1943, the Nazi wartime economy was in deep crisis. Industrial workers were in short supply and the rate of the mass murder of Jews had slowed down. On the other hand, the productivity of camp inmates increased dramatically. In early 1943, in his infamous speech at the Berlin Sportpalast, Joseph Goebbels had whipped up the German people to the point of accepting "total war." From then on, the entire economy was focused on increased weapons production. For us few remaining Jews, this was decisively important. In the fall of 1943, several ghettos and forced labor camps in the *Generalgouvernement* that produced mainly textiles were disbanded. However our camp, Kraków-Płaszów, remained open. In the main office of the camp, I was able to gain access to classified documents and was secretly involved in keeping the camp from being liquidated. Thus, several thousands of my fellow inmates were not deported to Auschwitz. Without this strategy, described in detail in the pages that follow, the rescue by Oskar Schindler one year later during the fall of 1944 would not have been possible.

When I paid a visit to the United States in the early 1970s, I met Jews who were surprised that I choose to live in Germany. But they were even more astonished that I had so much good to say about a certain former member of the Nazi party. My close friendship with Oskar Schindler began in 1943 and lasted until his death in 1974. Back then, his name was not yet widely known, and relatively few people knew of his exceptional rescue efforts in Płaszów and later in Brünnlitz. After being forced to work for Amon Göth and after having had the privilege of working with Oskar Schindler, I've often wondered what would have happened if there had been no war and no Nazi ideology with its racist mania. Göth would probably not have become a mass murderer, nor Schindler a saver of lives. It was only the extraordinary circumstances of war and the immense power granted to individual men that revealed the nature of these men to such an impressive and terrifying degree. Fate had placed me between the two of them, and it was like having an angel on one side and a demon on the other. Almost forty years ago, I was unable to convince most of my American friends that when talking about the past, we have to take great care when telling our story. Even the tiniest details must be correct, for any imprecision threatens the credibility of the entire narrative. I am strictly opposed to exaggeration. In this book, I confine myself to telling the truth. I prefer to write a couple of words too few than one word too many.

THE ROAD TO RESCUE

KRAKÓW IN PEACETIME, 1918 TO 1939

FROM THE MIDDLE AGES to the partitions of Poland, my native city of Kraków was a European metropolis and the capital of the great Polish–Lithuanian empire. Beginning in about the thirteenth century, Jews were already settling in Kraków.

I was born in 1920 and lived almost forty years in this architecturally and historically important city on the Vistula. When I was liberated from the camp, I had just turned twenty-five. After my mother's death in 1958, my father and I moved to Augsburg, Germany, where my brother had already gone immediately after the war. My family was long established in Kraków. Only my paternal grandmother was from Breslau (today, Wrocław), and that's why her children and grandchildren all spoke both Polish and German at home. It was unusual to grow up bilingual in Kraków, but it seemed quite normal in our house. For me, being bilingual opened a window onto the world, and right up to the present I've always felt equally at home in the cultures of the Poles, the Germans, and the Jews. Even as a little boy, I knew that just as some people were blond and others brunette, some big and others small, there were also different languages, different religions, and different cultures.

In Poland after the First World War, there was a powerful return to Slavic traditions. This was due to Poland's newly won independence from the powers that had partitioned her in years gone by: Austria, Russia, and Prussia. That's why I was named Mieczysław. It means "he who won fame with his sword," although in my whole life I've never had a sword in my hand, nor ever wanted to. In Polish, my first name gets shortened to Mietek and that's what my friends and relatives call me to this day. If a Jewish family in the early twentieth century did not give its children biblical names, it indicated a high degree of assimilation. My father's cousin was named Egmont; you can't get any more German than that. So I passed my early years in two cultural spheres—Polish on the one hand, German on the other—both integrated within Judaism.

In contrast to many Jews in Kraków, both my parents and my grandparents were assimilated in their habits and dress. Nevertheless, my family was observant and strongly rooted in their faith. During the First World War, my father even made a solemn vow to donate a Torah scroll if he survived. And he kept his promise. After 1945, one of the few Torah scrolls not defiled by the Nazis was returned to us. I don't know if it was the one my father had donated, but I brought it along when I moved to Germany, and

My family in the late 1920s. My brother Stefan is second from the left.

it is now in a synagogue in Hamburg, where my brother Stefan's family lives.

My parents, Jakob and Regina, were married in 1918 after my father was discharged from the Austrian Army and had returned to Kraków. During the First World War, his experiences with his German comrades at the front had been positive. One of my mother's brothers had also served in the Austrian Army and liked to tell about a certain sector of the front and the German units stationed there. To him, they were "no-nonsense, forthright comrades." He liked to refer to them as "honest Michels." Later, after 1933, when my family discussed Hitler, we were of course worried about political developments in Germany, but we were incapable of imagining their devastating consequences. When we talked about Germany, we considered the situation something of an aberration that would soon be over. Herr von Papen[1] is said to have made a similar remark. We were all convinced that what was going on at the moment in Germany must surely be connected to unemployment or to the economic crisis or perhaps even to the lost war. Incidentally, while not one German general committed suicide after the First World War, Albert Ballin, a Jewish ship owner from Hamburg and an advisor to Wilhelm II on naval matters, took his own life because he could not accept the German defeat.

I was rather delicate as a child and prone to illness. I also seemed to have taken hold of things the wrong way. I mean that literally, for I am left-handed—something that was regarded as a genuine handicap in those days. Even the simple act of shaking hands with a visitor caused me problems. My family and my teachers went to great lengths to correct my "handicap" by a program of systematic reconditioning. So I learned to suppress my spontaneity in favor of cautious deliberation. My interests also clearly set me apart from the majority of my classmates. Instead of playing soccer, I began to learn the violin when I was barely seven years old. But despite good progress, I gave up music lessons after a few years in favor of reading, my real passion. I was especially interested in books about history, first in biographies and later in primary sources as well. Thus, at a relatively young age, I was fascinated by historical events and their connection to politics.

On Saturdays, my father took me to the synagogue. On the High Holy Days I accompanied him to small prayer houses where rabbis from surrounding towns prayed with their Kraków congregants. This experience gave me a broader perspective on Judaism. I recall one rabbi by the name of Lipschitz from Wielopole, east of Kraków, who read aloud from the prayer book. In a whisper, I asked my father if the rabbi didn't know the prayers by heart. I must have been about ten years old at the time, and even I had already memorized some of them. Of course the rabbi knew the prayers by heart. He probably even knew half the entire book by heart, my father replied, but he didn't want to make anyone feel ashamed who didn't. That was the reason he read from the open prayer book, so the others wouldn't feel inferior. To this day, I think about his exquisite tact and modesty.

During my early years, we lived with my paternal grandfather at 3 Węgierska Street in the neighborhood of Podgórze. My grand-

The Old Synagogue in the Kazimierz quarter of Kraków, pre-1939.

father and father dealt in agricultural products and my grandfather was even called upon as an expert witness on matters concerning legumes and grains. My father purchased rye and wheat flour by the wagonload from the area surrounding Posen (today, Poznań) and sold it to bakers in and around Kraków. His office was always in our apartment, for he conducted business through trucking companies and needed only a small space for bookkeeping.

When I was seven, we moved to a larger apartment building right next to the parish church of St. Joseph. Our new apartment at 1 Parkowa Street, only a few steps from my grandfather's house, was not far from a large park, and our building stood almost directly on the market square of Podgórze. Podgórze means "lower mountain" and this quarter of Kraków is located on the opposite bank of the Vistula. If you stand with your back to the church, you see the market square in front of you. To the right was the beginning of the ghetto that was set up in 1941. There was also a Jewish-owned chocolate factory there. Most of the families in our apartment building were gentiles. Besides us there were only three other Jewish families. At school, too, there were only a few Jews in my class, and almost all my friends were gentiles. I liked my school. Learning was easy for me, and later on in high school, I built up the German collection of the library. For a short time, starting in about 1936, I even edited the school newspaper.

Many rural Jews who had only briefly attended public schools didn't speak Polish well. The language of their daily lives was Yiddish, the language of their religion Hebrew. That was one of the causes of anti-Semitic prejudice. The Poles felt insulted when country Jews didn't speak good Polish, and they often made fun of them. I am very grateful that I was exposed to hardly any prejudice from my Polish classmates or my high school teachers.

Still, there was widespread anti-Semitism throughout Poland. The fires of prejudice were fanned especially by the Catholic Church.[2] But that wasn't the only institution that propagated racism. Anti-Semitism was the glue holding together a new kind of Polish nationalism, increasingly in evidence after the death of the "gentle" dictator Marshall Jósef Piłsudski in 1935. The historian Saul Friedländer goes so far as to call anti-Semitism the point of "national cohesion" at this time.[3] After Piłsudski's death, there were riots at the universities, especially in Lwów and Warsaw, but also in Kraków. Fortunately, this virulent anti-Semitism did not affect me directly until I began to attend university.

Because I did very well on my university qualifying exams in May 1938, I was given permission to pursue my studies at two universities simultaneously. I don't say that to boast, but my early successes in learning are a possible explanation for the fact that later, in the ghetto and especially in the camp, I was able to understand and correctly assess certain political developments. But I don't want to get ahead of myself. Until the decree that closed all Polish universities in 1939, I studied law at the Jagiellonian University and at the same time business administration and accounting at the Academy of Economics. The latter was on Sienkiewicza Street in the part of Kraków with the most modern and elegant houses. After 1939, the owners were driven from their homes as it became the favorite place for the German occupiers to set up their quarters. Although some classes continued to be held underground during the entire occupation, they were only for Polish students, not for Jews. I was not able to complete my master's degree until after the war.

In the fall of 1938, the president of the Jagiellonian University ordered that Jewish students sit only on certain benches in the lecture halls. In protest, we remained standing during our lectures. A rule was immediately promulgated that students were forbidden to stand during classes. They wanted to force us to sit on the "Jewish benches." Not that these benches were badly located—in the back of the hall, for instance. But for us, it was a matter of principle. We regarded the rule as blatant discrimination, an attempt to introduce into Poland the Nuremberg laws that had already been in force in Germany since 1935, legalizing the exclusion of Jews. Moreover, once the "Jewish benches"

Father, Mother, and me, about 1938.

had been adopted, students from other institutions—from the School of Mines, for instance, which had no Jewish students enrolled—would come to the Jagiellonian University so as not to miss out on the fun of seeing Jews being humiliated. My fellow Jewish students and I were disciplined and had a warning recorded in our transcripts because we had "disobeyed the directive of the university president." This incident led me to adopt a more distanced attitude toward the Poles. I realized how fragile and superficial the veneer of coexistence can be. For the first time, I became aware that my native country didn't really want me, a Jew, to live there.

Until 1944, I still possessed a copy of my transcript with the disciplinary entry. I always carried it with me, along with my other papers, in the ghetto and later in the camp as well. That proved to be a mistake. I should have hidden it. For when we were transported by cattle car from the concentration camp Płaszów to Brünnlitz in October 1944, the transport was routed via the Gross Rosen camp, where we had to surrender all our possessions and clothes, and that's when I lost my transcript as well.

From the partitions of Poland at the end of the eighteenth century right up to the end of the First World War, the ancient Polish coronation city of Kraków belonged—with occasional interruptions—to the Danube Monarchy of the Habsburgs. Its inhabitants were under the influence of Austro-German culture and liberalism. Among Kraków's idiosyncrasies are the many Renaissance inscriptions in Latin found in inner courtyards, on churches, and on old walls, admonishing passers-by and exhorting them to reflection. On Grodzka Street, below the royal palace, there's a small church that stands at a slight angle to the roadway. During my youth, it was a Lutheran church and it had one of these inscriptions. Since at the time I hadn't yet learned Latin in school, I had to translate the phrase with the help of a dictionary: *Frustra vivit, qui nemini prodest*—"He who helps no one lives without purpose (in vain)." I've never been able to forget that inscription. Especially during the war, its significance for me was enormous, since there were so few people who selflessly helped persecuted Jews. But those few rescuers evinced a high degree of goodness and humanity. Another inscription that was meaningful to me was located inside the Kraków municipal administration building: *Praestantibus viris negligere virtutem concessum non est*—"Men standing before others (leaders, those at the forefront) must not neglect (forget) courage (fortitude, morality)." Thus I understood early on that a person who, by his own actions or through the influence of others, is in a privileged position, is not at liberty to simply carry out his tasks mechanically.

This venerable old city of Kraków was declared by the Nazis in 1939 to be *urdeutsch*—originally and essentially German—and as a consequence was hardly bombed at all during the war. Only occasional bombs fell near the train station, and even then not onto the building itself. Later, Kraków also became a hub of supply lines between the Reich and the troops on the eastern front. It thus proved advantageous to have preserved the modern university clinics in order to care for German casualties. The Kraków-Płaszów station had long been located southeast of the city. At the beginning of 1943, the complex was greatly expanded. Who could have foreseen in 1939 that from 1943 on, the Nazis would intern us in a forced labor camp not far from this train station?

In contrast to Kraków, Hitler ordered Warsaw to be leveled. The city was considered a "nest of resistance," a "symbol of Polishness." The western part of the country was absorbed into the German Reich. The Nazis declared the middle section—including Kraków and Warsaw—a Polish Generalgouvernement and the eastern part was annexed by the Soviet Union until 1941. At first, the German jurist Dr. Hans Frank had the title "*Generalgouverneur* for the occupied Polish districts." However, this designation disappeared after a few weeks and only the name Generalgouvernement remained. As his residence and administrative offices, Frank chose the venerable Wawel Castle, once the home of the Polish kings. The stately Wawel overlooks Kraków like a patron saint. Under the German occupation, flying hundreds of Nazi flags, it became the threatening *Krakauer Burg*—the Kraków Castle. At first, extraordinarily high spirits prevailed among the occupiers. That changed only when the German front was broken through at Stalingrad and Kursk in early 1943. Until then, the Nazis apparently thought Russia was on the verge of collapse.

The Germans introduced into Poland the distinction between *Reichsdeutsche*, German citizens of the Reich, and *Volksdeutsche*, ethnic Germans from beyond its borders. I recall my revered Latin teacher and the principal of my high school, Edward Türschmid. As a Polish patriot, he did not want his name entered in the *Volksliste*, the list of ethnic Germans created by the occupiers immediately after the invasion. Whoever could prove German ancestry was entitled, as a *Volksdeutscher*, to certain professional advantages and subjected to fewer restrictions in daily life. Principal Türschmid wanted to remain a Pole; that wish alone was considered an affront to the German occupiers. Türschmid was not allowed to continue teaching and had to put up with harassment and special privations. After the war, he helped me get new copies of my qualifying exams and wrote another recommendation, as he had in 1938, that I receive special permission to study at two universities simultaneously.

Because of the increased need for housing in the capital of the Generalgouvernement, the Jews were to be expelled from the city. This didn't happen from one day to the next, but gradually.

Even before this "evacuation" began, there was what became known as the "Polish operation" in Germany at the end of October 1938. Thousands of Polish Jews were deported back to Poland, even if they had been living in Germany for decades. The deportation was organized by the Gestapo and carried out by the *Schutzpolizei*, the security police. Later, from the report of Ruwen Gräber of Hamburg, I learned how the operation was conducted. As he described it, "The doorbell rang about six in the morning. . . . I opened the door. The policeman: 'Good Morning. Are you Mr. Ruwen Gräber?' . . . And then he explained that I, as a Pole, was to be deported. He requested that I hand my passport over to him. I simply didn't believe it. This can't be! I've been living in this apartment since 1911!"[4] Some eighteen thousand persons, schoolchildren among them, were forcibly transported to the Polish border west of Posen. Although the deportation failed in some cases and about a thousand Jews were at first able to return to their homes in Germany, about seventeen thousand found themselves from one day to the next in legal limbo. Germany wanted to get rid of these people, but Poland refused them entry. Chaim Yechieli, at the time a fourteen-year-old boy, born in Germany but with a Polish passport, described the situation in these words: "The SS drove us across the border into no-man's-land. They hit us with clubs. We stood between the two borders for six hours. It was drizzling. And the Germans stood on one side with revolvers drawn and Polish soldiers on the other with fixed bayonets."[5]

Thousands of these deportees were at last allowed to cross the border into Poland, and makeshift housing was found for them in Zbąszyń, a medium-sized town nearby. They were not permitted to travel from there into the interior of the country until the end of November. After the German invasion less than a year later, those who had not received a visa to emigrate to America or some other place fell into the hands of the SS. Among the Jews transported to Zbąszyń against their will was a couple named Grynszpan. Barely a week after the forcible deportation of his parents, their seventeen-year-old son Herschel shot and killed the German attaché in Paris, Ernst Eduard vom Rath. The Nazis used this act of desperation as a pretext for the *Kristallnacht* pogrom of November 9, 1938. In reality, preparations for it had already long been underway.

In late 1938, I was one of a group of German-speaking Jewish students who volunteered to help see to the needs of the deported Jews. Many of them spoke not a word of Polish, for they had grown up in Germany. Some had been born there, although perhaps their grandparents had emigrated from Poland. Now, here they were, utterly destitute and helpless. I helped them write letters to their relatives abroad. They all wanted to get out of Poland, no matter how, no matter where to. They just wanted to leave.

Many of the deportees were put up in the Hotel Royal in Gertrud Street by the well-organized Jewish community of Kraków. How often did I hear them warn me, "Young man, try to get out of Poland as soon as possible. Hitler will come to Poland as well." Back then, I considered such prognoses panicky exaggerations, but the deportees from Germany were convinced that Hitler's expansionism would not stop at the Polish border. In hindsight, I've often asked myself how all of us, especially those in Western Europe, could have been so blind as not to recognize the imminent danger. After the war, we learned that even the Allies had completely underestimated the likelihood of Hitler starting a war. Among the deportees who warned us in vain were David Gutter and his family. I did not know Mr. Gutter then. But four years later, in the summer of 1942, we met when on orders from the German security police, Gutter was named "provisional director" of the Jewish community in Kraków, for which I was working as a bilingual typist and stenographer by that time.

THE INVASION

FROM THE VERY BEGINNING, the Wehrmacht was involved in crimes against the Jewish population. In September 1939, shortly after German troops had invaded Poland, there was a massacre of Jews in Upper Silesia, in the Katowice region. How ruthlessly the German occupiers immediately began to treat us can be gathered from an interview with Hans Frank in the *Völkischer Beobachter*[6] on February 6, 1940. "In Prague, for example, large red posters were put up on which one could read that today, seven Czechs had been executed. I said to myself, if I'm going to hang up a poster for every seven Poles I have shot, then the forests of Poland will not produce enough paper for such posters.—Yes, we had to act harshly."[7]

On October 26, 1939, Hans Frank announced in Kraków that Jews in the Generalgouvernement would perform compulsory labor, while Poles had to report for work duty. Compulsory labor meant in practice that the Nazis could arbitrarily detain us and assign us to work details. During that time, Jews avoided showing themselves on the street, for we would often get rounded up and forced to perform physical labor. We would have to move furniture, shovel snow, and sweep the streets. It was open season on Jews, and even the four walls of our apartments offered us no protection. It could happen that a man in uniform would unexpectedly ring our doorbell, look around the apartment inquisitively, and then command, "You have three hours to clear out. You may take a suitcase with you. Your furniture stays here."

Once I myself was picked up on the street and along with some others had to move furniture from the fourth floor of a building into a truck parked in front; they beat us as we worked.

But it would be a mistake to lump all Germans together. Near our building in Parkowa Street, soldiers had been quartered in a school that the Nazis had closed. One day—it must have been in the fall of 1939—a small troop of soldiers approached our building. I was just about to step out the front door. Two little Polish boys ran toward the soldiers, pointed at me, and yelled, "Jew, Jew!" I stood in the door, frozen with fear. The children wouldn't have gotten the idea of denouncing me on their own. They must have learned it at home. Luckily, the soldiers, older men from the Wehrmacht, only shook their heads in disapproval and passed me by without a word. This reaction surprised me and made a positive impression.

Not until after the war did I learn that Poles, in far greater numbers than any other nation, had helped hide and rescue Jews during the Second World War.

Systematic round-ups of Jewish civilians began at the end of November 1939. At this time, almost two years before the introduction of the yellow star for Jews in Germany, the Generalgouvernement forced us to wear a white armband with a blue Star of David. For a while, I didn't leave our apartment. Then, when I finally had to run an errand in town, I was promptly picked up and assigned to shovel snow and sweep the street. It was especially humiliating that we were under the command of a municipal street sweeper who ordered us about in coarse language and even spoke abusively to older, educated individuals. Without a doubt, he was basking in his new position of power. By chance, my former schoolmate Roman Kula saw me shoveling snow. He was the son of a district judge in Kraków. Roman came up to me, greeted me with a few kind words, and expressed his regret at my situation. The Polish street sweeper immediately came over and yelled obscenities at him. But he couldn't intimidate my friend, who in turn chewed the fellow out. It made me feel very good.

There's a phrase in Virgil that often came to my mind in those days, *rari nantes in gurgite vasto*—"isolated swimmers in the vast chasm of the sea." Only a few individuals resisted the Nazis' orders. There were only a few brave swimmers in this incalculably vast abyss of evil. No one knew in 1939 what was going to happen. Yet I still can't understand why there were so few who possessed the courage of a Roman Kula.

On October 31, 1939, the propaganda minister Joseph Goebbels ordered the breakup of the Polish media. That was the end of a free press in Poland. In its place, there was the *Krakauer Zeitung*,[9] a publication of the Nazi occupation. Now we could find out what was going on only from the BBC. At that time, there were approximately 1.2 million radios in Poland. But listening to foreign broadcasts was promptly forbidden. On December 15, 1939, all radios were ordered confiscated. Although the Nazis were not able to carry this out completely, their jamming made the reception of foreign broadcasts practically impossible. But that was the case only in the city. Outside of Kraków, in the countryside, you could hear the BBC well. Early in 1940, groups of young resistors decided to transcribe the broadcasts of the BBC Polish-language service, type them up, and distribute them illegally in Kraków. Wiesław Wielgus, a friend of mine from school days, and I belonged to one of these groups. Wiesław lived diagonally across the street from us. His father was a train engineer, his mother a teacher. He was an only child. He established contacts with the resistance in the countryside. His comrades and he were Polish Christians fighting for the freedom of their country. What motivated them was their genuine sense of national consciousness and pride. Other members of the group listened to the BBC broadcasts and wrote them down in shorthand. It was my job to type the transcripts onto wax stencils. I did so by removing the ribbon from the typewriter and typing onto the stencil with "naked" keys. By that time, I could practically type blindfolded and hardly needed to use the shift key, since capital letters are

Der Distriktschef von Krakau

ANORDNUNG

Kennzeichnung der Juden im Distrikt Krakau

Ich ordne an, dass alle Juden im Alter von über 12 Jahren im Distrikt Krakau mit Wirkung vom 1. 12. 1939 ausserhalb ihrer eigenen Wohnung ein sichtbares Kennzeichen zu tragen haben. Dieser Anordnung unterliegen auch nur vorübergehend im Distriktsbereich anwesende Juden für die Dauer ihres Aufenthaltes.

Als Jude im Sinne dieser Anordnung gilt:

1. wer der mosaischen Glaubensgemeinschaft angehört oder angehört hat,

2. jeder, dessen Vater oder Mutter der mosaischen Glaubensgemeinschaft angehört oder angehört hat.

Als Kennzeichen ist am rechten Oberarm der Kleidung und der Überkleidung eine Armbinde zu tragen, die auf weissem Grunde an der Aussenseite einen blauen Zionstern zeigt. Der weisse Grund muss eine Breite von mindestens 10 cm. haben, der Zionstern muss so gross sein, dass dessen gegenüberliegende Spitzen mindestens 8 cm. entfernt sind. Der Balken muss 1 cm. breit sein.

Juden, die dieser Verpflichtung nicht nachkommen, haben strenge Bestrafung zu gewärtigen.

Für die Ausführung dieser Anordnung, insbesondere die Versorgung der Juden mit Kennzeichen, sind die Ältestenräte verantwortlich.

Krakau, den 18. 11. 1939.

Wächter

Szef dystryktu krakowskiego

ROZPORZĄDZENIE

Znamionowanie żydów w okręgu Krakowa

Zarządzam z ważnością od dnia 1. XII. 1939, iż wszyscy żydzi w wieku ponad 12 lat winni nosić widoczne znamiona. Rozporządzeniu temu podlegają także na czas ich pobytu przejściowo w obrębie okręgu przebywający żydzi.

Żydem w myśl tego rozporządzenia jest:

1) ten, który jest lub był wyznania mojżeszowego,

2) każdy, którego ojciec, lub matka są lub byli wyznania mojżeszowego.

Znamieniem jest biała przepaska noszona na prawym rękawie ubrania lub odzienia wierzchniego z niebieską gwiazdą sjonistyczną. Przepaska winna mieć szerokość conajmniej 10 cm, a gwiazda średnicę 8 cm. Wstążka, z której sporządzono gwiazdę, winna mieć szerokość conajmniej 1 cm.

Niestosujący się do tego zarządzenia zostaną surowo ukarani.

Za wykonanie niniejszego zarządzenia, zwłaszcza za dostarczenie opasek czynię odpowiedzialną Radę starszych.

Kraków, dnia 18. XI. 1939.

(—) Wächter

A decree for Jewish inhabitants of Kraków to wear armbands with the Star of David, November 18, 1939.[8]

rare in Polish, occurring mainly at the beginning of a sentence and in proper names, in contrast to German, in which all nouns are capitalized. The texts were then reproduced on two or three pages and published as *gazetki*—"little newspapers." There were several such illegal publications in Kraków at the time. On purpose, we didn't give ours a name, so the Nazis would have more difficulty finding out where it came from. If they had, our whole group would have been in danger.

I could type only in the evenings, for I was using my father's old Smith Corona. I remember that during this time, the weather was still summery and warm, the window was open, and now and then German soldiers would pass by outside my room, which was located on the raised ground floor. My parents were close to despair. "There are soldiers marching by out there. If one of them hears your clatter and gets a notion to investigate, then we're all lost." The heart of our *gazetki* were the transcripts of the BBC broadcasts. But there were always short introductory texts. After a few months, these sometimes contained a smattering of anti-Semitic remarks. As soon as I noticed this, I resigned from the group. I was prepared to run great risks for this type of intellectual resistance. However, I was not prepared to risk my life and that of my parents for anything smacking of anti-Semitic machinations.

Since the introduction of white and blue armbands with the Star of David on December 1, 1939, the Jewish community had distributed about 54,000 of them. With the exception of children under twelve years old, all Jews had to wear one. In the meantime, many Jews were living illegally in Kraków. They had come from rural areas and hoped to find accommodations and protection in the city. I intended to appear in public wearing the armband as little as possible. At the same time, I could not expose myself unnecessarily to danger by going into the streets without it, although my appearance was not what was generally considered "typically Jewish." There were considerable penalties for ignoring the new Nazi regulations, and besides, everyone in Podgórze knew I was a Jew. So I avoided leaving our building for many weeks. I sat alone in our apartment and began to practice German stenography. I had already taught myself the fundamentals of German shorthand. Now I set about perfecting my rudimentary skills through weeks of self-study. Unlike my Polish friends, I was firmly convinced that the war would last a few years. The First World War had been drawn out over four years, and this war, I thought to myself, will last at least that long. Since I had never possessed the physical endowments for heavy labor, and, in addition, had thyroid problems, I wanted to be as well prepared as possible for eventual office work. With my knowledge of languages, my typing ability, and my newly acquired capability of taking shorthand dictation in German, I applied to the Jewish community and was hired as an administrative clerk. The office was located in a building at the corner of 41 Krakowska Street and 2 Skawinska Street. Later the community had to move its administrative office from there into the ghetto. I typed letters and translated from German into Polish and vice versa. I was the only person in that department who wasn't from Germany. One of my colleagues was Heinz Dressler, from Dresden, who later would work in one of the offices of the forced labor camp. We met there in the community office and became friends.

The Jewish community in Kraków was one of the oldest in Poland. It was a centuries-old institution that not only looked after its members but also maintained a multifaceted social infrastructure with hospitals, old-age homes, student dormitories, schools, and kindergartens.

Beginning on September 21, 1939, Poland's previously autonomous Jewish communities had to form so-called *Judenräte*—Jewish councils—whose task was to receive orders from the German occupation authorities and see to it that all orders were carried out efficiently. In smaller cities where there had been no incorporated Jewish communities prior to the war, but only individual synagogues or prayer rooms, *Judenräte* were formed ad hoc. The

Judenräte greatly simplified the administrative work of the German occupation. In Kraków, the municipal president, Dr. Mieczysław Kaplicki, chose Marek Biberstein, a teacher who had already been active in several social organizations, as the chairman of the *Judenrat*. Dr. Wilhelm Goldblatt was his deputy. The executive council that they headed had twelve members. From then on, in occupied Kraków, the Jewish community and the *Judenrat* were one and the same. We office workers, confronted each and every day with new demands, orders, regulations, and laws, could barely keep up with the workload. Through this job, I soon became familiar with the structure of the German administration of the Generalgouvernement.

By the beginning of 1940, my family was forced to take in three additional tenants. According to the regulations concerning floor space for Jews, we supposedly had too much room in our apartment in Parkowa Street. The Liebling family had only recently come to Kraków from bombed-out Warsaw, and they moved in with us. The Lieblings' little son later became famous as the film director Roman Polanski. He had been born Raymond Liebling in Paris in 1933. In the course of the continuing world economic crisis at the end of the 1930s, his parents had decided to return to Poland. I remember the seven-year-old child as being very nervous. He had an especially close relationship with his mother, a woman of definite artistic interests. His father was a businessman specializing in plumbing supplies. Mr. Liebling wrote up bids for Polish workmen doing jobs for the German trustees of Polish companies and then wrote out invoices for them, since most of these workmen were not able to write them in German. I had close contact with Mr. Liebling because I loaned him our typewriter from time to time, and sometimes did typing jobs for him as well.

On April 12, 1940, Governor General Hans Frank announced, "The Jews must be expelled from the city because it is absolutely unacceptable that thousands upon thousands of Jews own

Jews under arrest in the Podgórze quarter of Kraków, December 1939.

apartments and continue to slink around in a city that has the honor to have been designated by the Führer as the seat of an important agency of the Reich."[10] At the time, of course, we had no knowledge of this nasty pronouncement, although we soon became aware of its consequences. On May 18, 1940, began what the Germans officially called a "voluntary" relocation. The number of Jewish inhabitants in Kraków had grown enormously since the beginning of the year—from 56,000 before the war to 80,000. Now 60,000 of them had to leave the city by the fall of 1940 to make room for the thousands of German officials, policemen, SS men, and war profiteers flocking to Kraków from the Reich. Local authorities granted certain privileges to Jews who left Kraków "voluntarily" by the end of the summer. They were permitted to settle anywhere else in the Generalgouvernement. The Jewish community supported Jews leaving the city "voluntarily" by giving them some money for food and travel expenses.

We in the Jewish community administration issued the necessary certificates for resettlement. Without official papers no Jew could show himself in the city any longer; having no valid papers meant certain arrest. Beginning in November 1940, the German security forces staged ever more frequent roundups of Jews without residence permits.

Up to that time, Oświęcim, known as Auschwitz in German, had been for me merely the name of a quiet, unremarkable town. My father's oldest sister lived there with her husband, a businessman named Grünbaum. Oświęcim had about 40,000 inhabitants. It had had an Austrian garrison and in the Middle Ages had developed a special relationship to the Catholic Church.[11] By 1940, the Germans had chosen this city as the location for a concentration camp. The Auschwitz camp opened that year. Later, the former Polish army barracks became known as Auschwitz I (*Stammlager*). Auschwitz II (Birkenau), the site of the gas chambers, was erected nearby on the orders of Heinrich Himmler and placed under the command of Rudolf Höss. The Auschwitz complex was to become the largest cemetery in history. By the end of the war, approximately a million Jews and one hundred thousand Poles had been murdered there—not to mention the many victims from other countries and ethnic groups.

We heard of the existence of a concentration camp in Auschwitz for the first time at the end of 1940, in connection with a memorandum from the rabbis of Kraków to Polish relief organizations. In it, the rabbis requested the Polish organizations to join in their efforts to get the German authorities to postpone the "voluntary" resettlement until the spring of 1941 so that the Jews still in the city illegally would not have to find new places to live in the middle of winter. At the time, we still didn't know what the German occupiers already had in store for us.

SS-*Untersturmführer* Oskar Brandt, head of the Office for Jewish Affairs of the Kraków security police at 2 Pomorska Street, was furious when he learned of this petition. When he subsequently heard that the Kraków rabbis had also appealed to the Prince Archbishop of Kraków, Stefan Sapieha—even though the latter was not at all considered philo-Semitic and it is unlikely he ever even read the memorandum—Brandt called a meeting in the Jewish community

Kraków around 1941. Jews being sent to do forced labor.

center. In the future, he commanded, petitions of any kind whatsoever had better be addressed only to him and the security police. He looked menacingly around the room at those present. "And who was it," he wanted to know, "who actually thought up this memorandum?" No one volunteered any information, whereupon Brandt threatened severe punishments for everyone. Then a distant relative of mine, the lawyer Dr. Isidor Leuchter, spoke up. He said he was the author of the memorandum. Brandt took him along in his car to be interrogated. Luckily, no one knew that I had typed the memorandum from Leuchter's draft.

Brandt then ordered the participating rabbis—S. Kornitzer, S. Rappaport, and M. Friedrich—sent to the Auschwitz camp immediately.

A short time later, a telegram arrived, signed by the "SS Camp Commandant Auschwitz," with the news that the detainee Isidor Leuchter had passed away. His ashes could be picked up for a fee of five reichmarks. In the course of the following weeks, several similar telegrams reached our office. Each one stated that the detainee number so and so had died of heart failure on such and such a date. "Upon the receipt of five reichmarks, an urn with the ashes may be picked up by members of the family." Gradually for us, Auschwitz became synonymous with death.

I wrote out dozens of requests to change złotys issued by the Generalgouvernement into reichmarks. We were very puzzled and disconcerted by the identical cause of death stated in each telegram, because many of those who had died so suddenly—supposedly of heart failure—were younger or middle-aged men who had never complained of cardiac problems. We soon agreed that something was amiss. I didn't find out until after the war that many of those sent to the camp at that time had in fact died of heart failure. In the Kraków Auschwitz trial of 1947, at which I served as an interpreter, one of the accused was an SS non-com by the name of Ludwig Plagge. His nickname among his fellow defendants had been "Calisthenics Plagge." All new arrivals at

Auschwitz were turned over to him. The arriving detainees were in a weakened condition, having already been mistreated in other prisons and torture chambers. Plagge would actually make these poor people do calisthenics for hours on the parade ground. Many collapsed and died of heart failure. Only those who survived this torture were then admitted to the camp.

IN THE GHETTO

On March 6, 1941, the *Krakauer Zeitung* reported the construction of a ghetto in the Podgórze neighborhood. The justification was as follows: "Sanitary, economic, and law-enforcement considerations make it imperative to house the Jewish population of Kraków in a special, enclosed section of the city, the Jewish residential district."[12] With the erection of the ghetto, the ostracization of the Jews was made even more comprehensive. For the non-Jewish Poles living in this district, the directive meant that they immediately had to vacate their apartments and give up their businesses and workshops as well. Fifteen thousand Jews were to be barricaded within an area that until then had accommodated three thousand inhabitants. The allocation of space was measured by windows. The basic rule was four people per casement window. Since many rooms had double casement windows, up to eight people lived in a single room. That often meant two families. There was hardly any room left for furniture. The rooms were so crowded that we often had to step over mattresses and blankets to conduct the routine head-count, which was always carried out at night because there was a curfew and every ghetto resident had to be in his quarters.

The Nazis closed the gates of the ghetto on March 20, 1941, but not all of Kraków's Jews had been permitted to live there. Only members of certain professions were allowed to move into what the officials called the "Jewish residential district." The

Jews forced to shovel snow in Kraków.

word *ghetto* was never used. At first, you needed a stamp on your yellow identity card proving that you had shoveled snow for a certain number of days. Then it became primarily workmen employed by German or Polish firms who received permission to live in the ghetto. Finally, preference was given to skilled factory workers producing goods important for the war effort, who were allowed to bring their families as well. This meant that those not working for a German agency or engaged in production essential for the war had to leave the city and find housing in smaller towns. There were exceptions, however. It was decreed that elderly Jews who were sick and could not be moved did not have to leave Kraków. On the basis of this provision, my grandfather, Arthur Gabriel Pemper, who was then eighty-five years old, obtained the necessary corroboration from a German public health officer. And so, on account of his age, he was allowed to die in his own bed in October 1941. But had he lived a year longer, he would have been among the first deportees sent to be exterminated at Bełżec. That's how swiftly and unforeseeably

Kraków Jews forced to build the wall around the ghetto.

an advantage could be transformed into a disadvantage, and vice versa. Any attempt to come up with a strategy against such systematic injustice was unthinkable, to say nothing of trying to make long-term plans.

I did not receive a permit to live in the ghetto, nor was my father able to demonstrate that as an independent businessman, he was "important to the war effort." And so my parents and younger brother moved in with relatives in Wiśnicz, about thirty miles south of Kraków, while I went to live with my maternal uncle, Zygmunt Weissenberg. He owned a trucking company in Zielonki, on the outskirts of Kraków. In my uncle's house, I helped out by tutoring my two cousins.

After a few weeks, I again contacted the Jewish community in Kraków and belatedly received permission to move into the ghetto. And so, beginning in the summer of 1941, I was once again working for the Jewish community, that is, for the *Judenrat*, and was thus able to follow the administration of the German occupation up close. I was already thinking that if there was anywhere

Jews would be able to make themselves indispensable, it was in the big cities, and that proved to be correct.

In March 1941, Hitler had announced that the Generalgouvernement was soon to be made *judenfrei*—free of Jews.[13] As a result of this statement of policy, an administrative struggle began over the "solution to the Jewish question." I would occasionally learn something about this from the correspondence of the Jewish community. Of course, I had no precise information, but I was able to glean from what I read or overheard, and from what I had to type that various interest groups were impeding each other's efforts. Such contradictions were extremely interesting to me. Perhaps, I said to myself, it can be useful for us Jews if the occupiers disagree with each other. Today we know that the SS in Berlin was competing with the civilian authorities of the Generalgouvernement in Kraków. Secret messages were sent back and forth between the two capitals, and new contradictory directives appeared constantly. Although the *Reichsführer* SS Heinrich Himmler and the governor general Hans Frank were both die-hard anti-Semites, they couldn't stand one another. Each wanted to solve the "Jewish question" in his own way, and both surely wanted to derive as much political and personal advantage from it as possible. So it was a question of jurisdiction, and also of what would become of the assets of the persecuted. Would the property of the Jews flow into the coffers of the Reichsbank in Berlin or those of the governor general in Kraków? In November 1941, Himmler emerged victorious from this struggle.[14] From then on, he and his lieutenant Reinhard Heydrich had the final say "with regard to the Jews."[15] That is, with regard to about two and a half million people in the Generalgouvernement alone.

By the end of 1941, almost a million Soviet citizens and people of Jewish descent had already starved to death or been murdered. I learned this only later, although various rumors were already circulating about it at the time. We also knew nothing about the plans the Nazis were formulating for the Generalgouvernement in mid-1941, which they then carried out in 1942. Today, this intensive campaign is known as *Aktion Reinhard*. On July 16, 1941, there was a conference in the "Wolf's Lair," the Führer's headquarters in East Prussia. On this occasion, Hitler made the infamous statement that any inhabitant of the occupied eastern territories who dared even look "askance" at a German should be shot dead.[16]

Two days later, on July 18, Heinrich Himmler traveled to Lublin and assigned SS-*Brigadeführer* Odilo Globocnik, the police chief of the district, and his chief-of-staff, SS-*Sturmbannführer* Hermann Höfle, the job of murdering all the Jews in the Generalgouvernement. Also present at this meeting was SS-*Obergruppenführer* Oswald Pohl, who in 1942 would be appointed head of the SS-*Wirtschafts-Verwaltungshauptamt*—the Economic and Administrative Main Office of the SS. Globocnik was to begin *Aktion Reinhard* in his own district. The Bełżec extermination camp, close to completion by November 1941, was located east of Kraków on the train line between Lublin and Lwów. Since the region was nearly uninhabited, it was perfect for what the SS was planning. Barracks to house the Jews were unnecessary. Immediately upon arrival in Bełżec, the Jews had to take off their clothes to get "showered." The SS would then lead them into the gas chambers, called "inhalation facilities and showers" and murder them with carbon monoxide, using the exhaust of diesel motors. Within eight months, an estimated 600,000 Jews were killed at Bełżec. In the ghetto in Podgórze, we knew nothing about it. However, we heard rumors and even some details from Polish railway workers and our own underground organizations: at the final destination of the trains, there was neither a large internment camp, nor a building site, nor highway construction, nor a factory that would have needed workers. Yet the trains returned empty. Polish farmers from the surrounding region reported that every time a "human shipment" arrived, a little while later they could smell burnt flesh.

During these months in the ghetto, I became aware of changes in the functions of the German civilian administration. Thanks to my work as a clerk for the Jewish community, it was easy for me to notice them. At the beginning of 1942, it was decreed that "Jewish matters" were no longer under the jurisdiction of the civilian administration—the municipal administrator Schmid and the district administration at large. From then on, the German security police would be in charge of us. They were the equivalent of what one usually called the Gestapo. But as far as I know, there were no state secret police[17] as such in the Generalgouvernement. I gradually began to see connections and recognize power struggles within the SS bureaucracy. By then, for instance, I had memorized the SS ranks, which were comparable to the ranks in the Wehrmacht, but unfamiliar to us at first. There was the *Höherer SS- und Polizeiführer Ost*—the "higher SS and police chief east"—the superior of all SS and police officers in the Generalgouvernement. At first, this position was held by General Friedrich Wilhelm Krüger, who was residing in the Wawel, on the royal hill. His adjutant was SS–*Hauptsturmführer* Count Korff. Within the Generalgouvernement, all the commanders of the security police and the security service, as well as of the traffic police, reported directly to General Krüger. At first, there were four districts within the Generalgouvernement: Warsaw, Kraków, Radom, and Lublin. In mid-1941, the district of Galicia with its capital Lemberg (Lwów) was added. Each district had its own SS and police chief. *Oberführer*[18] Julian Scherner was the SS and police chief of the Kraków district, with offices located in Oleander Street. Scherner's chief of staff was SS-*Sturmbannführer* Willi Haase, at whose trial in Kraków I later testified. Haase was sentenced to death. The later commandant of the Kraków-Płaszów camp, Amon Göth, got along famously with Scherner and Korff, and the two of them were often Göth's guests in 1943 and 1944 for drinking bouts in his villa.

Because of the shift in jurisdiction that emerged in early 1942, we ghetto residents now found ourselves under the supervision of the SS and the security police. At the time, I often thought of a line from Virgil that I had learned as a schoolboy: *Rerum cognoscere causas*—one needs to know the causes of things. I was convinced that something terrible was about to happen, I just didn't know what it would be. Then in the spring of 1942, all the Jews living in the ghetto had to report to the Savings Bank Building with their employment documents and identity cards. Some tables had been set up outside, and members of the security police were checking each person's documents. In some cases, they stamped the identity cards with the seal of the police authority; in others—especially for young people and the elderly—they did not. That was an ominous sign. The first transport from the Kraków ghetto of people to be exterminated in Bełżec took place on June 1, 1942. It was carried out by Willi Haase and his SS men. At the time, Bełżec did not yet have the connotation of an extermination camp for us, and we wondered why the Nazis were "evacuating" primarily the elderly, the sick, women, and young children to help with the harvest in the Ukraine, as they alleged.

In the second exterminatory transport from the Kraków ghetto on June 8, 1942, the newly chosen chairman of the Jewish community, Dr. Arthur Rosenzweig (Marek Biberstein's successor) and his family were sent to Bełżec. He was accused of not having exerted himself sufficiently during the first "evacuation" a week earlier, failing to herd even more ghetto Jews onto the square in front of the pharmacy, the departure point for the transports. After that, the Nazis named David Gutter as provisional director of the *Judenrat,* and that was the end of the elected executive board.

My parents and my brother Stefan were still living outside the ghetto at the time. My most urgent task was to figure out how to bring all three of them to Kraków, get them into the ghetto, and find them work in a business "important to the war effort." In spite of everything, it seemed to me more advisable for them to live in the ghetto than somewhere outside the city. It was relatively easy to secure work for my mother in a tailoring cooperative with a contract to make uniforms for the Wehrmacht. My younger brother

The main entrance to the Kraków ghetto. The building on the right was the headquarters of the Jewish community from 1941 to 1942, where I worked intermittently.

had always liked helping out at my uncle's trucking business and other transport companies. He simply clambered up onto the first horse-drawn wagon he saw and got into Kraków illegally.

Finding work for my father was much more complicated. He was already fifty-four years old and as a former self-employed businessman, had no vocational training. At that juncture, Olga Bannet, a young lawyer whose father was also a lawyer in Kraków, was able to help us. She was head of the office of demography and statistics in the Jewish community, whose duties included registering the inhabitants of the ghetto. She had connections to Polish judicial officials and for a few hundred złotys was able to obtain a fake subpoena for my father to testify in a trial in Kraków. I sent this document to my father in Wiśnicz. He took it to the local German police commandant who stamped it with the official seal. Now my father was entitled to purchase a ticket and travel by train. Without such documentation, Jews were no longer permitted to use public transportation. This entire enterprise had

A section of the barbed-wire fence that divided parts of the Podgórze ghetto from the rest of Kraków.

a very small window of opportunity: there was already an official announcement that the Jews in Wiśnicz were ordered to leave for Bochnia, the nearest district seat, which was an assembly point for "resettlement." According to what my father told me later, several hundred Jews had already set out for Bochnia—he had encountered them carrying suitcases and bundles along the road. All the Jews from Wiśnicz had to walk to the assembly point. It was a haunting scene. Only my father was able to walk to the station with a real train ticket in one hand and the document that saved him in the other. And so he reached Kraków quite legally.

Sadly, the young lawyer Olga Bannet did not survive the war years.

I had brought my family back to Kraków. My mother, furnished with official papers, was already at work in the large tailor shop in the ghetto. But I still had to get my father and my brother from the city into the ghetto, because they were in mortal danger living outside the ghetto illegally and without papers. Since November 1941, there was a standing order to shoot Jews in Kraków on sight; outside the ghetto they were fair game. Then chance came to my aid. One Sunday, I had work to do in the Jewish community, and David Gutter called me into his office. "This gentleman is from the Klug construction company. They are expanding the Kraków airport. The SS and police chief has authorized them to employ a certain number of Jews at the construction site. Be so kind as to help him fill out this form on your typewriter." Once I was alone in the room with the gentleman, an ethnic German, I got the impression that he had a certain amount of latitude in his choice of workers, because while talking, he was pulling various papers out of his pockets—first from the left and then from the right pocket. When I saw that, I summoned up all my courage. "I have a request," I said. "You've still got room on your list for a few extra names. I need one line—or actually, two: one for my father and one for my brother." "No," he replied, "can't be done." After some back and forth, he finally allowed me one line to fill out. Since at the time, I didn't know whom I could save, I entered the name "Pemper, Jakob Stefan" onto the line. I thought to myself, I can save either my father, Jakob, or my brother, Stefan. And so I was able to secure for my father a job "important to the war effort" with the Klug construction company. My brother later got a job with the same firm.

The third transport to the extermination camp, again euphemistically called an "evacuation operation," took place on October 28, 1942. Working in the office, I had learned how one could predict such transports. When the guards at the gates of the ghetto were confined to barracks, it was usually a sure sign that something was brewing. I was especially concerned about my father and feared that he would be put into a transport because of his age. So as a precaution, I called up his work detail at the airport, and thanks to a friendly official, got my father himself on the telephone. I advised him not to return to the ghetto that evening. He spent the night on the hallway floor of a Polish acquaintance. And so I was able to save him again.

In the course of this third deportation, more than half the people remaining in the Kraków ghetto were sent to their deaths in Bełżec. Such was the shock and helpless fury at the immeasurable brutality of the Nazis that Jewish resistance groups outside the ghetto started planning a major retaliation in the middle of the city. At Christmastime, 1942, they succeeded in setting off several bombs in the Café Cyganeria, a favorite spot for Wehrmacht soldiers, policemen, and the SS. Eleven Germans died and thirteen were wounded. The leaders of the resistance group, among them Dolek Liebeskind, were apprehended and executed. I was deeply shaken at the loss of these young people, but my grief could not alter my conviction that such desperate acts would have no positive effect on our fate. If we were to save as many of us as possible from certain death, we had to find different avenues. There's a saying in Latin: *Qui gladio ferit, gladio periit*—"He who fights with the sword perishes by the sword." Perhaps there were other ways to resist the German occupiers—without weapons, for we had no desire to perish.

It must have been the beginning of November 1942 when David Gutter returned from his daily briefing to the SS and police chief carrying two ring binders full of letters, each containing three or four hundred pages. This was the correspondence between the office of the SS and police chief of the Kraków district and various Polish and German firms and government agencies. Gutter assigned me the secret task of alphabetizing the letters by agency and company name, with cross-references to type of business. I set about the task in the evenings, after the other office workers had gone home. In their letters, various agencies and businesses asked for permission to continue to employ Jews. The reply of the SS and police chief in Kraków was usually that, as an exception, permission could still be granted for this or that Jewish worker, but the firms should begin to plan for the time when there would no longer be any Jews left in the Generalgouvernement. At the most, only a few would remain, "interned in forced labor camps or concentration camps," as one of the letters explicitly stated. My heart stood still. I was so dismayed I could hardly breathe. This, then, was to be our fate: the ghetto was not the final destination after all, as most believed. Instead, only a few of us all were meant to be spared as useful slaves, confined to camps. Of course, I could not share this information with anyone. Some of the letter-writers were even making positive efforts to protect their Jewish workers; their people spoke German or Yiddish and so they (the employers) could easily communicate with them. Moreover, they were well trained and it would take a long time to replace such reliable workers with Poles. Letters such as these made it clear to me that in the future, it would be extremely important for us to be employed in jobs the SS considered useful.

From David Gutter I learned that the man who had given him the binders, SS-*Unterscharführer* Horst Pilarzik, was a fairly primitive, uneducated type of person. I had not heard his name before. With a heavy heart, I carried out my task, put the letters in order and cross-referenced them by type of business.

A few days later, Pilarzik called the Jewish community office and said in a voice of military command, "Wash your chest!" Then he laughed out loud and asked, "You know what comes next?"

I tried to control myself and answered, "Yes, next comes, 'You're going to be shot.'"

"And how do you know that?"

"Well," I replied, "it's a German saying."

"*Jawoll*, so it is." Pilarzik seemed to be enjoying the conversation and continued in a patronizing tone of voice, "Well, this is Pilarzik. You were given that correspondence to sort. When do I get it back?"

I answered politely, "I'm almost done. Maybe one more evening, and it will be finished."

Then Gutter drove the community's horse-drawn carriage (Jews were not allowed to ride the streetcars) all the way across town to the office of the SS and police chief in Oleander Street to deliver the two binders to Pilarzik.[19] I doubt that Gutter even looked at the letters. But they set me onto the right path. Now I knew that sooner or later, we would be interned in camps. I met Pilarzik a few months later, when the ghetto was being disbanded. And then again, later, in the summer of 1943, when he turned up briefly in the Kraków-Płaszów camp.

In February 1943, a large—better yet, gigantic—SS officer appeared in our office. He was almost six and a half feet tall. I am small by comparison, only five and a half feet. This was SS-*Untersturmführer* Amon Göth. He came to us in the ghetto and demanded to speak with some doctors. Dr. Aleksander Biberstein, a respected internist and specialist for infectious diseases who had been our family doctor for years, gave details of this meeting in 1946, during Göth's trial for war crimes.

> About the middle of February [1943]—so, while the barracks were being built—the Jewish community instructed me, on orders from Göth, to go to the camp. I was on my way to the camp with Dr. Schwarz to discuss with the accused the construction of a hospital and sanitary facilities in the camp, as the Jewish community had informed us. We arrived at the camp under escort. We did not find the accused in the barracks where we were waiting. After a while, the accused came and asked us very politely to sit down, meanwhile offering us cigarettes. By the way, I wish to emphasize that the words "Jew" or "inmate" did not occur a single time during the entire conversation, in contrast to what Göth said later. Göth continued, saying that he wanted the workers to be well fed and have excellent medical care. He said he planned to have special barracks built for intellectuals. As for their clothes, he would construct a laundry building and they would receive freshly washed things each week. This conference made a good impression on some of our colleagues. But I thought it was a cunning, malicious lie.[20]

In February 1943, I got only a brief glimpse of Göth in the Jewish community offices. I didn't really become familiar with him until the fourth extermination campaign, during the dissolution of the ghetto on March 13 and 14, 1943. After that, we surviving Jews were herded into the Kraków-Płaszów camp, officially called a forced labor camp.

A few days before the ghetto was liquidated, my father had a serious accident on the construction site at the Kraków airport. He got caught beneath a truck and suffered a complicated fracture of his lower left leg and ankle, which had to be put into a cast. His leg never healed completely, and he limped a bit for the rest of his life. But at the time he was lying in the ghetto hospital and then in our miserable lodgings, hardly able to move. I knew the SS could deport him at any time. I realized that the dissolution of the ghetto was imminent when David Gutter directed me to issue certificates to members of the community's board of directors to affix onto the doors of their apartments. The text was something like, "This is the apartment of such and such and is therefore not to be evacuated." I produced about a dozen such letters of safe-conduct, stamped by the SS and the police. I was convinced that without a safe-conduct letter on your door, you were destined to die or be deported.

Without further ado, therefore, I removed a portion of my father's cast above his knee and lifted him onto the box of a horse-drawn brewery wagon. I knew Herr Klinger, the owner of the transport company. He had been my uncle's business partner. For months, he had been driving his wagon regularly between the ghetto and the Płaszów camp, transporting various goods: at first bread, later suitcases and other things. I asked him to take my father directly into the camp. "I'm happy to take your father along. However," he added in concern, "if a crate falls off the wagon and a policeman orders your father to put it back, it will come out that he can't walk. What then?" Undeterred, I stuck by my request and said, "I'll have to run that risk." I figured it was better than the certainty that if he stayed, he wouldn't be alive the next day.

My mother had already moved from the ghetto to the camp without any problems. She was now working in the tailoring and mending workshop of the Viennese clothing manufacturer Julius Madritsch, who had moved his business from the ghetto into the camp a few weeks earlier. At the time, Madritsch and Oskar Schindler employed hundreds of Jewish workers in their factories. My brother had also long since succeeded in getting into the camp. He had seized an opportunity to join one of the many transport squads that for weeks had been carrying people's few possessions from the ghetto into the camp barracks at the edge of town. He was seventeen, but still looked very young. On account of that, he might not have obtained an official authorization to go to the camp. Later, when assembling lists of prisoners, we always made him two or three years older than he really was.

Only about eight thousand people survived the massacre and the terror that were part of the liquidation of the Kraków ghetto on March 13 and 14, 1943. David Gutter kept me in the ghetto until the last minute, in case anything needed to be typed. On the afternoon of March 14, I was one of the last people to head for the Płaszów camp. As we left the ghetto, we still didn't know that a much worse situation had befallen us, that new depths of lawlessness awaited us.

SS-*Untersturmführer* Amon Göth, the camp commandant, had been transferred from Lublin to Kraków only a few weeks before, having earned himself a fearful reputation during the liquidation of the ghetto in the Lublin district. But we didn't know that at the time. After our shocking experiences during the last two days of the Kraków ghetto, we soon associated the name Amon Göth with the image of a brutal murderer who seemed to know no pity. Earlier, a very different rumor had been making the rounds, as Henryk Mandel, a former prisoner, confirmed in

After the liquidation of the Kraków ghetto, March 1943.

his testimony at Amon Göth's 1946 trial: "We heard a rumor that the new commandant was from Vienna and that the conditions in the camp would now improve. By the second day, we realized what sort of improvement this would be. The accused called a meeting of all the shop stewards and gave a speech. He declared that he was taking over the Kraków-Płaszów camp and would expect everyone to carry out his orders to the letter. To prove he meant what he said, he had a certain number of blows administered to each one of them. A few days later, two women were publicly hanged."[21] All the cruelties we had suffered up to then were now increased. Things got worse and worse. I wish upon no one the experience of finding out how much suffering he is capable of withstanding.

In the days after the bloody liquidation of the ghetto, the corpses were transported into the camp, where the dead were not properly buried but simply dumped into trenches and covered with dirt. During one of these transports, my brother helped rescue a child. A few days after having arrived in the Płaszów camp, my friend Izak Stern told me that his five-year-old nephew Menachem, the son of his younger brother Natan, had been smuggled into the camp in a rucksack by his parents on March 13. Now they had to smuggle the child out again and turn him over to Polish friends. (Poles could be executed for such a deed.) I asked my brother, who hadn't even met the Sterns at the time, to do everything possible to turn the child over to the Polish friends. Stefan gave a bottle of schnapps to the Ukrainian who was supposed to guard him during their trips between the camp and the ghetto. It didn't take long for the guard to get drunk, and in this way the little boy was taken out of the camp, hidden beneath some goods being transported. During a preplanned stop along the road, he was then quickly handed over to the Polish friends. Before the war, the Jaksch family had been customers of the Sterns' grandfather. Now they told their neighbors that little Menachem was the child of relatives who had been bombed out of their house in Warsaw. He was well received and looked after by this family, but was never allowed to bathe naked with other children, for he was circumcised. Today, Dr. Menachem Stern is a physician and lives in Tel Aviv. In 2004, he wrote, "I remember Stefan Pemper, the fourteen-year-old Jewish boy who helped me flee the camp in 1943."[22]

AMON GÖTH, OSKAR SCHINDLER, AND THE KRAKÓW-PŁASZÓW CAMP

IN THE THIRD WEEK OF MARCH, Amon Göth asked the typists already working in the camp to tell him who had written the letters for the Jewish community. They gave him two names: Heinz Dressler and Mietek Pemper. Heinz is a half year older than I. After the war, he moved to the United States. He went into Göth's office for a trial dictation. Heinz was much better qualified than I, having attended a commercial high school in Dresden. He had been taught perfect German shorthand, while I had learned it primarily through self-study. He emerged from the office after only a few minutes. Then it was my turn. When I entered, Göth told me that he was also looking for an interpreter, and since Heinz Dressler spoke hardly any Polish, he was choosing me. And so, against my will, Göth commandeered me to be his typist and personal secretary. In fact, during my first months in the camp, I was the only secretary in the commandant's office. I knew that Göth mistreated even the people who worked in his immediate environment. Some were cruelly tortured, others shot. Now, day in and day out, I had to work for a mass murderer. There was no possibility of escape from the job I was forced to do. My chances of survival were slim.

Those prisoners working in the commandant's barracks or other offices where they were in regular contact with German personnel were housed in separate quarters. The SS feared communicable diseases, and thought that by housing us separately, they could protect themselves from the recurrent infections that swept through the camp. I shared a three-man bunk in the barracks for "clerks and bookkeepers" with my friends Izak and Natan Stern, who worked in other offices. Every morning at dawn, I bid the Sterns farewell as if I were setting off on a dangerous journey, not knowing whether at day's end I would return unharmed, badly injured, or dead. My fellow prisoners could see me walk the few hundred yards down a hilly path to the office of the commandant, right next to the camp's main entrance. Every day, I spent several hours with Amon Göth. Every day, I feared for my life. The mental agony I suffered is almost impossible to describe. Words fail me.

One evening, after I had been taking dictation from Göth for a few days, I said to Izak and Natan, "Just imagine, we're inmates now. Today I wrote a letter to the Chamber of Foreign Trade in Kraków stating that such and such a Jew is unable to keep his appointment there because he is an inmate in the 'Jewish forced labor camp of the SS and police chief of the Kraków district.' So we aren't inhabitants of the ghetto with a field office on Jerozolimska Street in Kraków anymore. No, we're inmates in a forced labor camp." We had lost all our civil rights.

Under these changed circumstances, the first thing I had to do was help my father. He desperately needed a job where he could sit down and did not have to appear for the daily roll call. The slight limp he had from the accident at the airport had to be concealed at all costs. Early in the summer of 1943, an SS man showed up in the commandant's anteroom. As was often the case, Göth and his adjutant were somewhere else in the camp or had gone into town. At that time, we hadn't yet been issued prison uniforms, and I was wearing a simple shirt and sweater from my days in the ghetto. The young man said he was SS-*Rottenführer* Müller and had been charged with the establishment of a camp bakery. I struck up a conversation with him, and soon we were into technical details about how many pounds of bread you could make from two hundred pounds of flour, how much water you had to add, and how the amount of water depended on whether you used sixty percent flour from the first milling or seventy percent flour.

Finally, Müller asked how I knew so much about the subject and I told him about my father. "Hm," he said, "then your father could work as a baker for us . . ."

"No, he's not a baker. He's an expert on flour and grains. He could possibly work as . . ."

"All right, then, he could be our chief storekeeper." And so from then on, my father had a relatively secure job that protected him from being harassed by the SS. In addition, the bakery personnel were not required to stand on the parade ground for roll call.

I seldom saw my family while I was a prisoner in the camp. I assumed—and was later able to confirm—that Göth had people spying on me. He wanted to find out if I talked to other people about my work. But I knew that any conversation about what went on in camp headquarters would put me and my family in mortal danger. That's why I avoided any regular contact with my parents and said nothing about my work in the commandant's office. Via friends and acquaintances, my family was able to keep in discreet contact with each other and exchange news. It was also a great advantage that from time to time, my mother, my brother, and I would receive extra bread rations from my father. Otherwise, terrible hunger prevailed in the camp. At Göth's trial, Regina Nelken testified, "We were issued a loaf of black bread a week. The soup was inedible. In view of these circumstances, those who worked outside the camp felt it their duty to help those working in the camp. They brought bread, sugar, and cigarettes back into the camp from outside, and risked their lives to do so. Göth once shot to death an entire group of bakers—there were sixty of them—he had caught with white bread."[23]

We suspected that Göth and his SS team were misappropriating foodstuffs meant for us inmates and selling them on the black market. Dr. Aleksander Biberstein confirmed our suspicions in his postwar testimony:

> Each inmate was provided with provisions amounting to no more than 700 to 800—on rare occasions perhaps a bare 900—

> calories per day. But we were supposed to get 2,200 to 2,500 calories. So each inmate only got a third of that each day. To improve the meager provisions for the sick, I established contact with a warehouseman by the name of Fass with whom I had been acquainted before the war. I thus gained access to the warehouse. Every day, I visited the kitchen and storerooms, where I saw unbelievable amounts of all kinds of food that had been brought there from town. There was pearl barley, expensive liqueurs, and various kinds of vodka. Moreover, a patient I knew, a butcher named Feig, told me that large amounts of grade A meat got delivered to the camp. It was also well known that the accused often invited his good friends from the Gestapo and high-ranking SS officers to drinking bouts in his private quarters within the camp.[24]

Approximately ten thousand inmates were employed in the camp's workshops in 1944. This required an enormous administrative apparatus, with orders, confirmations, messages, and requests for repairs being constantly shuttled back and forth. Of course, there were telephones in the commandant's office and in all the shops and their offices, but the paperwork within the camp was always hand-carried by messenger. These young people performed their task with extreme reluctance because they feared the arbitrary harassment of the SS men they constantly encountered on their rounds. Some feared to catch sight of Göth even from afar, for that could be risky. Moshe Bejski, who became one of Israel's highest judges after the war, told a TV interviewer, "Quite often when Göth left his villa and walked down to the office, he would simply shoot a person or two in cold blood along the way."[25] As much as possible, the inmates hid, changed the direction they were walking, or otherwise inconspicuously avoided Göth. For this reason, I'm sure none of my fellow prisoners envied me my work in his office. This became apparent when I wanted to recruit some of my former colleagues from the Jewish community to help me with the secretarial work. "What?" they cried fearfully. "Please don't put in a request for us!" They even begged my parents to intercede on *their* behalf (not on mine!). They feared having to spend any time at all around Göth, to say nothing of having to work for him.

Wherever Göth happened to be standing—be it in front of the administrative building or next to the SS barracks—whenever he needed me, he sent a messenger to fetch me, and I had to appear before him immediately. I took dictation standing up and then returned to the office to make the telephone calls involved, see to obtaining whatever was needed, and type up what I had been assigned. I was in his presence day in and day out for over five hundred days: from March 18, 1943, until he was arrested in Vienna on September 13, 1944.

Göth had himself shaved every day, usually in his villa but now and then in the office. Sometimes he shouted so menacingly at the barber that the poor man trembled—not exactly helpful when you're shaving someone with a straight razor. Unfortunately, I've forgotten the name of his barber. I only remember that he intentionally injured his own right hand so that he wouldn't have to shave Göth any more. No such avenue of escape was open to me, however. I had to be at Göth's beck and call—every day, no matter what time or how long it would take.

I would sit in the commandant's office and take dictation from him. While he talked, Göth would watch the mirror outside his window, which he used to oversee the area in front of the barracks. Suddenly he would stand up, take one of the rifles from the rack on the wall, and open the window. I would hear a few shots and then nothing but screams. As if he had interrupted the dictation only to take a telephone call, Göth would come back to his desk and say, "Where were we?" These bland words spoken in a calm voice still bring back to me every detail of that time, over sixty years later.

The sheer amount of clerical work was so great that it would have been enough for at least two secretaries. But since none of

Plan of the Płaszów Concentration Camp

1 Commandant's offices
2 SS barracks
3 "Gray House"
4 "Red House"
5 Göth's villa
6 Pen for Göth's dogs
7 Latrines
8 Brick warehouses
9 Warehouse for personal effects confiscated from inmates
10 Stone quarry
11 Kitchen
12 Stables
13 Garage
14 Housing for Germans
15 SS infirmary
16 Baths for camp inmates
17 Yard for building materials
18 Inmates' infirmary
19 World War I Austrian fortification, used as an execution site
20 Barracks for inmates

industrial workshops

industrial workshops

garages

← to Wieliczka

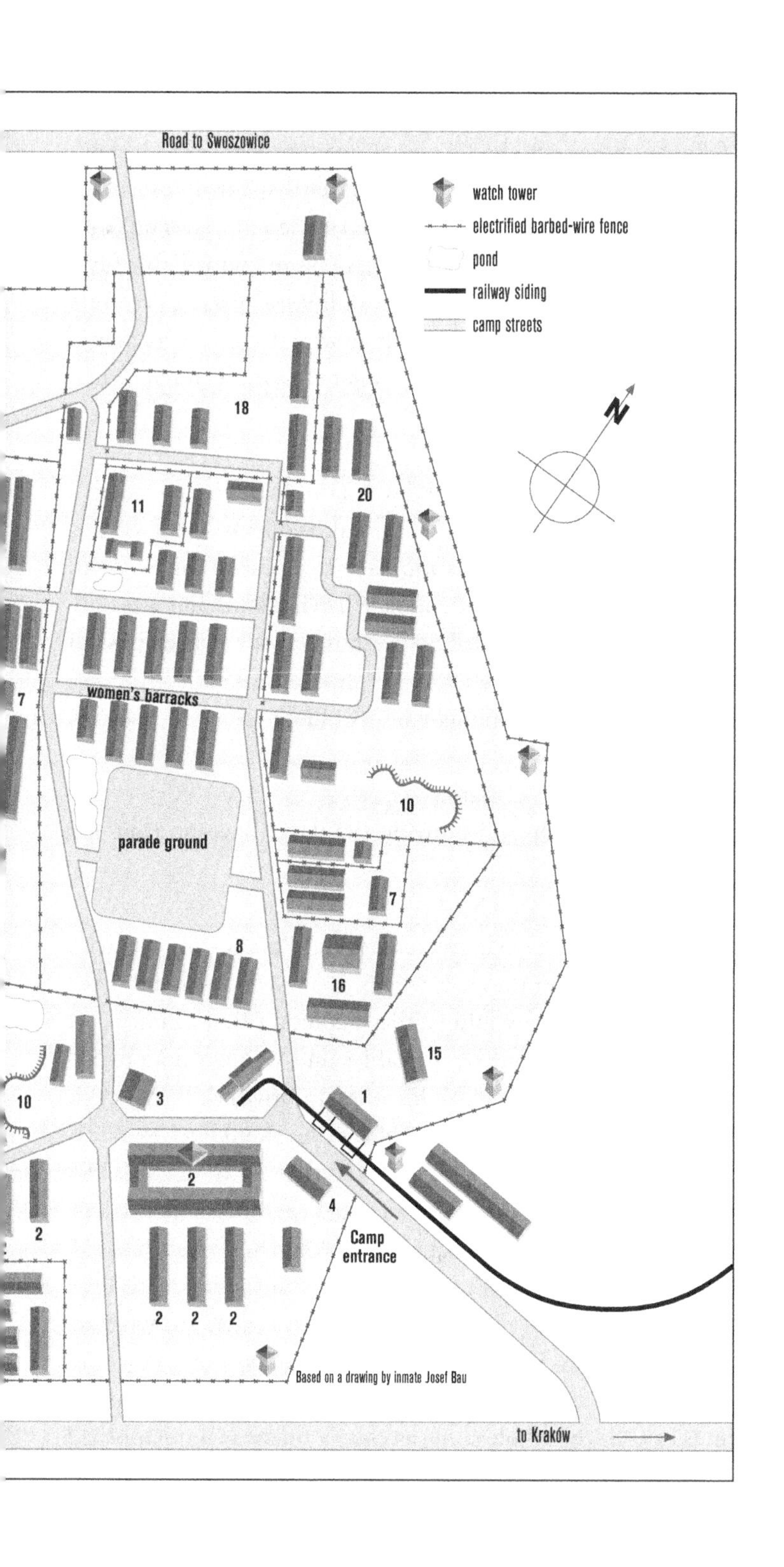

Road to Swoszowice
watch tower
electrified barbed-wire fence
pond
railway siding
camp streets
N
18
11
20
women's barracks
7
10
parade ground
7
8
16
15
10
3
1
2
4
2
Camp
entrance
2
2
2
Based on a drawing by inmate Josef Bau
to Kraków

my fellow inmates who had the qualifications wanted to be anywhere near Göth, I denied myself the request for an assistant. What if a fellow prisoner I had requested made a mistake and Göth in fact physically abused him or even, in his uncontrollable fury, killed him? I refused to take responsibility for placing even one more prisoner directly into the daily mortal danger I was in myself. I preferred to finish the accumulated work at night, when Göth was not present.

One night shortly after midnight, I was alone in the commandant's headquarters, finishing up work as usual. Suddenly, the door was flung open and there stood Göth, back from carousing in town. He peered sharply around the room. When he saw that it was only me, attending to the files piled on two tables that had been pushed together, his body relaxed and he almost looked a little disappointed. Perhaps he thought he would catch me at some illicit activity.

"Why are you doing that now?"

"There's so much to do during the day I have no time for the files."

"Then get someone to help you."

"Many thanks, *Herr Commandeur*, but I'm the only one who knows where certain things get filed. If someone else did it for me, then maybe there would be files I couldn't find again."

Göth sat down at one of the tables and wrote a note to SS-*Obersturmführer* Heinz Kühler, his administrative head: "My clerk Pemper often needs to work at night, so he should get extra rations." He was mumbling as if dictating the text to himself, "So and so many grams of fat and so and so many grams of marmalade per week." He looked at me inquisitively, "And how much bread?"

"Thank you, but I don't need bread," I answered truthfully. "My father is chief storekeeper in the bakery, where the workers get an extra ration. He gives some of that to me."

Göth leaned way back in his chair and looked at me in amazement. (I can see the whole scene as clearly today as if it happened yesterday.) Then he shook his head incredulously and said, "You're no Jew, Pemper! A Jew would have accepted it all and exchanged it later for something else." I accepted Göth's insult in silence, for I had to avoid getting involved in a discussion with him. It is all the same to a condemned man whether he gets a little more bread or a little less. All I could do was to try to delay my execution as long as possible in the interest of my family.[26]

The translations of official documents from German into Polish or vice versa that I had to do for Göth were for the most part similar to those I had done for the Jewish community. Once, however, Göth ordered me to accompany him to the interrogation of a fellow inmate. I was supposed to translate the man's "confessions" for him. But my dismay and horror at the cruel methods used by the SS upset me so much that instead of translating, all I could do was repeat word for word the fragments of what the tortured man was crying out in his pain in Polish. Göth was angry, but instead of punishing me, he sent me back to the office. After that, he chose other interpreters for his interrogations.

Göth's punishments were draconian. Inmates were beaten almost to death just for smuggling a little bread and sausage into the camp. During Göth's trial, my fellow prisoner Henryk Mandel described the punishment he and a number of other inmates received for smuggling in food. First he was berated at the main entrance by the guard who discovered his contraband: "Our soldiers are starving at the front and you want to gorge yourself on bread and sausage and butter!" Then the guard informed Göth, who had the senior Jewish inmate Wilek (Wilhelm) Chilowicz bring him the whips from the guardhouse. Two other trusties brought two tables and a bucket of water. Then the procedure began.

> We had to count out loud and they warned us not to miss a beat or the whole punishment would begin again. We really tried to count correctly. After a hundred lashes, we got an additional blow to the head if we didn't get down from the table

> quickly enough. Inmate Meitlis's turn came right after mine. He was an older guy, weak, and he screamed dreadfully. After thirty lashes, Göth ordered the count restarted in order to shut him up. In the process, Meitlis was also struck on the head countless times. So they began the count again, but Meitlis just screamed louder. Göth then picked up a brick and struck Meitlis so hard on the back of the head that he broke the brick in two. Meitlis got another hundred lashes. After the beating, each of us had to report to Göth, who then asked if we were satisfied and if we knew why we had been punished. Meitlis got down off the table, reported to Göth, and then turned away. At that moment, Göth pulled his revolver and shot Meitlis in the back of the head. Göth then ordered that none of us was to be bandaged or disinfected with iodine. Our bodies were torn from the beatings, we were all bleeding. Later came the order to get to work. At the time, a barracks was being built for the guards. We were given wheelbarrows and shovels and were supposed to bring dirt into the camp at a run. Some of the army guards, however, took pity on us and had thirty other prisoners take our place. It was only thanks to them that we survived that dreadful day.[27]

After Göth had shot or tortured someone to death, he had the names and camp numbers of that person's entire family looked up in the camp files, so that he could kill them as well. On one such occasion, he remarked, "I don't want anyone to be dissatisfied in my camp." What an absurdity! As if the rest of us in the camp were satisfied or content! But since hearing that remark, I knew I could not afford to make even the slightest mistake. For if he shot me, I thought, he would also kill my family, and that must not happen. It was a heavy burden for me to bear, but it meant that I never allowed myself to think of giving up. Helen Jonas-Rosenzweig, one of Göth's two housemaids, told an interviewer that worries about her family were always uppermost in her mind: "I never feared death. Göth always carried a small pistol with him. I was never afraid to die; what I feared was having to watch him murder my mother or my sister."[28]

Some of the witnesses at Amon Göth's trial in the fall of 1946 described him as a giant with a remarkably soft and gentle face. But appearances are deceptive. In the blink of an eye he could metamorphose into a raging beast. In the beginning, Göth sometimes took me along on his inspection tours of the camp. After a few such times, my fellow inmates told me to try to accompany Göth more often on his rounds. I was surprised by the remark, and asked them why. "Well," they replied, "if Göth has you along, he doesn't just pull out his pistol and knock someone off." Often, when Göth carried out an inspection or turned up somewhere in camp unexpectedly, he would just shoot some inmate to death whether he had an excuse to or not. I suddenly became aware of what I had been doing unconsciously up to then: I had learned to read and assess the signs of rising inner tension on Göth's face. I had quickly been forced to recognize when an outburst was imminent that could cost an innocent inmate his life. In such situations, I was able to distract Göth with some comment. I would cautiously remind him that there was a conference scheduled at an SS office in town that day, or there was a telephone call he needed to make, or a letter that had to be answered. Whereupon, he would calm down. Göth was like a bottle of soda water you have shaken before opening it—literally "eruptive." This also taught me that on no account should I redirect his anger toward *myself*, for who would distract him then? Who would prevent my own execution at the last minute?

Göth's dogs, a huge Great Dane named Rolf and a mongrel named Alf, would usually accompany him on his rounds through the camp and elsewhere as well. Alf was supposedly a mixture of German shepherd and Siberian wolf. In any event, it was an extremely aggressive animal. The dogs ran free through the camp with their master and were possibly his cruelest weapon. They were trained to attack on command, or to attack anyone who approached their master at a run from behind. Both of them were not just theoretically capable of tearing a person to death; they proved they could on several of my poor fellow prisoners.

One day, a few weeks after I began working in the commandant's office, Göth was standing with some other SS men outside the Red House, near the camp entrance. Before leaving for a conference in town, he had to sign a few letters. I approached him with the folder containing them. He gestured to me to hurry, and then turned around to continue speaking to the SS men. I began running toward Göth from behind, when the two dogs immediately rushed toward me to attack. I stopped short and had just enough time to back against the wall of the house, so the two dogs couldn't pull me down right away. The Great Dane bit my right upper arm and his teeth went through my heavy sweater, my shirt, my skin and muscle, right down to the bone.

At that moment, Göth looked around for his dogs, saw what had happened, and called them off. They then stopped attacking me, and I picked up the folder of letters and took them to Göth, knowing that the next bite probably would have killed me.

In the camp hospital, they could only patch up the wound; there was no medicine to fight a possible infection, nor for the sharp pains that began as soon as the shock had worn off. Immediately after my wound was seen to, I returned to work. Since I was unable to bend my right arm, I was forced to perform my duties standing up and with my arm stretched straight out. Later, Göth asked me why I stood up to work. When I replied that it was because of the dog bite, he had no further comment.

The second time I got injured was also the result of a misunderstanding. In the spring of 1944, Göth had been issued a large number of coupons to procure iron, probably because of his connections in the office that rationed metal. Metal was scarce, so these coupons were valuable. They were to go to the German workshop supervisor Bigell, but Bigell told me to bring them to the inmate who kept track of overall metal consumption in the camp. When Göth later asked Bigell what had become of the coupons, he gave him the vague answer, "Pemper passed them on." Göth sent for me immediately. "Where are those iron coupons?" he yelled.

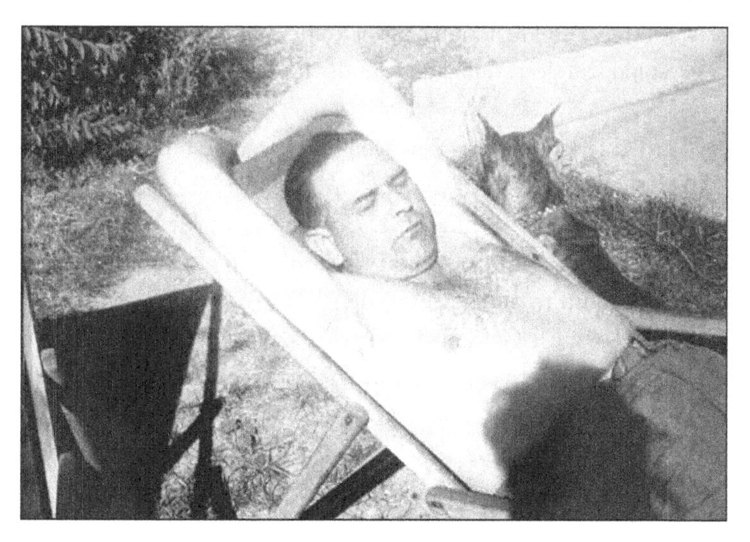

Amon Göth with his dog Rolf outside his villa on the grounds of the Kraków-Płaszów camp.

"Herr Bigell directed me to pass them on to . . ." Before I could finish my sentence, Göth struck me in the face with his riding crop, according to the principle, "Shoot first and ask questions later." He assumed that Bigell had misappropriated the coupons.

Bigell was more than just a rascal. He was an incorrigible, cold-blooded murderer. On February 15, 1967, Oskar Schindler made the following deposition:

> Karlheinz Bigell always wore civilian clothes. He was supposedly a war invalid. I know that Bigell shot the Gutter family to death, because SS men told me about it. According to them, it happened as follows: Bigell had been drinking with Göth and others. They were making fun of Bigell, saying he didn't have the guts to knock off a Jew. So Bigell sent for David Gutter and his family, whom he knew personally—David Gutter and his wife and two children. And then, in his drunken state, he shot all four of them in the main street of the camp. It must have been between two and four A.M. He obviously thought of it as a test of courage. I ran into Bigell in the main railroad

> station in Frankfurt am Main in 1946, and I asked him how he could still sleep at night. He said, "It's just four less Jews."[29]

As Göth's clerk, I not only observed his character, but also learned a lot about his personal life and his career in the SS. Amon Leopold Göth was born in Vienna on December 4, 1908. He attended primary school and a secondary school or *Realgymnasium*—a high school up to the tenth grade. By 1930, he had joined the National Socialist German Workers' Party (NSDAP) and the SS in Vienna. But three years later, when the party was legally banned in Austria, he fled to Munich. On March 9, 1940, he was sent to Katowice as an SS-*Oberscharführer* and administrative officer. In November 1941, he was deployed as an SS-*Untersturmführer* S (special leader of SS and police). And on August 10, 1942, Göth was promoted to *Sonderführer* (special leader) of the Waffen-SS. As the leader of a special squad, Göth participated in operations in the Lublin ghetto under the command of the infamous Odilo Globocnik, SS and police chief of Lublin. There, he distinguished himself in the eyes of his SS superiors to such a degree that as part of his new assignment in Płaszów, he also directed the liquidation of the Kraków ghetto on March 13 and 14, 1943.

Even after he was transferred to Płaszów, he still received correspondence about the earlier operations. One of these letters had to do with a place named Bełżyce. In the course of targeting people to be exterminated, Göth had apparently confiscated and then misappropriated a large number of tanned hides. Something must have gone wrong, for several letters were exchanged with regard to the matter. By chance, I also saw that Göth possessed a special permit from Globocnik to inspect "classified construction projects of the Reich" and it was in this context that I first came across the name "Wirth." After the war, I learned that for a period, Christian Wirth had been the *Lagerleiter* or commandant of Bełżec. That meant that Globocnik is likely to have authorized Göth to inspect the construction of the three death camps at Treblinka, Sobibor, and Bełżec. He may also have been one of the SS men under the command of Globocnik's deputy, SS-*Sturmbannführer* Hermann Höfle, all of whom swore an oath in the summer of 1943, "not to impart to people outside the circle of one's colleagues, under any circumstances, whether orally or in writing, information of any kind whatsoever about the progress, execution, or occurrences during the resettlement of the Jews." For all matters pertaining to "Jewish resettlement were '*Geheime Reichsache*'"—top secret.[30]

On July 28, 1943, Göth got a promotion that jumped him two ranks, to SS-*Hauptsturmführer* F (Specialist SS and police leader). He received his letter of appointment at the instigation of General Krüger, supported by SS and police chief Julian Scherner.[31] On April 20, 1944, he was finally able to get himself named SS reserve leader, a request that had earlier been denied because he had not served in the army and had no combat experience whatsoever. Around June 1944, Amon Göth was promoted again. Now he was officially in the officers' ranks.[32] The chief of the main SS personnel office in Berlin, General Maximilian von Herff, even added a handwritten "Congratulations!" to the letter of appointment. Göth was exceedingly proud and in better spirits than I had ever seen him before. He liked to show the letter around and even showed it to me. You could hardly believe this was the same Göth who tortured prisoners and set his dogs on them. The fact that in 1943, Göth could rise to the post of camp commandant as a *Untersturmführer* was likely the result of lack of personnel and the fiasco on the eastern front.

In 1943, the forced labor camps in the Generalgouvernement were officially under the jurisdiction of the local SS and police chiefs. But there were hardly any standardized guidelines, much less definitive rules, for running a forced labor camp. Judging from what I was able to learn in the commandant's office, Göth possessed the authority to act on his own, a master over life and death. And so we prisoners lived in constant uncertainty and mortal fear. There are no words to describe our condition. Halina Nelken, a young woman who was a fellow inmate of mine, later called

Płaszów a "planet within a surreal cosmos."[33] When the work details returned to camp in the evening and wanted to know what had gone on in the camp during the day, the other inmates would call out what sounded like soccer scores to them, "Three to nothing" or "Four to nothing." In fact, it meant that Göth had already shot three or four prisoners that day. This was the code to let everyone know how the day had gone so far.

Göth almost always meted out the harshest punishments, even for the slightest offences. One particularly harsh punishment was to spend the night in a *Stehbunker*—"standing bunker"—and then have to report for work the following day. The *Stehbunker* were tiny, walled-in cells in which it was impossible either to lie down or stand upright. Even sitting was impossible. They were located in the basement of the so-called Gray House, which still stands today on the site of the former camp. The noncommissioned officers lived on its first and second floors. In 1944, after Göth was arrested by the SS for malfeasance, I was put in solitary confinement there for two weeks and saw the *Stehbunker* with my own eyes.

In his letters to his father, Göth mentioned several times that he was busy with the expansion of the camp and had discovered how much fun he had with the planning and architecture involved. He was toying with the idea of attending university after the war and becoming an architect, but it was clear to him that it wouldn't be easy at his age. At the same time, day in and day out, he couldn't help observing the Jewish engineer and camp architect Zygmunt Grünberg, whose enormous skill went far beyond anything Göth could ever hope to achieve, even in some distant future. For every challenge and issue related to construction or building technique, Grünberg had the answer. Where others gave up, Grünberg could always find a solution. Göth was visibly impressed. But he must have envied Grünberg tremendously and hated him for it, too. He constantly struck him and cruelly tormented him. I was present when Göth had a row of houses just outside the camp torn down and then wanted Grünberg to tell him how many bricks could be salvaged. Grünberg immediately began to do the calculation in his head, but Göth wanted an instantaneous answer. "Faster, faster," he screamed while striking Grünberg mercilessly. At his trial in 1946, Göth was asked by the prosecutor, "Did the accused have the right to beat the engineer Grünberg?" Without the least sign of remorse, he answered, "I did have the right to."[34] Göth tried to rationalize his cruel methods by citing the acute lack of personnel. Most of the men in the guard details were former Russian POWs who had been given brief training in Trawniki, an SS training camp near Lublin. Göth explained that they were not as reliable as his German personnel. That was why he had to maintain a "strict regimen" within the camp.

Göth liked to display the success of this "regimen" to official visitors. In the summer of 1943, three or fourth months after the ghetto was emptied, General Friedrich-Wilhelm Krüger held an inspection in the Kraków-Płaszów camp. It was the first time I had seen a German SS general from close up. Krüger was accompanied by SS men with carbines at the ready—one on his right and another on his left—who would have shot on the spot anyone who got too close to him. Before the inspection, we had to work day and night to get the camp "whipped into shape." The camp streets were swept; everything had to look "tip-top." Of course, the inmates had to stay out of sight while Krüger was walking around the camp. In the main office, I too tried to make myself as inconspicuous as possible.

Göth was enormously ambitious. In order to hasten his rise through the ranks of the SS, he attempted to distinguish himself through excesses of terrible violence and was in fact partially successful. For example, he was able to advance to *Hauptsturmführer* without having been an *Obersturmführer*, and until the SS arrested him in 1944, he was well launched on his career. But in his drive to succeed, he would often bypass the deputies of his superiors, which made them very resentful. Even while still in Lublin, he made enemies with his ruthless behavior and provoked the hostility of his immediate superior, SS-*Obersturmbannführer* Hermann Höfle.

Probably for that reason, and also to avoid further conflicts, Göth was transferred to Kraków. There it was SS-*Sturmbannführer* Willi Haase whom Göth would have liked to shove aside immediately. He took every opportunity to bypass him and sought direct contact with Haase's boss, SS-*Oberführer* Julian Scherner. Scherner participated in the drunken evenings in Göth's villa. There, on the wall of the trophy room, hung the framed saying, "Whoever shoots first gets more out of life." I saw it when I was waiting to be interrogated after Göth's arrest in the fall of 1944. Sayings like that were typical of Göth's sense of humor. I was standing next to him once while he was overseeing inmates who were carrying one huge rock each from the quarry by the road for the foundation of a new barracks. He turned to the other SS officers in attendance and laughed, "This is my new Einstein theory!" (In German, *ein Stein* means "one stone.") It was important to Göth that people laugh at his jokes, that no one contradict him, and that he possess absolute power over the people around him. His high level of energy and criminal intelligence were a dangerously explosive mixture.

In my darkest hours in the camp, when despair threatened to crush me, there were three things I would recall to lift my spirits and give myself courage: Winston Churchill's "blood, toil, tears, and sweat" speech, the progress of the German invasion of Russia, and the Japanese attack on Pearl Harbor. Churchill delivered his speech before Parliament on May 13, 1940, shortly before the anticipated fall of France. It was very pithy, promising to defeat Germany, whatever the cost:

> I have nothing to offer but blood, toil, tears and sweat. . . . We have before us many, many long months of struggle and of suffering. You ask, what is our policy? I can say: It is to wage war, by sea, land and air, with all our might and with all the strength that God can give us; to wage war against a monstrous tyranny, never surpassed in the dark, lamentable catalogue of human crime. That is our policy. You ask, what is our aim? I

> can answer in one word: It is victory, victory at all costs, victory in spite of all terror, victory, however long and hard the road may be; for without victory, there is no survival.[35]

Even before I had read the end of the speech, I had tears in my eyes. I was crying like a baby as I typed it out for our *gazetki.*

To be sure, Churchill's speech did not prevent the signing of the cease-fire between France and Nazi Germany on June 22, 1940. France broke up into three parts. Northern France was occupied by the Germans, southern France was ruled by the Vichy-regime under Marshal Philippe Pétain, and General Charles de Gaulle led the free French regime into exile in London. A year later, on June 22, 1941, the German Wehrmacht invaded the Soviet Union. This was followed by the Japanese attack on the United States fleet in Pearl Harbor on December 7, 1941. Four days later, on December 11, Germany declared war on America. It was clear to me that Hitler now had no chance to win. He could not conquer the whole world. The only question was whether by the time he was defeated, we Jews would have been annihilated.

In the winter of 1941, we were still in the ghetto, and we could see how badly planned the campaign against Russia was, for we had to surrender all our fur coats, fur collars, and fur hats. Some Jews who tried to hide their furs were shot on the spot or sent to camps. That's how I lost my cousin Halina Liebeskind. She had tried to hide a fur coat she had inherited from her mother, who had passed away. Halina was very attached to the garment, which held many memories for her. She was taken to the camp in Lublin and died there.

It was clear to us that they needed our furs for the German soldiers on the eastern front. At the time I thought to myself, did the strategists really think the Wehrmacht could overrun Russia without having to encounter the proverbial Russian winter? Hadn't they learned anything from history? Napoleon's campaign of 1822 also began in June, and it was the terrible winter that forced the *Grande Armée* to retreat. And from these things I derived hope.

It was good we found sources of hope then, for we would need them more than ever when events took a further turn against us in 1942. As a result of the Wannsee Conference in January of that year, Jews were placed in mortal danger. It was at Wannsee that the Nazis coordinated the murder of all Jews in areas under German control as soon as possible. On January 25, 1942, Adolf Hitler declared to his *Reichsführer* SS Heinrich Himmler, "The Jew must get out of Europe. I'm only saying he must go. If he gets destroyed in the process, I can't help it."[36] At the same time, there was a contradictory strategy, stemming from the needs of the war, that had been beneficial to us in the ghetto and continued to be so now that we were in a forced labor camp. Only a day after Hitler's declaration quoted above, Himmler issued a directive to General Richard Glücks, at that time the inspector-general of all concentration camps, that in the coming weeks, he was to accommodate a hundred thousand additional Jewish men and fifty thousand Jewish women in his camps. With this directive, Himmler was by no means deviating from his ultimate intention to murder all Jews, but the ominous developments and losses on the Nazis' eastern front had caused an acute shortage of workers in the German Reich, and the adverse course of the war forced Himmler to adopt a new policy. In the three months from November 1941 to January 1942, half a million Russian POWs had died in German camps. These men were no longer available as workers in German industries. Now the Nazis spoke bluntly of "extermination by work."

Today, we have access to the minutes of meetings of the Generalgouvernement at that time, in which the shift in policy is clearly evident. Chief Arms Inspector Major General Maximilian Schindler, whose office was in Kraków, told Governor General Frank that it was ill-advised to remove Jewish workers from industry. In principle, he was in favor of "evacuation" (i.e., eventual extermination), but he recommended keeping the Jews on "as workers for the remainder of the war."[37] On July 15, 1942, the official diary of Governor General Frank notes that "almost all repairs of uniforms and boots" for soldiers on the eastern front were carried out by Jewish forced laborers.[38] Ten months later, in May 1943, after returning from a meeting with Himmler in Berlin, General Schindler even expressed the view that "in the final analysis, the wishes of the *Reichsführer* SS" would probably "not be able to be fulfilled." Himmler would have to "give up on the removal of these Jewish workers."[39] That was exactly four months after the German capitulation at Stalingrad.

Having followed such news as I could while in the ghetto, I tried to keep up once I was in the Płaszów camp as well. Whenever Göth and his adjutant were on errands in town, which was often, I was alone in the office and had access to three German newspapers: the *Völkischer Beobachter* from Berlin, the *Krakauer Zeitung*, and the more intellectually sophisticated weekly *Das Reich*. Göth subscribed to these papers and kept them in his anteroom. I was especially interested in *Das Reich* and enjoyed reading the columns of Joseph Goebbels. The propaganda minister was both a masterful writer and an evil demagogue.[40]

By the early summer of 1943, as a vigilant observer and critical reader of those publications, I became aware of how things stood for the Germans on the eastern front. In addition, there were many scraps of uncensored information that trickled through to me. I gleaned them from the conversations of the SS men who often gathered in the commandant's anteroom. Both my desk and that of Göth's adjutant were there. The SS men coming in for a chat had comrades at the front and would talk about the transports of badly wounded men arriving in Kraków every day from Russia. Also in the anteroom was a large cabinet with compartments into which I sorted all the mail that arrived for the SS men. Some of them had arranged with me to give them a signal if mail from home had come. Then they could enjoy the anticipation of news from their families on their way to the office. Most of them were respectable older men, not all of whom had volunteered for the SS. When they read their letters while still in the anteroom, they sometimes talked about Germany or about the situation on the western front. Contact with these men was often safer than with the guards from the Ukraine, Lithuania, or Latvia, who were former Soviet POWs the Nazis had trained to be guards. They were often inebriated and tended to be violent.

Early in the summer of 1943, a guard escorted a middle-aged man into the office. After the guard left, the prisoner and I were alone, he in a uniform unfamiliar to me and I in my inmate's clothes. He told me he was a Jew the Polish police had discovered during a security check at a train station. He was being sent to prison. I looked the man over and thought to myself, "You haven't a clue that you will be dead in a few hours." From my friend Heinz Dressler, who worked as a clerk for the chief of the camp's detention center, I knew that Göth "cleaned out" the camp prison from time to time by simply having the incarcerated shot to make room for new arrivals. "What's your profession?" I asked the man. "Watchmaker," he said. Hearing this, I remembered that the other day, I had overheard SS-*Untersturmführer* Leo John say he was looking for a specialist to repair old watches. The SS had probably pocketed some antique watches on one of their usual raids and wanted to get them cleaned and put in working order. "Can you repair old watches as well?" I asked. "It depends on what kind they are," the man answered cautiously. I looked him straight in the eye. "You *can* repair old watches. You've got to be able to." Now all I had to do was find out if Göth had already visited the camp prison, meaning there would be no more danger of a "clean out" that day. I called up Heinz and asked, "How does it look?" "Not yet, but it'll begin soon," he answered.

So until then, I had to hide the man. There was a small, empty room behind Göth's office that was almost never used. I put the prisoner in there and told him to just wait quietly for the time being.

When SS-*Untersturmführer* John came into the commandant's office later that afternoon, I told him I'd found someone who could repair old watches. He was delighted and had the man brought to the watch repair shop.

A few days later, I called Mr. Licht, the Jewish supervisor of the shop, to ask about his new colleague. He told me briefly that the man had quickly learned the ropes. I never talked to that man again, for I didn't want to endanger him or myself by giving him an opportunity to thank me for saving his life. It would have been much too dangerous for both of us. That was another diabolical thing about the camp: you could neither give nor receive any thanks. Unfortunately, I lost track of the watchmaker and don't know what became of him. But even his temporary rescue was an encouraging sign for me. I saw that I was able to do something, even if it was only a drop of water on a hot stone compared to the terrible afflictions all of us faced on a daily basis. It reinforced within me the well-known Talmudic teaching from my childhood: what counts is only what we do for others. It is more important than anything else.

In the office, I took care of the incoming mail, did filing, and for a while—at least in the beginning—maintained the records of how much ammunition the SS guards used. With the help of these records, I could calculate the number of inmates in the camp who had been shot within a certain period of time. From a personnel evaluation I was able to read, I learned that a certain Arvid Janetz, an SS man from Latvia, was a particularly "zealous" participant in executions. Until about the end of 1943, I had access to the personnel files of all the SS men within the camp. When the forced labor camp was converted into a concentration camp in January 1944, however, Göth had to appoint a special SS personnel officer to type up the files. But until then, I learned from Göth's dictation which guards were being commended or disciplined, who got his leave lengthened or shortened, and who was to be confined to barracks on the weekend. During this time, I felt like a condemned man who knows he must die, but not exactly when he will be executed. I was utterly convinced that Göth would allow me to live only as long as the camp existed and he needed me. My being constantly at his beck and call made things easy for him.

I even typed Göth's private correspondence to his SS friends—mostly comrades he had known during his time in Lublin—and to his father in Vienna. The letters to the senior Göth were addressed to his company on Mariahilfer Strasse 105, Vienna IV/56. In his letters, Göth would inquire whether his father had hay fever again or how his business was going. Amon Franz Göth ran a printing shop associated with a small company that published "military and technical works," and his son had detailed, specific ideas about the day-to-day business of the company. He suggested a series of postcards with Alpine scenes that he thought would be a hit on the market. He advised his father to ask General von Eisenhart-Rothe to write a foreword for a book his company was planning to publish. These were quite ordinary letters that gave

Amon Leopold Göth.

no hint of how violent a man Commandant Göth could be. But I do remember one letter to his wife, who lived in Innsbruck. I guessed that she had written him about their son Werner hitting his little sister Inge. With a good deal of manly pride, Göth dictated the reply to me: "Like father like son. Werner is really following in my footsteps."

Göth found it difficult to take orders and was always in conflict with his immediate superiors. He didn't get along well with Höfle, for example, who in his capacity as Globocnik's chief-of-staff had directed the liquidation of the Warsaw ghetto in May 1943. Göth was too independent for Höfle. He wanted to be his own boss and have his own camp. It wasn't enough for him to be the commandant of some satellite camp. He wanted to be his "own *commandeur*," as he put it. He always used the French word, although the official SS term was *Kommandant*. In his letters to his father, his old comrades in Lublin, as well as to his friend Egon Jaroschowitz, he emphasized again and again, "Now at last, I'm my own *commandeur.*"

At the end of March 1943, one of the first letters I typed for *commandeur* Göth was from the SS-*Hauptscharführer* Albert Hujer to Oskar Schindler. I had recently encountered Hujer during the liquidation of the ghetto on March 13 and 14, as he ran through the streets in a murderous frenzy, shooting wildly in all directions. He had even murdered patients lying in their hospital beds and their physician, Frau Dr. Blau, as well. And now Hujer was dictating to me a letter to Schindler, informing the factory director that his Emalia workers would no longer be allowed to walk the two and a half miles from the camp to his factory:

> TO: The German Enamelware Co., Kraków, Lipowa Street.
> IN RE: Custody of Jewish workers to and from the factory.
>
> By the order of the SS and police commandant, those requisitioning Jewish workers are responsible for providing armed civilian or military guards to accompany the Jews to

> and from their place of work. This order, issued as a pure matter of security, has been completely ignored by you.
>
> I personally carried out an inspection on March 28, 1943, and discovered that the civilians accompanying the Jews were not in possession of firearms.
>
> I hereby inform you that the Jewish workers assigned to you will immediately cease to be allowed to come to your factory. Signed, Göth.[41]

At that point in time, Göth had not yet met Oskar Schindler, who was the same age as he. But the genial Schindler immediately got in touch with Göth. He became outwardly friendly with him, and the two of them were soon addressing each other with the familiar *du*. From then on, Oskar Schindler came and went freely in the Płaszów camp.

Schindler was tall, powerfully built, and could hold his liquor. He visited Göth in the camp, supplied him with expensive cognac, partied with the SS men, and treated them to schnapps and cigarettes. In a uniform and on parade, he would have looked like a perfect Nazi, but he always wore tailor-made suits and had a bounce in his step. "Schindler was a handsome man," Göth's former housemaid said after the war. "He smelled wonderful. We heard his shoes; they made a special sound. He had an attitude like, 'Heads up! Here I come!' He wanted people to know who he was. He wanted to be admired. He had enormous self-assurance. He was self-satisfied, but in a pleasant way."[42]

My friend Izak Stern had known Schindler since 1940 and would remain his friend during and after the war. Before the war, Izak Stern had been active in Zionist youth work. He had been the office manager of the Jewish clothing manufacturer J. C. Buchheister, where Joseph Aue was the German trustee. Schindler had wanted to take over a Jewish clothing factory as a trustee, and so he came into contact with Izak Stern. Fortunately for us, however, nothing came of his plans. During the summer or fall of 1943, even clothing manufacturers producing uniforms for the

Wehrmacht, although they were "important to the war effort," were not considered "crucial for victory" and could be liquidated. If Schindler had not purchased the metal-working plant instead, Schindler's List would not have been possible.

Stern later told me that Schindler's business visits to Buchheister had led to conversations between them about Jewish philosophy. Schindler had shown off his scraps of knowledge on the subject. After we had been in the camp just a few weeks, Stern told me, "Oskar Schindler is a special person. You can speak openly with him. He wants to help us. He only looks a hundred percent Nazi, but he really isn't. He's very humane and not prejudiced against us Jews." In the camp, Stern was in charge of the workshop accounting office. Even though he never worked in Schindler's factory, it is possible that he was able to meet Schindler a few times in Lipowa Street. It was through Stern that I later came into contact with Schindler myself.

From March 1943 on, Schindler pretended to be Göth's loyal friend and fellow Nazi. In reality though, he exploited his contacts with Göth to protect his Jewish workers. Schindler continued to maintain this fiction even after Göth's arrest in the fall of 1944. He didn't want to run the risk that at the last minute Göth could somehow still harm his workers. Göth still thought he had a friend in Schindler in 1946, when he asked the court in Kraków to summon Oskar Schindler as a character witness (unsuccessfully, I might add).

In the fall of 1944, for tactical reasons, Schindler even offered to transport all of Göth's private belongings—shoes made to order, suits, furniture, carpets, and objets d'art—from Kraków to Brünnlitz. It was a huge favor, for trains were needed to transport the troops and the wounded and, of course, also for the deportation of Jews and opponents of the regime. The fact that Oskar Schindler was able to get a large shipment of personal effects onto the rails at that time is a clear indication of his talents. With the eastern front getting closer, Schindler obtained permission to move his armaments factory from Kraków to Brünnlitz, not far from his birthplace of Zwittau in the Sudetenland (today, Svitavy in the Czech Republic). He was allocated a number of boxcars for the move, and needed at least two of them to transport Göth's loot. Sure enough, Göth paid a visit to Brünnlitz in the spring of 1945, shortly before the German capitulation, to arrange for his booty to be shipped on to Austria. When the chief judge at Göth's trial in 1946 asked Edek Elsner, the head of Schindler's warehouse, how much stuff had been Göth's, Elsner gazed around the enormous courtroom with its two-story high ceiling and said, "About half this room full." Spectators in the courtroom laughed out loud and even shook their heads in disbelief.

By June 1943, more than two million Jews had already been murdered in the Generalgouvernement. There were only 120,000 left, distributed among fifty or sixty forced labor camps. With 12,000 inmates, Płaszów was one of the largest.[43] As other camps that only produced clothing began to be liquidated, it became clear to me that this was the Nazis' reaction to the eastern front closing in on them. They were obviously concentrating their interest on factories "important to the war effort." That was the new catchphrase.

Oskar Schindler's German Enamelware Company (DEF) on Lipowa Street produced kettles, tureens, pots, and pans for the canteen kitchens of the Wehrmacht. Schindler earned most of his money in black-market deals and invested those earnings, among other places, in bribes and presents, while also using some to cover expenses for "his" Jews. Later, he financed his rescue operation with that money. In a 1996 interview in the *Frankfurter Rundschau* newspaper, Schindler's former secretary in Kraków, Elisabeth Tont, described his business methods: "He took over the abandoned factory in Kraków, along with its foreman. They started producing cookware that they sold on the black market. I would go to Tschenstochau and bring the illegal earnings back to Schindler, wrapped in a newspaper. He also sold some things openly. His girlfriend had a shop in Kraków."[44]

At first Göth tried to force Schindler to relocate this important factory to the new industrial section of the Płaszów camp. That would have consolidated Göth's power and enhanced his reputation among his superiors. Göth even threatened to take away Schindler's Jewish workers if he refused to move. But Schindler couldn't be intimidated. He possessed unshakable self-confidence and parried Göth's attempt to coerce him with a joke: "But you don't expect me to drag my heavy enameling furnaces into the camp on wheels, do you?" So the matter was dropped.

The distance from the ghetto to Schindler's Emalia factory had not been very far, but from the Płaszów camp the inmates had to walk several miles. Their workday was already twelve hours long, and Schindler felt sorry for his people. He could see how weak they were and knew that when they returned to the camp, they sometimes still had to stand on the parade ground for several hours before they were allowed to enter their barracks. Schindler used the haggard state of his workers as an argument to Göth for the need to erect barracks to house them on his own factory grounds. Thanks to Göth's intercession with the SS and Police Chief Julian Scherner, Schindler accomplished that enormous feat: he obtained permission for himself and three or four other German factory owners to erect separate, small satellite camps right on the grounds of their factories. The Emalia factory was surrounded, of course, by a barbed-wire fence and guarded by SS men, but the conditions in it were significantly better than in the dangerous and terrible Płaszów main camp. I don't know how many additional cases of French cognac that may have cost Schindler. From then on his Jewish workers could work at the factory and also sleep there, largely protected from the fatal assaults of Göth and his subordinates. But I know all of this only from hearsay, for neither I nor anyone in my family ever worked or even set foot in the factory on Lipowa Street in Kraków-Zabłocie.

Since Schindler's Emalia was now officially a satellite camp of Płaszów, his car was often seen driving through the camp gate and past the commandant's office. He needed tools for his workers and had our tool-making shop make replacement parts for his machines. As the director of a satellite camp that processed metal, Schindler was dependent on ration coupons. The metal rationing center only allocated such coupons if their purpose had received a stamp of approval from the armaments inspector. Fortunately, the chief arms inspector was Major General Maximilian Schindler. Oskar Schindler, with his personal charm, was already acquainted with his namesake. They were not related, but that didn't stop Oskar Schindler from letting interlocutors in various agencies and in the SS believe they were. After the war, he expressed gratitude to the general and even some SS men. He said they had been among the "unfortunately small number of Germans" who had had the courage, in spite of their uniforms and with no quid pro quo, to espouse "humane treatment of the Jews."[45]

Whenever Göth was away inspecting the other satellite camps of Płaszów, Schindler would get word to me and we would meet each other at the main camp, in the hallways of the administration building, but never in Göth's anteroom. This gave us the chance for a brief uninterrupted conversation. Schindler wanted to hear from me what was going on in the camp, how he could protect his workers, or if there were some new danger in store for them. He was also interested in the situation of Jewish workers in other satellite camps. At the time, I knew nothing about the contacts he had in town, but clearly he felt he could not rely on them alone to warn him of threats to his Lipowa Street workers. In my experience, no other manufacturer worried about his workers as Schindler did. No one but him ever asked me, "What can I do to protect my Jewish workers?" He was always eager for news, but could only meet with me when Göth was not in the office. When we did meet, Schindler always greeted me with a handshake, which was unusual, and perhaps even illegal, between a German and a Jewish inmate. He was never brusque or curt with me.

At the time, I didn't know that before 1939, the Sudeten German Schindler had worked in Breslau for several years under Admiral Wilhelm Canaris as a spy with the German eighth counterintelligence general command. Schindler, although a German patriot, always struck me above all as a man who regarded us without prejudice and did not think we were *Untermenschen*. Perhaps influenced by his religious upbringing, perhaps by having had Jewish friends in his neighborhood as a young man, he had a different relationship to us oppressed creatures. In any event, in the summer of 1943, I saw in Schindler the road to rescue I had been searching for since the beginning of the war. With his help, I thought, we would have to try to organize our survival. No one except Schindler evinced any interest in our fate. His courage restored my faith in humanity. When I met him in the camp, I knew there was another world worth living for. In all the years of darkness, I never met another person who organized such a large rescue operation, over such a long period of time, with so much courage and resoluteness as Oskar Schindler. He was certainly no saint, but rather very human and often a bit reckless. But we Jewish inmates could count on him. He never abandoned us.

As recently as 1994, Schindler's former secretary Elisabeth Tont said, "I still can't explain where he got his courage from."[46] Schindler himself wrote to the New York journalist Kurt R. Grossmann in 1956, "A powerful motivation for my actions was my sense of moral obligation to the many Jewish schoolmates and friends with whom I had enjoyed a wonderful boyhood, free of racial prejudice."[47] In the 1950s, Grossmann was one of the few journalists interested in Schindler's unique rescue efforts. Back then, he was already calling him one of the "unsung heroes" of the Holocaust.

Since the fall of 1943, the forced labor—and later, concentration—camp Płaszów had several satellite camps. The Lipowa Street camp housed workers from Schindler's enamelware factory, from the New Condenser and Airplane Factory (NKF), and from another shop producing goods for the Wehrmacht. There was also another camp housing the workers from a large Polish cable factory. Two more satellite camps were located in Wieliczka and Zakopane. All were under the command of Amon Göth and, thus, of the SS. The growth of the Płaszów camp, which reached its high point in the summer of 1944 with more than 24,000 Jews and a relatively small number of Polish inmates, required considerable administrative effort. Göth was not an office person, preferring to spend his time inspecting the camp or visiting downtown Kraków. He therefore delegated many office tasks to his adjutants, who in their turn passed the work on to me. After the German defeat at Stalingrad, however, all able-bodied German men were called up to the front, and there was a shortage of qualified workers in the offices and administrative units of both the Reich and the Generalgouvernement. Vacant positions, therefore, were almost always filled by people one or two ranks lower than their predecessors, since no one with the appropriate training was available. Officially, the position of concentration camp commandant corresponded to the rank of *Standartenführer* (colonel). Göth was only an *Untersturmführer* in the SS in 1943. That same year, he was promoted to *Hauptsturmführer*, still three ranks below *Standartenführer*. His adjutants, who often left and had to be replaced, were also somewhat underqualified for their assignments according to the internal guidelines of the SS. Unlike them, I had no trouble composing complicated letters, so they entrusted me with tasks they officially should not have turned over to me. In this way, I gained access to classified information about the future of the camp and its inmates.

In the early summer of 1943, Horst Pilarzik arrived to take up the post of one of Göth's first adjutants. However, it wasn't very long before he disappeared from headquarters as abruptly as he had arrived. It was said that Pilarzik had been present in an officer's mess in Kraków, in an inebriated state. Unable to find a free seat, he had called out, "Surely there's still a seat left for a Knight of the Iron Cross!"[48] whereupon he was quickly offered a chair. Since he was not a Knight of the Iron Cross, however, he got demoted and I never saw him in the camp again after that.

Göth's next adjutant was SS-*Hauptscharführer* Gerhard Grabow from Hamburg. Our desks in the headquarters anteroom faced each other. He always treated me courteously and sometimes even offered me something to eat, which was very unusual for an SS man. Grabow was a typical north German: blond, lean, and very strong. He had been a shipyard worker with Blohm & Voss, and after we had gotten to know each other a bit, he said to me, "What was I supposed to do? I lost my job and then they came from the SS and offered me work here." The Płaszów camp was apparently the first place Grabow had ever encountered Jews in his life. Once, out of curiosity, he went to the *Appellplatz* (parade ground) to have a look at roll call. When he returned, he said in astonishment, "Man, Pemper, I've never seen so many Jews all together in my whole life!" Grabow was a rather simple but decent guy. He had only an elementary-school education and really started to sweat when Göth would tell him to compose a letter just from some keywords he had given him. Grabow found this quite daunting, but every time Göth gave him such an order, he would respond with a resounding "*Jawoll*!" As soon as Göth had left the premises, Grabow came over to me. "We've got to write a letter now. But don't tell anyone, because it's a classified matter."

"But the letter refers to such and such previous correspondence, with which I'm not familiar."

"Yes, hmm," he would mutter, "that letter is very classified."

Then I would tell him that I would be able to compose the letter according to Göth's specifications, but only if I was informed about the whole matter. Grabow would briefly ponder what I had just said, then would nod in agreement and go and lock all the doors to the commandant's office. Then he would open the safe where the files of classified camp correspondence were kept. I would leaf slowly through the letters, memorizing their contents as much as possible.

From time to time, Grabow would interject, "No one is to know about this!"

"No," I would reassure him, "of course not." In this way, I gained access to the secret documents of the camp. Göth, of course, had no idea what I was doing.

On January 10, 1944, Płaszów became the newest of some twenty concentration camps under the jurisdiction of the Economic and Administrative Main Office of the SS in Oranienburg, near Berlin. An inspector from that office must have noticed that important business in the commandant's anteroom was not being handled by a qualified SS man, but rather by an inmate—even worse, by a Jewish inmate. This situation came in for criticism, of course—criticism that Göth could not ignore.

With Płaszów now a concentration camp, new regulations applied. For example, it was forbidden to employ inmates in positions where they might gain access to confidential or, worse, classified documents. And so one day, a young woman about my age showed up in the anteroom. It appeared that Göth had known her in Katowice, for they addressed each other with the familiar *du*. Her name was Ursula Kochmann, and she worked in the office for three hours every morning. But Göth was a night person, unable to dictate letters at a set time. It was very convenient for him to be able to send for me to take dictation at any time of day or night, whether in the office or at his villa. That was probably why he continued to ignore the regulations and dictate things to me that he really wasn't supposed to. Sometimes he warned me in so many words not to tell anyone about it. When I then assured him that I would never do such a thing, he only responded, "Yes, yes, I know you wouldn't," which was confirmation for me that Göth was having me watched. To be sure, he seldom dictated extremely top secret correspondence to me. One of his SS noncoms who could type would take care of that.

Frau Kochmann was married to a German judge from the Kraków *Sondergericht*—one of the "special courts" set up by the Nazis—who was a good deal older than she. I saw him once or twice, and on those occasions he looked at me as if I were some kind of exotic animal. In contrast, she was quite a friendly, sympathetic person. I can still remember how she and I watched the arrival of a group of Jewish women from Hungary in the spring of 1944. Their heads had been shaved and they were wearing striped camp uniforms as they trudged past the commandant's office in a melancholy trance. I remarked to Frau Kochmann that this group reminded me of a Greek tragedy and she replied, "My husband always says, 'Woe to us if we lose this war.'" I didn't respond to her remark, for it was something she should not have said at all in the presence of a Jewish inmate.

One time, Göth had an important meeting in the city. He was waiting impatiently for a letter to be finished that he still needed to sign. He paced up and down the anteroom and was constantly looking at the clock. His hectic demeanor made Frau Kochmann so nervous she began to tremble and that caused a mishap: she put the carbon paper into the typewriter backwards, and Göth scolded her loudly. She was close to tears while she typed the letter a second time. When Göth had finally gone, I tried to comfort her. "Why don't I prepare the pages for you from now on, with the carbon paper already held in place by paper clips, so that such a thing can never happen again?" She immediately agreed. What I didn't tell her was that I would use a new piece of carbon paper for each page, so that when I was alone in the office, I could read the impressions left on the carbon paper, and in that way find out the contents of the classified correspondence. In retrospect, I would like to apologize to Ursula Kochmann for pulling the wool over her eyes for so many months and being dishonest with her. But there was nothing else I could do. My priority was the welfare—the possible survival—of all us prisoners. We had to find out what the Nazis had in store for us. There are situations in which one is justified in ignoring ethical norms, and even required to do so.

THE TRICK WITH THE PRODUCTION TABLES

THE MURDER OF ALL EUROPEAN JEWS had been generally agreed upon, but until the *Endsieg*—final victory—the work of the cheap slave workers was to be exploited. But then why were some ghettos and labor camps in the Generalgouvernement liquidated between the fall of 1943 and the spring of 1944, while others were not? The historian Dieter Pohl has tried to solve the riddle. In 1998, he wrote that up to now, "no one has been able to explain definitively how some camps were chosen for liquidation." He assumes correctly that the decisive factor was the importance individual factories had for the war effort.[49]

After I had succeeded in gaining access to classified documents in the commandant's office in the summer of 1943, I was able to come up with a plan to prevent the liquidation of the Płaszów camp for as long as I could, hoping that as many of us as possible would survive until the end of the war and not be sent to other camps for extermination. The best possibility seemed to be to emphasize our "importance to the war effort." I could not have carried out this plan, however, without the enormous help of Oskar Schindler. It looks like a surefire strategy in hindsight, but at the time it was unrealistic to have much hope for its success. There was hardly time to weigh and compare events strategically, as they deserved. By good fortune, however, each stone of the mosaic fitted with the others. But right up until the last minute of the war, we were never certain whether we would survive or not.

I want to make one thing absolutely clear: without Oskar Schindler's courage and his continuous efforts on behalf of the Jews in Kraków-Płaszów and later in Brünnlitz and elsewhere, we would not have been able to survive. Schindler gave me the courage to resist; he helped wherever he could. I had access to the classified information and drew my own conclusions. I then discussed many things with him, but only hinted at what I knew from the documents. Schindler had contacts within the arms inspection agency and the Wehrmacht. He also had cash for the expensive bribes and presents that helped effect favorable decisions from the authorities. In all situations, Schindler took decisive actions rooted in the profound humanity of his intention to help "his Jews" survive at any price.

Schindler's former secretary Elisabeth Tont confirmed that his efforts extended beyond just the Jews who worked for him:

> I saw how he helped everyone, without exception. One day I got a call from my former landlord and landlady, who were Jewish. My landlady told me that they were in a terrible camp, where each night so-and-so-many Jews would be shot. She said, "Please ask Schindler to get us out of here. He's already saved the lives of so many Jews." I called him up—it was two years since I had worked for him—and asked him this favor. Shortly thereafter I get another call from my landlady. She was now in Schindler's factory, working as a chambermaid in the SS guardhouse, while her husband worked in the factory.[50]

Today, it's hard to appreciate the risks Schindler ran every day, for years, in order to help us. And so it was that he and I, each from different vantage points, accomplished something well-nigh impossible: at the end of 1943, the forced labor camp Kraków-Płaszów, where about eighty percent of the production was in textiles and tailoring, did not get shut down, but continued to function. Schindler's unremitting efforts of these years were decisive for the final feat of the rescue operation known as Schindler's List that began in the late fall of 1944. He battled to the very end for our welfare and our lives. Through him alone we finally gained the freedom we all constantly yearned for, but often thought impossible to achieve.

In the administration building, in the wing where the production offices were located, the foremen of the various workshops and production units would appear regularly to deliver their weekly reports. Before placing these reports on Göth's desk, I read them myself to determine which camp workshops were producing well, where the bottlenecks were, and where orders were falling off. I was not able to take any notes, but since childhood I've had a very good visual memory on which I depended during my years in the camp. Until the summer of 1943, factory work of any kind offered a certain protection from being selected and shipped off to one of the extermination camps. Thus, from the beginning of the German occupation, work was synonymous with survival, even if the work was physically grueling and often much too strenuous for us inmates. By chance at the end of July 1943, while scanning classified documents, I came across something unexpected that made one thing clear to me: I had to take immediate action if I wanted to delay our destruction.

After the capitulation of the Wehrmacht at Stalingrad at the end of January and the beginning of February 1943, the Russians had begun a counteroffensive. During that summer, the Red Army had already advanced close to the border of prewar Poland. In the newspapers I had access to, I read of decisive changes in the areas around Kraków and Lublin, where Jewish work camps producing only textiles were being shut down. Moreover, I had noticed that Göth was less and less interested in the reports and statistics from our clothing, knitting, and glassware workshops, while devoting increased attention to those producing metal goods such as plumbing supplies and locks. Göth's different reaction to these reports confirmed my worst fears. In view of Germany's deteriorating military and economic situation, what mattered now

Women being herded to work in the Kraków-Płaszów camp.

were only those areas of production geared toward the war effort. I knew that except for our tailoring shop that made uniforms for the Wehrmacht, Płaszów produced little of direct and immediate value for the front or for winning the war.

In my next conversation with Oskar Schindler, I asked him for the spec sheets with technical data for his metal processing machines. I did not go into details. And Schindler knew better than to ask further questions. Once I had these sheets in hand, I "neutralized" the data sheets, so to speak, doctoring them so that no one could trace them back to Schindler and his factory. Then I showed them to the foremen in our metal-working shops and asked them to come up with specific suggestions as to which of the items that would have immediate use at the front they could produce with their machines. I asked for precise details—how many units per day, assuming we could obtain the orders and the necessary raw materials. My recurring question was, "What is the manufacturing capacity of our machines?" When the foremen asked me why I wanted the information, I answered, "Headquarters is negotiating important contracts." After that, the foremen asked no further questions.

They knew me and trusted me. However, I was doing this on my own, completely aware of the risk I was taking. Since I was a condemned man anyway, I had nothing to lose. If Göth had asked me how I dared to collect information from the foremen without his knowledge, I could have reminded him of a similar situation in our paper processing plant with which he was familiar.

An acquaintance of my father's, Benjamin Geizhals, was the technical director of the paper plant in our camp. One day he came to me in despair, saying he was at his wits' end. There were no more orders for his entire production unit. Specifically, they manufactured office binders but could no longer get any of the metal ring book mechanisms. If his unit was closed for lack of orders, the lives of his workers would be at risk. After Mr. Geizhals had explained the situation to me, I obtained from the Generalgouvernement's board of foreign trade the addresses of pertinent manufacturers and asked them for cost estimates for such ring book mechanisms. It was all done very officially, written on stationery with the letterhead "Forced Labor Camp Kraków-Płaszów of the SS and Police Chief" and, of course, signed by Göth. My letters actually succeeded in eliciting bids on these metal mechanisms from some companies, and the paper production plant was able to obtain enough orders again. Since this successful intervention, the workshop supervisors and foremen were convinced of my initiative, and so without further ado, they now prepared the itemizations of manufacturing capacity I had requested. When I thereupon asked the foremen for a further itemization of products they could manufacture that would be of interest to the Wehrmacht, they again made various suggestions, according to their area of specialization.

From several letters Amon Göth had dictated to me for convenience's sake in his villa in the evening, I learned more about the Nazis' plans. It was still the summer of 1943. The Russian front was drawing nearer and nearer, and that meant that Göth's days as commandant were numbered. Simultaneously, I was in increasing danger, for I knew that Göth had already disposed of several inconvenient witnesses and accessories to his crimes. I was firmly convinced that I would never know a life of freedom again, because Göth would certainly shoot me shortly before any possible liberation of the camp. Oskar Schindler later confirmed my fears in Brünnlitz and again after the war, "Göth would never have permitted you to survive to tell anyone outside the camp all the things you had witnessed there."

Consequently, in the office, I made myself as inconspicuous as I could. Whenever Amon Göth had superiors from Kraków or Berlin visiting the camp, I kept my eyes and ears open but made myself as "invisible" as possible. It helped that I had always insisted on wearing the plain, striped prisoner's garb. I did not want to think of myself or have others regard me as "privileged." Nevertheless, some of my fellow inmates tried to persuade me to wear the gray uniform of the *Ordnungsdienst*,[51] a camp police force made up of Jewish inmates. Perhaps they thought that if I were an "OD man" like themselves I would supply them with classified information from the office. That's something I never did. I always maintained my distance and kept what I saw and heard to myself.

Some so-called camp police were very keen to wear this special OD uniform. They would even get their inmates' uniforms custom fitted by a camp tailor. They considered themselves something special, although we were all in the same miserable situation. The pride and arrogance evident in a few prisoners was appalling to me. Unfortunately, in the dreadful daily rut of the camp, more than a few Jewish inmates harmed their fellow inmates in their eagerness to curry favor with the SS. It's difficult to address the topic of Jewish informers and collaborators in the SS camps. They were convinced that of all the prisoners, only they would survive the war. Yet many of them did not; almost all were sooner or later killed by the SS as accessories to their crimes.

Wilek Chilowicz, the senior Jewish inmate of the Kraków-Płaszów camp, was practically Göth's personal slave. He and his *Ordnungsdienst* men believed nothing would happen to them, but they were wrong. Chilowicz tried several times to draw me into his circle by offering me an OD uniform. I refused. I was convinced that one day I would be shot anyway by Göth. And if it had to be, I wanted to be remembered as a decent human being. I had to struggle against being forced to wear the OD uniform of privilege.

Chilowicz pressured me doggedly, and someone was always leaving an OD uniform jacket and policeman's cap on my wooden bed. They would be there when I returned to the barracks in the evening. I would lay the gray uniform aside and continue to insist on wearing my simple striped prisoner's garb. That's why I had no inhibitions or problems at all testifying at Göth's trial in 1946. Others who had worn the gray OD uniform in the camp advised me at the time not to testify against Göth. Izak Stern also advised against it. But I knew that I hadn't sullied myself. I could in good conscience swear the oath and Göth would not be able to say anything in court that would compromise me.

Finally, I obtained Göth's express permission to continue wearing my inmate's stripes. I had to resort to trickery to get it, but from then on, I was free of Chilowicz's importunities. I told Göth that I often found myself alone in the anteroom of his private office. An SS officer from outside the camp might enter and not recognize my garb as that of an inmate because he assumed that no Jewish prisoner would be working in the commandant's anteroom. If he tried to shake hands with me, it would be an embarrassment to discover that I was a Jew. I well remember Göth's skeptical look when I told him this story. He was by no means stupid, and I began to fear that he had seen through my ploy this time. But he just mumbled something like, "Yes, well, maybe so . . ." which I took as his consent.

"OK," I said, "then I can tell Chilowicz I have your permission to keep wearing my blue-gray stripes." Perhaps others in the camp thought I was a fool because I had turned down—even vehemently refused—the "privilege" of wearing an OD uniform.

As for the manufacturing capacity of our machines, Göth didn't have the slightest inkling of what I was up to behind the scenes.

When I was absolutely certain we would have to add some kind of arms production to our manufacturing program in order to keep our camp open, I told Oskar Schindler about the liquidation of clothing and uniform factories in other parts of the Generalgouvernement. "Well," Schindler tried to reassure me, "it's not a threat to my people, since I'm in metal ware, not apparel." Despite his encouraging words, I was convinced I was right. Every time I leafed through incoming official correspondence, I came across more new information. Events were coming thick and fast, and I was driven by the conviction that speed was essential. I read reports from meetings called by the higher SS and police chief east in Kraków, where among other things, they discussed whether Jewish work camps should continue to exist, and if so, which ones. And if the situation on the eastern front continued to worsen, which camps would have to be liquidated or moved farther west. In these meetings, it was finally announced that General Oswald Pohl, the highest authority over the whole SS economic empire and now head of the Economic and Administrative Main Office of the SS in Berlin-Oranienburg, had decreed that the only Jewish work camps to be retained were those who could prove that their production was *siegentscheidend*—crucial for victory. I was struck by the word. In all the letters, telegrams, and documents I had read thus far, I had never encountered this term. I understood it as the comparative degree of the word *kriegswichtig*—important to the war effort. The production of uniforms and boots for the Wehrmacht was *kriegswichtig*. Even the envelopes we licked for the SS in the camp were *kriegswichtig*. But weapons production alone was *siegentscheidend*.

As a result of this insight, I had a very important conversation with Schindler. For the sake of caution, I didn't tell him I had read this information myself, since Schindler was sometimes a bit careless and too trusting. So I told him only that, based on various scraps of conversation I had overheard, I was almost certain that to guarantee the security of the Jewish contingent in his factory, it would be absolutely necessary to develop arms production in addition to his enamelware production. Schindler again murmured something about being "in metal ware," and I became impatient and involuntarily let slip a somewhat impertinent remark: "Herr Direktor Schindler," I said, "you can't win a war with just pots and pans. It would help if you would start producing some arms in your plant to keep your people safe." Whether or not that was news to Schindler, he now began to expand arms production in his factory, especially the manufacturing of grenade parts. They were recorded under the code name "MU" for *Mundlochbuchse*, but I'm not sure to this day what that word meant.

A year later, in the summer of 1944, when the transfer of important factories into the territory of the Reich was being discussed, the Economic and Administrative Main Office of the SS decided that only the section of Schindler's factory that produced the grenade parts, the MU, would be moved to Brünnlitz in the Sudetenland. For that reason, most of the people who got onto Schindler's List were the workers in the MU department, not those working in enamelware production. If Schindler hadn't begun production of grenade parts in 1943, there would have been no Schindler's List and no rescue effort. For pots and pans, while *kriegswichtig*, were not *siegentscheidend*.

Oskar Schindler took determined action immediately. Production of the MU got under way. By now it was not just a question of preserving Schindler's satellite camp, but the central camp as well. The scheme had to succeed. Of course, I could not tell even my friends Izak and Natan Stern about the letters, telegrams, and classified documents I had read. For we never knew when any of us might be tortured. And so I just alluded in general to some of the information I had. I spoke to them of the consequences of Stalingrad, and that they were much more far-reaching than we could imagine. I said our camp might be on the brink of liquidation. I ended my little presentation with the words, "I think the only solution will be to become associated with a concentration camp in some way. Because that kind of camp will surely continue to exist until the war is over." The two Stern brothers were speechless. They looked at me incredulously, almost with concern, and probably thought, "The poor guy has lost his mind." How could they know that for me, because of my position as Göth's stenographer, all this was by now fairly certain? I also knew from the office correspondence that within the system of Germany's thousands of prison camps, the approximately twenty concentration camps such as Auschwitz, Dachau, Buchenwald, Bergen-Belsen, and Mauthausen had the highest priority, both in terms of supplies and continued existence. If we could succeed in turning our forced labor camp into another concentration camp, then perhaps we had a chance to stay alive longer. In the end, this supposition proved to be correct.

Something else had become clear to me in the meantime. The preservation of our camp was of decisive importance not only for us Jewish inmates, but for Göth as well. Göth was aware of his dilemma: the camp produced mainly brushes, glassware, clothing, and shoes—obviously nothing that was "crucial for victory." The closing of the camp would have meant losing his many perks and privileges, having to forgo luxury and debauchery, perhaps even being sent to the front. He had no desire for that, because by now he weighed about two hundred sixty-five pounds and had bad diabetes. Preserving the camp would allow him to continue being his "own *commandeur*." And so ironically, and only on this one issue, our interests as inmates coincided with his as SS camp commander.

In late summer 1943—in August, I think it was—at the same time as Schindler was attempting to restructure his factory, Göth demanded from me an itemization of what our metalworking shops were manufacturing or could manufacture if necessary. This was confirmation that he now thought they played the most important role in the camp. He didn't ask how many shoes, sweaters, or uniforms we were able to produce. He explicitly asked about metal products. I found this enormously significant. In the past, Göth had given me tasks without telling me exactly how I was to carry them out, and that was also the case this time. He was interested only in results. Since I possessed some insight into the long-range plans of the Nazis from my reading of classified information, I had Schindler again give me data sheets on his machines and their capacity, and I went back to the technical directors of our workshops and asked them to give me several updated examples of products that their machines, with the necessary modifications and adjustments, could produce. It was particularly important to me that the shop supervisors not just name products they could make, but give me information about requisite materials, formats, and alternate configurations. I quite intentionally demanded such multifarious data so that when I itemized each product, it would take up an entire line of a standard sheet of typing paper in landscape format. With such a plethora of information and precise detail, I wanted to impress Göth and capture his attention. And I succeeded.

Each line began with the name of a product and the number of units that could be produced in a month and ended with the abbreviation "*od.*" Then came the next line, again with all details, and again at the end the two letters "*od*," and so on, line for line. I put together the production lists mostly in the evening and at night, so that no one would see what I was actually writing. It was not unusual for me to work deep into the night, so no one was surprised to see a light on so late in the headquarters office.

After a few days, I showed Göth the itemization. At first, he reacted with impatience. "We wouldn't be able to produce that."

Whereupon I answered, "*Herr Commandeur*, I have documentation for everything."

Now he even got a bit gruff, "The totals are too large. We can't produce all these things."

"You're right," I answered, "but they're alternatives."

Now Göth was suddenly getting interested. "What do you mean by 'alternatives'?"

"Well, that's indicated at the end of each line by the letters '*od.*' It's according to the Duden[52] dictionary. '*Od.*' stands for '*oder*'" ("or"). I showed Göth the page in Duden as if that were the most important thing. The trick worked. Göth was impressed by the data and the additional reference to Duden, just as I had anticipated, for I had learned how he reacted to such things. For a few seconds, Göth just sat there, saying nothing and peering intently at me. Time seemed to stand still. Suddenly a terrifying thought popped into my head: "Now he's either going to pull out his pistol and shoot you because he thinks you're trying to make a fool of him with all these tedious details. Or he's thinking, Pemper knows something that he actually can't know, namely, that these lists are exactly what I need." Of course, Göth couldn't ask me to provide him with falsified information, for then he would have made himself vulnerable to blackmail. However, he quickly realized the value of these itemizations for himself and for the camp. Here was a plan, a stratagem that would enable him to remain the camp's *commandeur*, and that's all he cared about.

Göth had only one more brief question, "How many copies do you have?" I showed him the original and two copies. He nodded, put all three items into his pocket, and set off for town without another word. He may have guessed that it was a trick. But he had taken possession of the lists and thus had taken the first step. I had calculated that if Göth presented my inflated production tables to his superiors, they would react just as he did. They would be impressed by the tangled mass of statistics running across the page and hardly anyone would stop to ask unnecessary questions or discover the deceit contained in the two little letters "*od.*"

It turned out that Göth really did take the souped-up production tables to meetings in town, because the preparation of these lists of the supposed arms production capacity of our camp coincided with discussions at the office of the higher SS and police chief east in downtown Kraków. Although Göth was not of high enough rank to participate in those discussions, I surmise that he presented my production lists either directly to the relevant authorities or to their adjutants, thereby documenting the importance of our camp for the war effort and preventing it from being liquidated. Of course, I have no idea what exactly occurred at the high-level meetings in the rooms of Minister of State and SS General Krüger and then in subsequent discussions with General Oswald Pohl at the Economic and Administrative Main Office of the SS in Berlin-Oranienburg. I never again saw the inflated production tables I had so carefully prepared, although I conducted an intensive search for them after 1945. They may have been destroyed at the end of the war, or are perhaps still stored in some archive.

I later learned that crucial negotiations about which camps would be preserved and which disbanded did in fact take place in Kraków on September 3, 1943, and then in Oranienburg on September 7. Most smaller camps with no "production of crucial importance for victory" were liquidated, which meant certain death for their inmates, who would be sent to extermination camps such as Sobibor and Auschwitz. But the Kraków-Płaszów camp and a few others remained in operation. Otherwise, without the inflated production lists from late summer 1943, our death would have been imminent and Oskar Schindler's rescue operation of October 1944 would probably have never happened. However, because of the advancing Russian troops, in July and August 1944 many of Płaszów's inmates started to be transferred to other camps such as Mauthausen and Stutthof. But between the fall of 1943 and the summer of 1944, some twenty thousand Jewish and Polish inmates got a reprieve, a chance to stay alive at least a while longer.

We know about General Pohl's decision to liquidate smaller camps and consolidate others from an official document dated September 7, 1943:

> Subsequent to the discussion with SS-*Obergruppenführer* Krüger of September 3, a discussion took place on September 7 in the Economic and Administrative Main Office of the SS. In attendance were SS-*Obergruppenführer* Pohl, SS-*Gruppenführer* Globocnik, SS-*Brigadeführer* Glücks, SS-

Brigadeführer Lörner, SS-*Obersturmbannführer* Schellin, SS-*Obersturmbannführer* Maurer, SS-*Sturmbannführer* Florstedt, and SS-*Obersturmführer* Dr. Horn. The following decisions were taken:

1. The approximately ten remaining work camps of the SS and police chief in the Lublin district will be transferred to the Economic and Administrative Main Office of the SS as branch camps of the Lublin concentration camp. With this change, they become the responsibility and come under the supervision of the Economic and Administrative Main Office of the SS. SS-*Sturmbannführer* Florstedt will have direct command over them and see to their security and orderly administration.

2. With their transfer to the Economic and Administrative Main Office of the SS (Working Group D), the inhabitants of these work camps become concentration camp inmates. The Reich assumes responsibility for the necessary expenditures.

3. Apart from these approximately ten labor camps in the Lublin district, it is in the interest of a general cleanup that all the labor camps in the Generalgouvernement be transferred to the Economic and Administrative Main Office of the SS. SS-*Sturmbannführer* Florstedt is charged with the responsibility for the transfer of these camps to the authority of Working Group D of the Economic and Administrative Main Office of the SS. Details are to be discussed with SS-*Obersturmbannführer* Schellin, SS-*Obersturmbannführer* Maurer, and SS-*Obersturmführer* Dr. Horn.

4. Our aim is to liquidate those camps with small numbers of prisoners as well as those whose production is neither crucial for victory nor important for the war effort.

Signed, Oswald Pohl, SS-*Obergruppenführer* and General of the Waffen-SS.[53]

Kraków-Płaszów. Commandant's headquarters and the main street of the camp. In the right foreground is the "Gray House" in which I was kept in solitary confinement for two weeks in September 1944.

The final decision to keep our camp in operation was made a few weeks later, at the end of October 1943. Pohl wrote that, among others,[54] the Kraków-Płaszów camp would not only remain open but become a concentration camp. The transfer would be dependent on General Krüger not withdrawing his men from the camp, because Pohl was unable to provide any personnel to serve as guards. So the former forced labor camp guards should continue to man their posts in the newly designated concentration camp. "Arranging this," said the letter, "should present no problems."

At the time, of course, I was not able to breathe a word to anyone about the interconnections I was able to discern from the classified information, my inflated production lists, and the preservation of the Płaszów camp. Even after the war, I maintained public silence, speaking about these things with only a few close confidants. But I was grateful that fate had placed me in a position where I could do something to save human lives during the war.

A SURPRISING REVELATION DURING THE TRIAL OF GERHARD MAURER

KRAKÓW-PŁASZÓW officially became a concentration camp on January 10, 1944. Oswald Pohl was the head of the entire economic empire of the SS, but he personally had nothing to do with the specific details of transforming Płaszów. These changes were taken care of by Working Group D of the Economic and Administrative Main Office of the SS in Berlin-Oranienburg, headed by General Richard Glücks. SS-*Obersturmbannführer* Gerhard Maurer was responsible for transmitting all decisions and directives from Oranienburg to Płaszów. Maurer also directed the department D II, which controlled the work assignments of the prisoners in all twenty-plus main concentration camps within Germany and the conquered territories in Europe. Maurer, who had been born in Halle an der Saale in 1907, was a true believer who had joined the National Socialists in 1930 and the SS in 1931.

When the war was over in 1945, I resumed my university studies and received a degree in business administration in 1948. In January 1950, I began to work as head of the accounting department for state enterprises in Kraków. Soon thereafter, I received a telephone call from the investigating magistrate Dr. Jan Sehn. Coming right to the point, he asked me if the name Gerhard Maurer meant anything to me. "But of course," I replied and immediately headed for his office in the center of town. There I wrote down a facsimile of Maurer's signature, which I knew very well from the many letters he had sent to Göth beginning in January 1944, once our forced labor camp had been designated a concentration camp. Sehn was overjoyed, since up to then he had not been able to find anyone who knew who Maurer was and could serve as a witness against him at his war crimes trial. Sehn, who had prosecuted Amon Göth in 1946, had been assigned to prepare Maurer's case as well. Five years after testifying against Göth, I was again asked to serve as the chief witness for the prosecution. The trial took place in Warsaw in 1951. Maurer was one of the SS leaders who, with great dedication and efficiency, had directed the persecution of the entire Jewish inmate population in Germany and occupied Europe from his office in Berlin-Oranienburg. He had known exactly what was happening in the concentration camps, for he emphasized in his testimony that he had personally inspected all of them. If I remember correctly, he also visited Płaszów at least once.

Before the trial, I said in my deposition in Kraków: "My informants, the SS officers in Płaszów, often described Maurer as an especially energetic personality. One indication was the fact that it was he who spoke for Glücks and was allowed to sign letters as his personal deputy and not just 'by order of,' although normally, Glücks's deputy should have been the head of the D I department. The SS officers sometimes remarked ironically that there was actually only one thing in Working Group D that Maurer couldn't do all by himself, and that was to sign the authorizations for long-distance trips by motor vehicle, since they required a general's signature."[55] Maurer's rank was only *Standartenführer*—the SS equivalent of a colonel.[56]

In my opinion, Maurer's prominent role in organizing the persecution of the Jews and the administration of the entire system of concentration camps has not yet been documented as thoroughly as it deserves, with the exception of the studies of Gerald Reitlinger and Johannes Tuchel. On November 18, 1943, General Pohl had informed all divisions of the Economic and Administrative Main Office of the SS that following the transfer of SS-*Obersturmbannführer* Artur Liebehenschel to the position of commandant of Auschwitz I, SS-*Obersturmbannführer* Maurer

would become the permanent deputy of General Glücks, the head of Working Group D.[57] Rudolf Höss, the former commandant of Auschwitz, confirmed Maurer's function within Working Group D in notes he made in Kraków in 1946: "After Liebehenschel's departure, Maurer became Glücks's deputy. With this promotion, Pohl basically turned over the inspection of the concentration camp system to Maurer, and little by little, Glücks left almost all important matters to him. Glücks was only nominally still the inspector. Since from that time on, according to the wishes of the RFSS [*Reichsführer*-SS Heinrich Himmler], arms production by the prisoners was the most important thing, it was natural that everything was regarded from that point of view."[58]

After the war, both Oswald Pohl and Gerhard Maurer were able to obtain false papers, disguise themselves as laborers, and go underground. Pohl wasn't tracked down and turned over to Allied tribunals until May 1946. In November 1947, he was sentenced to death for war crimes and crimes against humanity in the so-called Economic and Administrative Main Office of the SS trial in Nuremberg. He was executed in 1951. Meanwhile, the Americans extradited Gerhard Maurer to Poland in 1947. At his trial in Warsaw in 1951, I testified against him just as I had at Amon Göth's trial in 1946—drawing on my knowledge of his involvement in the roundup of Hungarian Jews.

The German Wehrmacht invaded Hungary in March 1944 and occupied the land of their former ally. From then on, the Germans pressured their Hungarian regent Miklós Horthy until he finally turned over several hundred thousand Jews to the "Eichmann Commando." The elderly and children among them were murdered immediately upon their arrival in Auschwitz.

On March 18, 1944, my mother suffered a hemiplegic stroke in the Płaszów concentration camp. There was no medical help for her, and from then on, she could only walk with the help of a cane. At the time, I had a lot to do in the commandant's office and often worked late into the night. One evening, I waited for an opportune moment to let Göth know how important it was for me to stay in the same place as my mother for as long as possible. Göth gave no clear response to my hints. So I decided to do something on my own, and spoke directly to the German camp physician, Dr. Max Blancke. I informed him that Göth agreed that my mother, Regina Pemper, would be able to remain in the camp for as long as I was there. Of course, Blancke knew that I was the commandant's stenographer, so he had no doubt that I was telling the truth. I was counting on that, and my calculation proved correct. Blancke and Göth had the same rank: SS-*Hauptsturmführer*. For that reason, I figured Blancke would not ask the camp commandant if an inmate were lying to him or not. If he had asked Göth about it, however, I wouldn't be alive today. But I had to take this risk to save my mother from being deported. And so despite her compromised mobility, she was not selected to be sent to Auschwitz during the so-called health roll call of May 1944.

On Saturday, May 6, 1944, I was in the commandant's office late at night as usual, finishing up some outstanding tasks. A health roll call had been announced for the following day. When Göth stopped by, long after the official end of the working day, I asked him, "*Herr Commandeur*, since I still have a lot to do here in the office, do I have to appear at the roll call tomorrow?" Göth took an unusually long look at me, apparently turning something over in his mind. Finally he said, "No, since we'll only be assigning people to jobs according to their physical capabilities. You're here in the office anyway, so there's really no need . . ." His sentence remained unfinished, which worried me a bit. Would I need to show up for the roll call or not? Later that evening, in the special barracks for administrative personnel, I told Izak and Natan Stern about my conversation with Göth. "I can't believe that at this point, in the fifth year of the war, after all they've done to us, the gentlemen of the SS are still thinking about how to employ us according to our physical capabilities. I don't like the smell of things. It would make me laugh if it didn't make me cry."

But what could we do? Natan Stern was quite tall, about 6' 2", but because of his back problems, he was a bit stooped. I suggested that he should stand up straight and march lively to show that he was quite capable of work.

The next day, a Sunday, all the inmates had to pass by a committee, men and women on two separate roll-call grounds so that they couldn't see each other naked. They called the entire exercise "The Right Job for Everyone."[59] Since Göth had given me permission not to participate in it, I only know what happened during the procedure from what my fellow prisoners told me afterward. The committee consisted of the German camp physician, Dr. Max Blancke, and his deputy, an SS medic. SS guards entered Blancke's comments about each male inmate onto a file card; female guards did the same for each woman.

Each inmate received an annotation. But no one knew the reason for these entries. "What's the point? What are they going to do to us?" I was besieged by numerous questions. But I didn't know anything either.

Not until two weeks later did I get a chance to take a look—a forbidden one, of course—at the documents produced during this event. Gerhard Maurer had sent a telegram to all the concentration camp commandants under his command asking how many Hungarian Jews they could accept on a temporary basis, until barracks could be built and fenced in at various arms factories where they were needed as workers. Göth had immediately replied that he could house eight thousand of them, provided he received permission to double up people on each sleeping pallet. He intended to organize two twelve-hour shifts and operate his shops round-the-clock, so that one group of inmates could sleep on the pallets while the other group worked. After a few days, Maurer's refusal arrived via telex. The health inspector in Oranienburg had reservations about the double occupancy because there would be too much danger of epidemics in the summer. Kraków must not be exposed to this danger because of its importance as a rail intersection between the Reich and the eastern front. Moreover, there were some six hundred SS and policemen employed in the camp whose health must not be jeopardized.

If Göth had simply accepted Maurer's refusal and taken no further action, no one would have been able to charge him with anything. But Maurer's refusal continued to preoccupy the eager commandant. A few days later, Göth fired off another telegram to Maurer, in which he lowered the number of prisoners he could accommodate to six thousand. Göth also informed his superior that he could accept that many new arrivals provided he was allowed to send current inmates no longer capable of full-time work to Auschwitz for *Sonderbehandlung*—"special treatment." He received immediate permission from Maurer. At the same time, the commandant's office in Auschwitz was alerted to prepare to accept a special transport from the Płaszów concentration camp. The result of this agreement was the "health roll call" of May 7, 1944.

By 1951, I had already been on the witness stand three times. Now I was being called back again after Göth had declared during his trial that he could indeed remember this transport but he had not been aware that the prisoners sent to Auschwitz were to be killed. "For us in the camp," I had told the judge presiding at Göth's trial in 1946, "there was no question that these people were being sent to their death. The transport on May 14, 1944, consisted mostly of young children and the very elderly. At the last minute, patients from the infirmary were added. It was clear to us that these people were going to be killed in Auschwitz." In the published transcript of Göth's trial, I recently discovered another statement I made at the time: "About 1,400 people were sent to Oświęcim [Auschwitz], including 286 children. Göth sent a telegram to Oświęcim that stated the exact numbers of children, the sick, and the elderly. I did not personally take care of this correspondence, but did see some of the telegrams later on. The entire operation was kept very hush-hush."[60]

A few days after May 14, 1944, two or three young Jewish men on a work detail at the Płaszów railroad station threw away their jackets with the letters KL (*Konzentrationslager*—concentration camp) painted on the back and fled. Unfortunately, they were captured and did not survive. At that time, it was almost impossible to hole up anywhere, because the punishments for Poles who hid Jews or helped them escape were draconian. A few days later, Göth sent a telegram to Auschwitz that said something like, "To prevent further escape attempts from work details, I would like to supply all work details with striped prisoners' uniforms." He therefore requested Auschwitz to "return the uniforms from the May 14th transport of special treatment prisoners." This telegram is clear evidence that contrary to his testimony, Göth knew very well what the concept *Sonderbehandlung* meant. After my testimony, the presiding judge asked the accused whether he had any further questions. "No more questions," was Göth's answer.

I would like to emphasize again the difference between an issue of logistics and the question of personal guilt. As an administrative matter, Maurer's initial inquiry about how many Hungarian Jews Göth could accommodate on a temporary basis had no criminal intent. However, Göth's suggestion in response was clearly criminal.

In my deposition of February 23, 1950, during the judicial inquiry against Gerhard Maurer, I spoke of my work in Göth's office. "From March 1943 until October 1944, as prisoners in Płaszów, other inmates and I were assigned to office work in the camp commandant's office, where I worked as a clerk and stenographer. My work gave me access to camp files and correspondence and also the opportunity to read classified letters to and from the office." I described in detail the extraordinary circumstances that I was able to exploit in order to do this.

In this deposition, I basically repeated what I had already stated at Amon Göth's trial. In Maurer's 1951 trial, however, the accused declared categorically that "the witness cannot have seen what he claims to have read." He said he had personally inspected all twenty main concentration camps and not one of them had a

Jewish inmate as the stenographer working for the camp commandant. That might have been the case in a small satellite camp, he said, but never in a concentration camp. Thereupon, the presiding judge asked me if I could prove my assertion. At first I responded that they could review my sworn testimony from the Göth trial. My testimony was part of the official transcript and had been published. But then I mentioned something that almost took Maurer's breath away. In the summer of 1944, he had sent all concentration camp commandants a black-edged card announcing the deaths of his wife and three children in an enemy air attack.[61] I had seen this card as part of my daily work in Göth's office. Maurer sat there for a moment in stony silence, then briefly consulted his Polish attorney. He then rose and said quietly, "That is correct. I shall no longer challenge the veracity of the witness. But I still can't understand how he did it." He sat down, shook his head, and reiterated his amazement. A Jewish inmate as the stenographer of a camp commandant! Finally he began to swear rather loudly and even curse the former commandant. "How could Göth have acted so independently and impertinently! How could he have flouted all the rules and regulations!" I then explained to the court that Płaszów was very different from all the other concentration camps such as Dachau, Buchenwald, Mauthausen, and Sachsenhausen, which the Nazis had filled with prisoners from all over their empire. Our camp had initially been just the continuation of the Kraków ghetto and I had been taken over as part of the "inventory" of the ghetto administration, so to speak. That was the explanation for my unique role.

During the recesses, I talked with the presiding judge about the organizational structure of Working Group D. The D I department had charge of general prisoner affairs and D II of work assignments. D III had charge of prisoners' health. D IV was charged with general administration. As a prisoner, I of course was not supposed to know anything about these organizational structures. How extremely classified this was is apparent from the fact that Eugen Kogon, an acknowledged expert on the concentration camps and himself a former inmate of Dachau, did not know that *D* did not stand for Dachau, but referred to the Working Group within the Economic and Administrative Main Office of the SS. He wrote in his book *The Theory and Practice of Hell* that he had seen incarceration orders of the security police that had been stamped with the letter *D*. He and his fellow prisoners surmised that *D* stood for "Dachau." But the SS used *Da* when referring to the Dachau camp. From the correspondence and organizational charts I saw in the commandant's office in Płaszów, I was able to figure out the entire structure of the Economic and Administrative Main Office of the SS in Berlin-Oranienburg with its five working groups: *W* stood for the business undertakings of the SS, *D* for the concentration camps, *C* for construction projects, *A* and *B* for other areas. When the presiding judge heard me outline this structure, he exclaimed, "What? You knew all of this? I wish I had witnesses like you in all my trials." I took that as a great compliment, for it emphasized something that had always been important to me: a witness should not draw his own conclusions. He should just say what he saw or experienced. That was the maxim I always followed.

PŁASZÓW BECOMES A CONCENTRATION CAMP

DURING MY YEARS IN THE CAMP, a quotation from Machiavelli was always present in my mind. The great Polish poet Adam Mickiewicz uses it as a motto for his verse epic *Konrad Wallenrod*: "You have to be both fox and lion." We Jews were not able to be lions, for we had no army to back us up. So we had to be foxes, on the lookout for hidden opportunities. We had no need to prove to ourselves or anyone else that we were against the hated Nazi regime. What we had to do was save as many lives as possible.

What always struck me about the Nazis was that, while many things ran efficiently, there were still certain contradictions and irregularities. Even in this diabolical system of extermination, there were some loopholes and gaps. We just had to find them. It had been difficult, but not impossible, to sneak my father, mother, and brother into the ghetto. In the camp, the road to rescue appeared by chance in Oskar Schindler, a man full of idiosyncrasies. Whatever anyone may say about Schindler, one thing is certain: he saved people's lives, and what could be more important than that?

If, like me, you have accepted the fact that you are *moriturus*—about to die soon—and convinced that sooner or later you will be shot dead, it changes your way of thinking. A few years ago, I discovered an important sentence in a book by Ruth Kluger, who survived the Holocaust as a child. Her sentence perfectly reflects my attitude at the time: "Only despair gives us courage, while hope makes cowards of us all."[62] This is why I was able to remain so curiously calm and composed in the camp while striving to help my family and others as long as I was able to.

There were other camp inmates who also courageously opposed our oppressors—not with weapons, of course, for that would have been just a form of suicide. One was Natan Stern, Izak Stern's younger brother. At the end of 1943, he composed a handwritten report on the conditions in the camp for the American Jewish Joint Distribution Committee, an organization founded in 1914. In November 1943, Oskar Schindler took this report with him to Budapest where he met with two representatives of the AJDC, or "Joint," as it was called. The younger Stern brother had made a name for himself before the war as an astute and circumspect lawyer. He had been a junior partner in the well-known law firm of Dr. Ignacy Schwarzbart, a legislator and representative of the Jews in the Polish parliament. During the war, Schwarzbart became an official of the Polish government in exile in London. In the ghetto and later, in the camp, Natan Stern had a leading position in the Jewish Self-Help and Social Service Organization. At the meeting in Budapest, Schindler had to prove that he was a legitimate emissary from the Jews in the camp. That is why Natan Stern had given him a handwritten report about Płaszów. The assumption was that this document would be passed on to the leaders of the Polish government in exile. Of course, Stern could not sign the report, because that would have put his life in jeopardy. But he was sure that in London, Schwarzbart would recognize the handwriting of his former junior partner and be able to attest to the legitimacy of the "Stern Report." Schindler brought back about fifty thousand reichsmarks from Budapest for the Kraków Jews in the camp. With this money, inmates on daytime work details outside the camp could covertly buy a little food for themselves and their families or acquire things to trade. Any alleviation of our lot, no matter how small, helped us to persevere and survive.

I did not learn of Natan Stern's report until after the war. We always had to reckon with the possibility that on some pretext or other, we would be tortured, and so we didn't want to endanger each other unnecessarily. Our best protection was always to know as little as possible about what others were doing. So this report that was a possible risk to the Stern brothers was not discussed with me. Nor did I, at the time, discuss with them my trick with the inflated production lists. The best thing was for each of us to do what he was doing by himself. Schindler, as I later learned, traveled to Budapest several times. In his luggage he always had new reports of the situation in Poland and letters for the Joint. Schindler's contact man was a dentist originally from Vienna, Dr. Rudolf Sedlatschek, and via Schindler, he sent sums of money and letters from relatives in Palestine that were then distributed to Płaszów inmates by a network of contacts within the camp.

With the 1999 discovery of Schindler's suitcase in the attic of a house in Hildesheim, Germany, other documents came to light having to do with the Kraków-Płaszów camp and Schindler's rescue efforts. In the suitcase was a seven-page typescript entitled "The Confessions of Mr. X." It is a report by two members of the Joint code-named "Israel" and "Schmuel"—most probably Dr. Rudolf Kastner (Rezsö Israel Kasztner) and Joel Springmann—who had had a meeting with what the report calls "a tall, broad-shouldered, blond man from the other side" in order to learn the truth about the fate of the few Jewish camp inmates remaining in Poland.[63] The "man from the other side," referred to only as "Herr X," is clearly Oskar Schindler. The report of the two Joint members mentions the contents of a letter that Schindler always carried with him as additional proof that he was a legitimate friend and not a foe: "According to regulations, Jewish workers on their way to and from work—in this case the factory—must be escorted by guards with loaded weapons.[64] During an inspection, the SS officer who signed the letter had discovered the workers returning from the factory to the camp without armed escort." The letter also informed Mr. X that "no further Jewish workers would be put at his disposal."[65] It is apparent that this is the letter dictated to me by SS-*Hauptscharführer* Albert Hujer on March 28,

1943. It is this letter that motivated Schindler to seek immediate contact with Amon Göth. "According to Mr. X," the Joint report continues, "his friendship with this SS officer was difficult and expensive to maintain," for the SS officer had a "great liking for French cognac. When I visit him, I have to bring him at least five or six bottles at a cost of two or three thousand Zlotti [*sic*] per bottle. I go hunting and on drinking sprees with him. I've tried to convince him, in the course of killing at least two bottles of schnapps, that murdering Jews is actually senseless and unnecessary. I think I've had some effect on him. At least I succeeded in convincing him to allow me to delegate Jewish workers for my factory. I can pick and choose myself which ones I want. That is a real accomplishment."[66]

Upon returning from his trip to Hungary in late 1943, Oskar Schindler performed another bold stroke: he persuaded his supposed friend Amon Göth to give Dr. Sedlatschek a tour of the Płaszów camp. Göth always did things he thought would be to his advantage. He liked having influential people around him and clearly considered Schindler such a person. That probably explains why he didn't turn down Schindler's somewhat unusual request to give Sedlatschek a special tour.

On October 22, 1943, General Pohl in Oranienburg had directed that Kraków-Płaszów along with other camps be taken over as a concentration camp. Göth learned of the decision two or three days later. After receiving this piece of good news, Göth was in a splendid mood. Perhaps his excellent disposition was also due to the arrival of his bosom buddy from Vienna, SS-*Untersturmführer* Josef "Pepi" Neuschel, who had been appointed director of the camp factories and workshops. In any event, on the day of Neuschel's arrival, Göth was unusually chipper. That is why I can recall the following incident so vividly. He obviously wanted to impress his friend Pepi with the extent of the absolute power he enjoyed. So he carried out an inspection in the administrative offices of the headquarters barracks, in the course of which a few pieces of sausage came to light in the desk drawers of some Jewish clerks. They probably had gotten them from German contractors who sometimes slipped them something while visiting the camp. The Germans held the camp repair shops in high regard because they did excellent work for little money. In turn, we inmates were thankful for any work. In addition, a defective pistol was discovered. Even though there was a repair order for it and a receipt with the name of the owner attached to it, all according to regulations, Göth wanted to create an incident to demonstrate his power. He had about fifteen Jewish prisoners from these offices lined up. Ten of them were led off to be shot. The executions were to be carried out by Ferdinand Glaser, a Sudeten German and state police constable.

One of the ten was the girlfriend of a former schoolmate of mine from elementary school. I had not been present during the inspection of the desk drawers, and now my friend hastily informed me that his girlfriend and some other prisoners were about to be shot. Since I wanted to help him, I tried to think of a pretext to interrupt Göth. I found him standing near the headquarters building with Neuschel and several subordinates. I told him about several telephone calls containing news that would please him. Then I inquired if I could ask him a personal favor. When he nodded his head, I said that the woman from the workshop accounting department had absolutely nothing to do with the defective pistol they had discovered. I even listed a couple of reasons why.

To my astonishment, Göth acted magnanimously. "OK, then go bring her back." The group being led off to be shot, however, was already more than two hundred yards away from where we were standing. I gathered up all my courage and spoke to Göth again. "Forgive me, *Herr Commandeur*, but Constable Glaser will never believe me if I tell him he is to release the woman." Then a young, slightly lame SS man named Ruge spoke up without permission. He had heard this last remark and suggested that he could quickly catch up to the group and relay Göth's decision. He wanted to do me a favor because we'd had our desks in the same office for several weeks and got along well together. So he hurried off to the group and brought back the woman. The others were executed by Glaser. If I had run after them, Glaser would probably have simply added me to the candidates for execution. By his spontaneous offer of help, Ruge saved the woman's life. (After the war, she moved to Israel, where she died in 2004.) The fact that Göth granted my wish and allowed at least one person to be saved was possibly connected to the good news we had just received: the camp would continue to operate. That meant that he would not be sent to the front in the fall of 1943 and could continue to be his "own *commandeur*."

Many of the German SS men had never seen Jews before coming to Poland, since by the early 1940s, entire regions of German territory were *judenfrei*—free of Jews. So it is easy for me to understand how the omnipresent propaganda and the anti-Semitic school curricula could have such resonance. After the war, I discovered one of these perfidious screeds:

> The *Untermensch*—biologically apparently fully our equal, with hands, feet, and a sort of brain, with eyes and mouth—yet an utterly different, abominable creature, only a sketch of

Kraków-Płaszów camp, quarry.

> a human being, with humanoid features, but intellectually and spiritually lower than any animal. Within this being, a barbarous chaos of wild, unbridled passions, a nameless destructive will, the most primitive cravings, the most naked bestialities. He is and will remain nothing but an *Untermensch!*[67]

Indoctrinated by such inflammatory pamphlets, young SS men thought of Jews as creatures who only looked like human beings, but appearances being deceptive, the *Untermenschen* were not even the same species as they themselves, the *Herrenmenschen*—the Master Race. How easy it then was to conclude that the sufferings of these Jews were also a deception and not comparable to the suffering of the *Herrenmenschen.*

In my opinion, the real criminals were not just those who shot people but also the authors of such propaganda, infusing the minds of young people with their anti-Semitic poison. In present-day discussions, I always mention a young SS man named Dworschak. He came from the Sudetenland and was the very image of an ideal SS man: about 5'9", blond and blue-eyed. Perhaps that explains how he became a member of the SS-*Leibstandarte Adolf Hitler*, Hitler's personal bodyguard regiment.

One time in the early summer of 1943, Göth was about to leave for one of his frequent meetings in downtown Kraków. His BMW was already waiting by the camp gate, which had not been opened yet, and I was quickly taking down some notes for a letter as he dictated them while walking to his car. He then added a few words of instructions about what had to get done while he was away from the camp. At this point, the SS man Dworschak, who was an officer of the guard, came up to Göth with a report that the police had just arrested a woman carrying forged Polish documents in downtown Kraków and brought her to the camp. She was Jewish. The woman was standing about 150 yards from us with a child in her arms.

"Shoot her!" said Göth without so much as a glance in the direction of the woman and child.

Dworschak flushed, then said quietly but clearly, "I can't do it." For a moment, Göth was speechless. Then he started to roar at Dworschak, threatening him with all the torments of hell. I was practically struck dumb as well. Dworschak's response amounted to a refusal to obey orders, the orders of Göth, a superior officer who thought of himself as lord over life and death, to whom a human life meant nothing! Dworschak simply kept stammering, "I can't . . . I just can't." Finally Göth dismissed him.

More than sixty years later, I still remember the note Göth dictated to me for the man's personnel file. Dworschak was to be punished because he had "lied to his superior." I thought long and hard about this formulation. All punishments in the camp had to have a justification that was written down in the personnel files. But I had never before encountered "lying to a superior" as a justification. He had never used it before. I surmise that if one could have asked Göth to clarify his reasoning, he would probably have answered something like this: "Dworschak lied to me. Because it's a lie that he *couldn't* shoot the woman. He just *didn't want to* shoot her."

Dworschak was confined to barracks for a couple of weeks and blocked from receiving a promotion for a few months. Nothing else happened to him. So what one heard after the war over and over again from former soldiers or SS men—"If I hadn't obeyed the order, I would have wound up in a concentration camp myself"—was by no means true. That wasn't how it was, or wasn't always how it was. But no one knew what was in store for him in any given situation, and this uncertainty and fear alone kept them mute and obedient. And of course, I don't know what would have happened if the refusal to obey orders had happened near the front, or if a soldier had refused to execute partisans.

Above all, I wondered how a man like Dworschak, a soldier in an elite SS unit, facing an unknown punishment, could still refuse to obey the order of a camp commandant. What had induced him to do so? Perhaps the woman reminded him of someone near and dear to him. Perhaps he had a sister or a fiancée whom he recalled at that moment. Could it be that he felt sorry for the little child? I don't know his motivation. I only know that Dworschak didn't carry out the order. He didn't shoot the Jewish woman and her little child.

In the many talks I've given since 1994, only one schoolgirl has ever asked me what happened to the woman and child. They were shot, of course, that same afternoon by Senior Police Constable Wenzel. He had seen the whole incident from a short distance away and knew that I had also witnessed it. Perhaps that made him feel a certain need to justify his action the next morning. For when he picked up the mail for his company in the headquarters anteroom, as he did every morning, he said to me without being asked, in an almost whiny tone of voice, "What could I do? It was an order." I said nothing. For young Dworschak it had also been an order, a very strict one, in fact.

I know that SS men did not volunteer in droves for the execution squads, although those who did got extra schnapps and cigarettes. It was always the same ten or twenty men who were willing to do it. They were the ones who executed condemned camp inmates and captured Polish resistance fighters, usually on the so-called Execution Hill in the camp.

The guard details in the camp now belonged to an SS guard battalion under the command of SS-*Hauptsturmführer* Raebel. It consisted of the same SS and policemen who had been there when Płaszów was not yet a concentration camp, because the Economic and Administrative Main Office had no guard details of its own. Some so-called *fremdvölkisch*—ethnically foreign—troops were also part of these details. They came from the SS training camp Trawniki near Lublin. Most of them had been Russian, Lithuanian, Latvian, and Ukrainian POWs. They wore black uniforms and we inmates feared them because they were especially brutal. They assaulted us with rifles, carbines, and leather whips. As far as they were concerned, there was no clear distinction between strict treatment according to camp regulations and ruthless killing. The guard details in Schindler's factory on Lipowa

Street also consisted of such men. But Schindler bribed them with schnapps and cigarettes, so the workers—especially the women—could sleep somewhat more soundly.

Once Kraków-Płaszów had been converted to a concentration camp on January 10, 1944, Göth stopped dictating personnel notices to me. It was one of the few new regulations he strictly observed. I also no longer had access to the personnel files of the SS. Instead, Göth appointed a non-com from Alsatia as his personnel officer. Charles Ehlinger was a former accounting officer in the French army who had been taken prisoner by the Germans in 1940. His father was German and his mother French and he spoke German with a slight French accent. When he was captured, they told him, "Your name isn't Charles, it's Karl—Karl Ehlinger." They did not intern him in a POW camp but instead declared him a *Volksdeutscher*—an ethnic German. Against his will, as he later told me, they then stuck him in the SS "to consolidate his worldview." That's how he wound up in Płaszów.

In 1960, shortly after moving from Kraków to Germany, I traveled to Mühlhausen in Alsatia, now part of France again. I had learned that after the war, France had treated Alsatians who had "changed sides" during the Nazi era very harshly. They apparently overlooked the fact that many, like Charles Ehlinger, had been forced to do so. I wanted to help him and attest to the fact that he had always treated me decently. Unfortunately, I was unable to find him at the address he had given me. I then called all the Ehlingers in the telephone book—sadly to no avail.

Back on April 30, 1942, General Pohl of the Economic and Administrative Main Office had already informed General Richard Glücks, the head of Working Group D in Berlin-Oranienburg, as well as all current concentration camp commandants, plant managers, and agents of the *W* (business) offices, about the regulations for camp commandants. Under point four, Pohl wrote, "The camp commandant has sole responsibility for *prisoners' work assignments*. These assignments must be *exhaustive* in the literal sense of the word in order to attain the highest possible output." Furthermore, Pohl defined the division of responsibilities between the camps and Working Group D in Berlin: "The *allocation of contracts* is made solely by the chief of Working Group D in the central office. The camp commandants are not permitted to accept any contracts from third parties on their own, nor to negotiate such contracts." Under point eight, the final point, Pohl outlined the qualifications for camp commandants: "Carrying out this order places considerably more demands on every camp commandant than has previously been the case. Since the camps are so dissimilar, we have dispensed with uniform regulations. Instead, the camp commandant himself must take the initiative. He must combine precise expertise in military and economic matters with intelligence and wisdom in leading groups of people who are to be brought to a high degree of performance."[68]

A month before that, Pohl had already informed the concentration camp commandants that "As of March 16, 1942 therefore, the entire Inspectorate of Concentration Camps is integrated into the Economic and Administrative Main Office of the SS as Working Group D."[69] These orders from 1942 were already well known in other concentration camps by the time Płaszów became one itself in early 1944. But for Amon Göth, now the commandant of the "Płaszów Concentration Camp," these regulations were something entirely new, and there were several administrative matters he needed to catch up on. For that reason, he liked visiting other concentration camps and always returned with new ideas and suggestions. He seemed especially impressed by the wrought-iron gates in other camps with their cynical mottos such as *Arbeit macht frei*[70] and *Jedem das Seine*.[71] He brought a piece of paper back from one of these trips and told me to have the camp draftsmen copy the saying out in large letters. I knew the text and mumbled it to myself sotto voce in Italian. "What was that?" asked Göth. "It's the last line of the inscription over the gates to hell in Dante's *Divine Comedy*. '*Lasciate ogni speranza, voi ch'entrate.*' It's often translated as, 'Abandon hope, all ye who enter here.'" Göth remained silent. I'm not sure what made him change his mind, but in any case, Płaszów did not adopt this motto, or any other for that matter.

Göth returned from another trip with the idea of setting up a brothel in the camp. His plan was to reward inmates who did outstanding work with brothel visits. While he was talking about his new plan, I found myself almost incapable of grasping such a monstrous idea. A brothel? Here in the camp? Where such hunger prevailed and our people could barely stand up they were so weak? But of course, there were a few privileged inmates who certainly would not have been averse to amusing themselves in a brothel. And whose daughter, whose sister, whose wife would draw this lot? But on no account was one allowed to argue with Göth's ideas. Cautiously, I inquired if I was allowed to say something.

"*Ja, ja*," he answered.

I said, "There are probably brothels in other concentration camps because prisoners were sent there individually. But our camp is a continuation of the ghetto. We have entire families here. I think that if you want to introduce a system of rewards for good work, our people would be more pleased with some extra rations—bread or soup they could give to their families. That's more important for our prisoners than going to a brothel." Later, Göth had a plan to build a brothel just for the Russian guards, but it was never carried out either. For quite some time already, the SS men in the camp had been receiving vouchers for a brothel in town that the SS had set up for its own people in the former House of Jewish Academicians.

Another time, Göth had in mind to tattoo the Płaszów inmates after visiting the Mauthausen concentration camp. He told me to order metal number punches from zero to nine from the camp's metal shop. To save time, each inmate was to be tattooed with a single impression of three to five individual number punches held together in a metal clamp. "Not just inmate numbers in the SS files anymore," I thought in horror. "No, now we're going to have our number tattooed into our flesh as well. From slaves to livestock—visibly branded for all to see, for the rest of our lives." Again, I cautiously asked if I might say something. I explained my reservations about being able to tattoo with this kind of metal punch.

"Why won't it work?" Göth asked in irritation. "They tattoo Jews in all the other camps, and with this stamp we can do it faster and more efficiently than with a single needle."

"The practice of the fakirs in India is to lie down on a bed of nails without injuring themselves," I carefully replied. "They do it so cautiously and evenly that not even one point pierces their skin." Göth gave me a skeptical look and said nothing for a while, while I assured him that I would of course order the stamp punches, "but the skin will present too much resistance to be tattooed with a stamp like that." Göth replied only, "Nonsense. You've just got to press harder." My remarks, however, must have set him thinking. He must have asked the German camp physician, Dr. Max Blancke, who seems to have confirmed my surmises that his idea was not feasible. Later, Göth inquired if I had already ordered the metal punches. I told him that I had. "Then cancel the order. We're not going to tattoo."

Helena Hirsch, a former domestic servant in Göth's villa in the camp, testified about his hubris at his 1946 trial. He had told her more than once that "when he gave an order, it was like the word of God."[72] Göth reveled in his absolute power and enjoyed intimidating people. Any inmates who could have threatened him were liquidated without further ado. He thought of himself as the "uncrowned king" of Płaszów and expected absolute obedience.

Such arrogance was typical of many SS men. They not only flaunted their power over the inmates, but also tried to outdo or trump each other as well. One day SS-*Sturmbannführer* Willi Haase, SS-*Oberführer* Julian Scherner's chief of staff, brought his two daughters into camp headquarters and sent for a barber. Göth was not in Płaszów at the time. He and Haase couldn't stand each other. Haase insisted on having his girls' hair cut in Göth's private office, where there was a long-haired sheepskin rug, dyed red, on the floor. I was scared to death that some of the cuttings would remain on this rug. If Göth found out that Willi Haase had used his office as a beauty salon for his children, there would be hell to pay. I had the floor carefully covered with towels, which I later shook out thoroughly.

I had learned one thing very quickly from the correspondence and telegrams I presorted and placed on the commandant's desk: if you pleased him, you lived; if you didn't, you died. I later read in the trial records of Rudolf Höss—the commandant of Auschwitz who had organized the entire machinery of murder on Himmler's orders—that there was no evidence that Höss had personally tortured, shot, or even struck a single inmate. Göth, however, had done so repeatedly. Seen in this light, he was worse than Höss. His personal behavior was more extreme and brutal than that of other commandants. At his trial, the presiding judge asked Göth whether he had had explicit instructions from his superiors for every death sentence that had been carried out. Not in every case, answered Göth. Instead, his general guideline had been to treat prisoners severely. And besides, he hadn't had enough reliable German personnel to work with.

As far as I am concerned, Göth was a perfect example of how the elements that make a person uniquely human—specifically one's conscience and self-control, to say nothing of one's compassion or empathy—can be lost. I don't know what motivates someone to become a murderer. Göth did more than just follow the orders of his superiors. He always thought up ways to be even more cruel and merciless. Göth's behavior seemed like the negative reflection of my own ethical convictions.

After January 1944, however, Göth had to keep his violent outbursts somewhat under control, for his harsh punishments and constant abuse impinged on production quotas and decreased the profits of the SS. As arms workers of a new concentration camp, our production was now considered "crucial for victory." Our value for the war effort increased and we were somewhat better protected from Göth's indiscriminate acts of torture and murder. From now on, D II department was in charge and it organized the work assignments of the camp inmates. In my February 1950 deposition for Maurer's trial, I explained what that meant in practice: "Requests, supported by written confirmation from various authorities and offices (documenting, for instance, the necessity of fulfilling the production program of the factory making the request, or its shortage of civilian workers), would be forwarded from the camp to the D II department of the Economic and Administrative Main Office in Berlin-Oranienburg on preprinted forms with several carbon copies. Receipt of the requests was confirmed by the personal signature of Gerhard Maurer, the head of the D II department. Sometimes, especially when only a small number of prisoners was involved, it was taken care of by Maurer's deputy, SS-*Obersturmführer* Sommer, who in 1944 was promoted to *Hauptsturmführer*. The head of work details in the camp—in Płaszów it was SS-*Hauptscharführer* Franz Müller—organized the work brigades, assigned tasks to various prisoners, received daily receipts from the employers for the number of prisoners brought to the workplace, and carried out inspections of the premises. He also checked to make sure the prisoners were working effectively, at the jobs specified in the request, that the factory was following the regulations for preventing prisoner escapes, and that the armed escort was really overseeing the prisoners and keeping them hard at work."[73]

D II department thus examined, processed, and carried out almost all matters having to do with prisoners. This was primarily the result of the fact that in 1944, all concentration camp inmates were integrated into the larger system of production for the war. It's difficult for me to state exactly the entire scope of responsibilities of the D II department, but it was enormous.

> For all practical purposes, it was Working Group D that apportioned prisoners for work. Only in rare instances was the

> camp commandant authorized to assign work details himself, for example, in particularly urgent cases, or when a job was short-term and involved a small number of inmates. Then the submitted requests would be processed in the camp, and it was also the commandant's responsibility to oversee the security situation. "Security" in this case meant not workplace safety nor protection from accidents, but rather safeguarding against escape attempts and partisan raids to free the prisoners, ensuring that the inmates were kept separate from civilian workers in the factory in question, and the prevention of any possible contact with the outside world.[74]

In view of the steady deterioration in the situation of the German army on both fronts, on June 17, 1944, Heinrich Himmler explicitly ordered that the task of "securing the concentration camps and their satellite labor camps" be turned over to the higher SS and police chiefs.[75] The Higher SS and Police Chief East General Wilhelm Koppe (successor to General Krüger) became the most senior security commissioner in the Generalgouvernement, able to intervene immediately in an emergency without first consulting the Economic and Administrative Main Office. I would guess it was Koppe who in mid-June 1944 ordered Göth to develop a security plan for the concentration camp Płaszów. On June 6, 1944, the Allies had landed in Normandy and on July 20, 1944, there had been an assassination attempt against Adolf Hitler. I learned of these events from the newspapers I read when I was alone in the main office. The military situation in general did not look good for Germany. In addition, the SS was worried about possible attacks by partisans or a prisoners' uprising.

Now, when Göth called me to take dictation at night, I could see he was struggling against leaden fatigue. One of the Jewish camp doctors had told me that Göth had diabetes and severe liver problems. Whether because of exhaustion caused by his illnesses or simply for the sake of convenience, he continued to entrust me with some internal SS affairs even though this violated the official rules and regulations for concentration camps. By June 1944, he had become outright negligent. One evening he gave me the "Alarm and Defense Plans" of two or three other concentration camps with the remark that no one must find out he had done so. He gave me the assignment of modifying these plans to fit our camp. It was mainly a question of detailing how many watch towers we had, how many minutes it took to change the guard, where the telephone lines ran, how an alarm could be quickly and securely communicated, who was to be contacted in an emergency, and where the camp gates and other exits were located. So there I sat, all by myself, and was charged with doing something I did not know anything about. I, a Jewish camp inmate, had access to and even had to draw up plans that were supposed to be top secret. How highly classified and secret the "Alarm and Defense Plans" really were I only realized after Göth's arrest in September 1944. The SS got suspicious of my work in the office and I was incarcerated for two weeks in the basement prison of the infamous Gray House.

Since the first months of the forced labor camp, in the spring and summer of 1943, Göth had wielded absolute and arbitrary power. He had tortured and shot people at will, had prisoners flogged and hanged or worse, ripped apart by his dogs, without having to be accountable to his superiors in Kraków. From January 1944 on, however, as the commandant of a concentration camp, Göth had to obtain official permission from Berlin-Oranienburg to punish an inmate. The application form had a space for the number of requested strokes on the bare buttocks, and another space for the number of nights a prisoner had to spend after work in the *Stehbunker* before reporting for his normal shift in the morning. We kept a stack of the blank forms in the commandant's office. The forms had to be filled out in triplicate and in various colors. Two copies went to the D II department and one carbon copy remained in the camp. The punishment could only be carried out once permission had been granted from Berlin. But to assume that

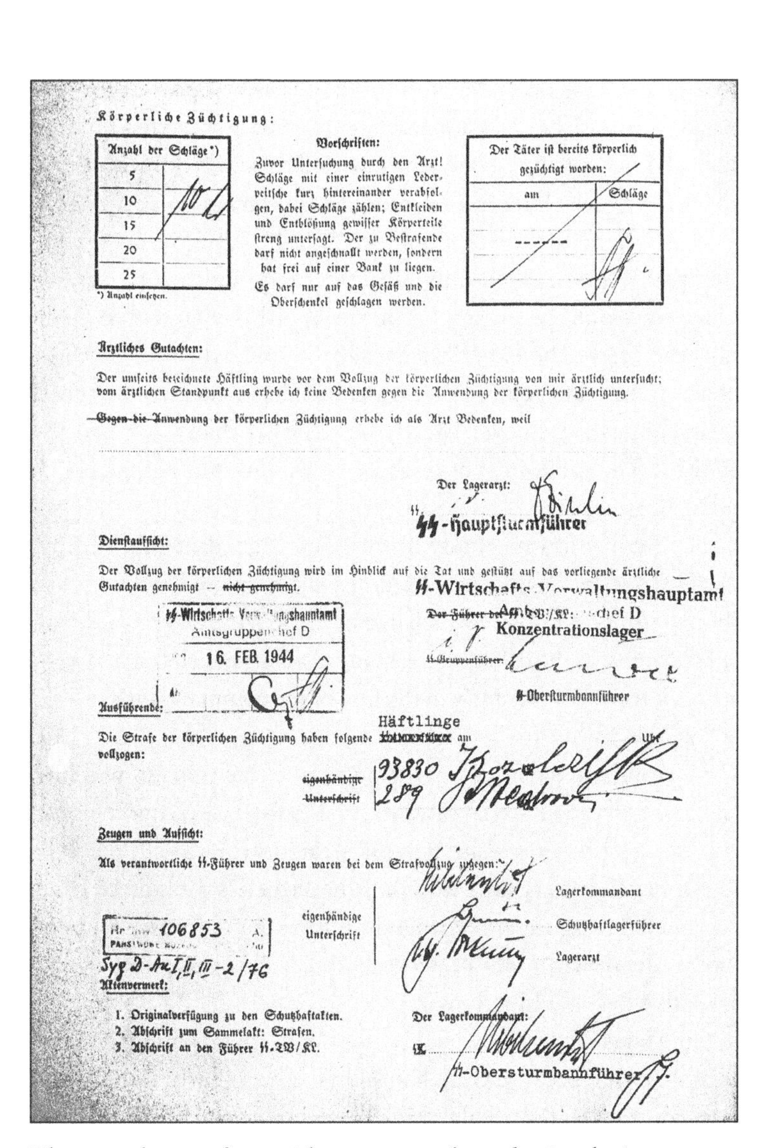

Körperliche Züchtigung:

Anzahl der Schläge*)	
5	
10	10
15	
20	
25	

*) Anzahl einsetzen.

Vorschriften:

Zuvor Untersuchung durch den Arzt! Schläge mit einer einrutigen Lederpeitsche kurz hintereinander verabfolgen, dabei Schläge zählen; Entkleiden und Entblößung gewisser Körperteile streng untersagt. Der zu Bestrafende darf nicht angeschnallt werden, sondern hat frei auf einer Bank zu liegen.

Es darf nur auf das Gesäß und die Oberschenkel geschlagen werden.

Der Täter ist bereits körperlich gezüchtigt worden:

am	Schläge

Ärztliches Gutachten:

Der umseits bezeichnete Häftling wurde vor dem Vollzug der körperlichen Züchtigung von mir ärztlich untersucht; vom ärztlichen Standpunkt aus erhebe ich keine Bedenken gegen die Anwendung der körperlichen Züchtigung.

~~Gegen die Anwendung~~ der körperlichen Züchtigung erhebe ich als Arzt Bedenken, weil

Der Lagerarzt:

SS-Hauptsturmführer

Dienstaufsicht:

Der Vollzug der körperlichen Züchtigung wird im Hinblick auf die Tat und gestützt auf das vorliegende ärztliche Gutachten genehmigt — ~~nicht genehmigt~~.

SS-Wirtschafts-Verwaltungshauptamt
Amtsgruppenchef D
16. FEB. 1944

SS-Wirtschafts-Verwaltungshauptamt
~~Der Führer der~~ Amtsgruppenchef D
Konzentrationslager
i. V.
~~SS-Gruppenführer~~
SS-Obersturmbannführer

Ausführende:

Die Strafe der körperlichen Züchtigung haben folgende Häftlinge am vollzogen:

~~eigenhändige Unterschrift~~ 93830 289

Zeugen und Aufsicht:

Als verantwortliche SS-Führer und Zeugen waren bei dem Strafvollzug zugegen:

eigenhändige Unterschrift

Lagerkommandant

Schutzhaftlagerführer

Lagerarzt

Nr. 106853

Syg D-AuI,II,III-2/76

Aktenvermerk:

1. Originalverfügung zu den Schutzhaftakten.
2. Abschrift zum Sammelakt: Strafen.
3. Abschrift an den Führer SS-TV/KL.

Der Lagerkommandant:

SS-Obersturmbannführer

The second page of a punishment report from the Auschwitz concentration camp. Maurer's signature is in the middle of the page on the right-hand side.[76]

because of these procedures things had really improved for the inmates would be delusional. Things were not better by any means! True, an application form would be sent to Oranienburg and a few weeks later a form would arrive granting permission to give an inmate a certain number of lashes. But for any given inmate, the new system only meant getting punished twice, for prisoners would be beaten up on the spot by whatever SS man happened to be there, and then a second time when the permission to punish arrived back from the D II department. Sometimes Oranienburg would even specify more lashes than Göth had requested. The random shootings by Göth and other SS men did cease, however.

The permission-to-punish forms were signed or initialed by Gerhard Maurer. Sometimes Maurer's deputy would sign with the abbreviation "o.V.i.A.," which meant "*oder Vertreter im Amt*"—or his deputy in the office. I saw many of these signed forms arriving back from Oranienburg in the files of the commandant's office.

Thus from January 1944 on, the punishment of inmates was bureaucratically regulated. However, in August 1944, Amon Göth, who had to fill out a written application in triplicate to the D II department for every little whipping, nevertheless was able to have the senior Jewish inmate Wilhelm Chilowicz and fourteen others shot to death without a previous inquiry. This was another one of Göth's evil machinations.

On August 13, 1944, a Sunday morning, friends came to me in great agitation because Göth had shown up very early at the camp gate, contrary to his usual habits. I hurried over to headquarters.

Göth was sitting in his office, surrounded by some SS officers, among them SS Officer Richartz, in civilian life an Austrian dentist from Carinthia, but then working as an SS judicial officer. The interrogation of one of the inmates was already under way. He had been accused by the camp guard Sowinski of trying to bargain with him to obtain a weapon. The inmate, a tall young man, vehemently denied it, but Sowinski persisted in his accusation. Finally, Göth ordered the inmate to exit the building through one of the windows on the corridor. The inmate obeyed, and just as his feet touched the grass outside headquarters, Göth drew his revolver and shot him in the head.

He then turned to me. "Now we will need several interrogation transcripts about the escape attempt of the Chilowicz group. And by the way, Chilowicz said that Pemper also intended to escape." I knew immediately that my death sentence would now be carried out, and this would be the official reason given for it. I was trembling inside, but outwardly I remained calm and replied, "Chilowicz lied. It's not true. In his tailor-made suit and custom shoes, he wouldn't attract attention in Kraków after his escape. But I'd be recognized immediately as an inmate"—pointing to a split seam on the right pant leg of my threadbare striped prison uniform—"and brought back to the camp." Göth laughed and said I should stick around to take dictation.

That afternoon, the dictation took place in Göth's villa. Again, SS Officer Richartz was present. He gave his blessing to the dictated sentences and attested to the fact that Göth was not acting arbitrarily, but rather "in order to prevent a large rebellion in the camp."

Taking dictation from Göth, Richartz, and the others lasted several hours. They described in great detail the preparations for the rebellion—how weapons were obtained, for example. This uprising supposedly would have made it possible to open the camp gates for a short time and give a large number of inmates a chance to escape. Hiding places outside the camp had already been arranged as well. All of it, of course, was a fabrication.

Finally the dictation came to an end, and I set off from the commandant's villa to the main office to type up the long reports. But then Göth opened a small side window and called out to me. I went back the few steps. "In the appendix, leave one space blank at the bottom of the list of names." My heart stood still. He meant the list with the names of the "ringleaders of the just prevented camp insurrection" who were to be executed. And my name would be added on the last line! I had no doubt of it, especially after Göth's remark of that same morning. Now I had to type the report of my own execution.

So I returned to the office. It was late afternoon, and I had a good two hours of typing to do before the mail was sent off by courier with the night train to Berlin—the mail that would contain the notice of my execution, among others.

On my way back, I was accosted by the Russian guard Wasniuk. Since he was falling-down drunk, he obviously didn't remember that I had permission to move freely within the camp. "My God," I thought, "if he knocks me off now, at least I won't have to type this report!" But he let me pass. I delivered my work by the deadline, with the last line left blank, as ordered. Fourteen men and women would be shot that day. I waited . . .

It was clear that Göth intended to eliminate disagreeable accessories to his black-market dealings and to cover up his tracks. He wanted to shoot me, too, so that no witness to his arbitrary murders and brutal actions would remain alive. If by 1944, even the flogging of a single camp inmate had to be authorized via a paper trail by the D II department, the murder of fifteen people, I figured, would certainly have required a special permit and a preliminary investigation, in the course of which the inmates to be executed would have revealed things about Göth's regime—his random acts of violence, his way of life, and his black-market activities—that could have endangered his position.

Chilowicz, a simple journeyman furrier, was Göth's voluntary personal slave. If he had survived the war, he, as a Jew, would have been indicted along with Göth. I can't say whether he would have been condemned to death. It's true that he helped some of his fellow prisoners, but it's also true that he harmed all too many others. He was utterly convinced that he and his family would make it and survive the war. He frequently and grossly overestimated his own capabilities. As Halina Nelken has written, "The inhumane conditions had affected people's character. Bad people became completely evil; good people were transformed into saints."[77] Wilek Chilowicz carried out all orders without a second thought. It was rumored in the camp that on Göth's orders he had even hanged his own mother. Fortunately, that was not true, since she was already dead by that time.

How cleverly Göth had contrived to murder Chilowicz and the other "insurrectionists" I learned a week thereafter, when SS-*Hauptscharführer* Grabow again asked for my help in composing a difficult letter. While leafing through the files, I stumbled upon the precise details of the plan.

At the beginning of August 1944, Göth had made an appointment to speak with General Wilhelm Koppe, the higher SS and police chief east and by then also the senior security commissioner for the Generalgouvernement. Göth informed him that an uprising was being planned in the camp, and he could prevent it, provided he was allowed to carry out a surprise raid and do so immediately, without having to inform Oranienburg ahead of time, without conducting the usual official inquiry, and above all, without a judicial proceeding. He already knew who the ring leaders were. Based on Göth's claim, General Koppe gave him written permission to proceed. Göth now recruited one of the guards, a Pole named Sowinski, from a village near Zakopane, who claimed to be an ethnic German. Sowinski approached Chilowicz and got him involved in a plan to escape, claiming that he had already arranged a safe hiding place for him in Kraków. But Chilowicz became suspicious and asked for a pistol as a sign of Sowinski's good intentions. After consulting with Göth, Sowinski got him a pistol but had its firing pin filed down in such a way that it looked like a working pistol, but it wouldn't fire. Chilowicz didn't notice anything wrong and of course had no opportunity to try the pistol out in the camp.

Early on the morning of August 13, Chilowicz, his wife, and a few other prisoners had planned to leave the camp, hidden in a truck with a wood-burning engine. Of course, Sowinski had informed Göth of this plan. While the commandant hardly ever showed up on weekends before ten o'clock, on this day he was up before seven, standing at the camp's main gate. He ordered the truck searched. As expected, they found Chilowicz and his group. They also found diamonds with which Chilowicz had planned to finance his escape. I was astonished to learn that such valuables were still to be found in the camp. Chilowicz and the others must indeed have been involved in black-market dealings to be able to acquire diamonds, for the normal currency in the camp was bread and cigarettes. Göth ordered the approximately fifteen people in Chilowicz's group "liquidated" that same afternoon. In order to implicate the camp's entire leadership team in this murder and thus ensure their collective silence, he assigned each of his senior SS officers one person to shoot. He probably also thought this would suggest to his superiors in Berlin that by quick and concerted action, all the leading SS officers had prevented a camp insurrection.

A little later, I learned the reason for leaving the last line of the list of names blank. One of the people in Chilowicz's group was Alexander Spanlang. He was a Jew and the technical director of the carpentry and cabinet-making shop. When he was already stripped and standing on Execution Hill, he told SS-*Untersturmführer* Anton Scheidt (from Ibbenbüren in Westphalia) that he had some saddle horses and a large supply of expensive wall tiles hidden with a Polish farmer outside Kraków. Such ceramic tiles were much sought-after by the Germans.

Spanlang promised to tell Scheidt where they were if he didn't shoot him. Scheidt informed Göth, and they decided to let Spanlang live for the time being, because that Sunday, for reasons unknown to me, they couldn't go to the farmer to pick up the tiles. So Göth didn't add Spanlang's name to the list until after I had delivered the typed report to him for his signature. I assume that Göth's mistress, Ruth Kalder, typed it in. She sometimes typed letters for him, especially when they were extremely urgent or top secret. Göth probably wanted to ensure that I couldn't warn Spanlang, who then might not reveal where his treasures were hidden.

The next day, Spanlang led some SS men to where the farmer lived. They loaded up all the tiles and the horses. When Scheidt then shot Spanlang, his name was already on its way to Berlin as well as in the files of the higher SS and police chief in Kraków. Göth was enormously sly, with a highly developed criminal mind that spared no one, not even collaborators like Chilowicz and Simche Spira, the former head of the Jewish police in the ghetto. These opportunists thought they would be the only ones to survive the war. But they were no match for Göth's criminal energy.

Whoever hoped to use Amon Göth for his own ends needed to be very clever about it. It was a strange irony of history that, in the fall of 1943, it was in Göth's own best interest to preserve the camp from being liquidated. That's why my trick with the inflated production tables worked. Yet in spite of this, Göth could dispose of me whenever he wanted. Oskar Schindler alone was the equal of Göth, his supposed friend. And to our good fortune, personally and morally Schindler was Göth's infinite superior.

OSKAR SCHINDLER, ONE OF THE RIGHTEOUS AMONG THE NATIONS

IT WAS ABOVE ALL Steven Spielberg's film that made Schindler's rescue operation famous. According to the Shoah Visual History Foundation, more than 300 million viewers all over the world have seen *Schindler's List* since it was released in 1993. The film is the Jewish director's homage to his mother who survived the war in a camp in Eastern Europe. Spielberg was born in the United States in 1947. The film's dramatic structure contrasts the figures of Amon Göth and Oskar Schindler, who face each other like demon and angel, one a mass murderer, the other a rescuer. I knew both of them intimately, a rare and remarkable experience. It was a precious gift for me to discover that a true human being like Oskar Schindler could exist even in the darkness of hell.

Both Göth and Schindler were born in 1908. In contrast to Göth, Schindler was never combative or aggressive. He exuded a personal warmth that opened many doors for him. He hailed from Zwittau in the Sudetenland, which became part of Czechoslovakia after the First World War and is today Svitavy in the Czech Republic. Even as a young man, he was a German patriot, but his uninhibited *joie de vivre*, his love of freedom, his wit, and his lively intelligence quickly led him to doubt the tenor and truth of German policies after September 1, 1939. In the mid-1950s, he wrote to the Jerusalem historian K. J. Ball-Kaduri, "Once I had experienced the first few months of the German occupation in the protectorate of Bohemia and in Poland, it became crystal-clear to me that I, like millions of other ethnic Germans outside the

Reich, had fallen for an extremely effective propaganda campaign. We had fallen under the sway of a gang of sadistic murderers and hypocritical swindlers who had fraudulently taken over the government of a great nation."[78]

Schindler spoke exceptionally beautiful and vivid German, and his surviving letters attest to his cordiality and innate kindness. In his conversations with me, he often used the Wehrmacht ranks instead of the newly coined SS ranks.[79] His politics tended to be conservative and he possessed strong ethical principles. Schindler once formulated his inner struggle this way:

> During the war, I was often under a lot of mental stress from the discrepancy between my ethical beliefs and what was happening politically. It cost me a lot of effort, but at last I was able to completely overcome the imperative of unquestioning obedience with which I had been inculcated, that is, my respect for law and order. I no longer accepted anything uncritically, and came to trust only my own judgment, my own humanity and sense of empathy. The sufferings of the persecuted that I witnessed every day, as well as friends who thought the same way I did, helped me overcome the conflict within myself.[80]

Göth and Schindler were like two opposing poles. Both enjoyed certain privileges within the German Wehrmacht and Nazi bureaucracy, but each used this freedom of action in his own unique way. Göth wanted to tattoo us with numbers and murder our families; Schindler requested workers by their first and last names, not by their camp numbers, and when his factory was moved to Brünnlitz, he insisted on bringing their families along as well.

To us, "his Jews," as he called us, Oskar Schindler was a sort of father figure. His moral transformation did not occur from one day to the next. Instead, Schindler grew into his new role step by step. He certainly didn't come to Kraków as a rescuer; he came as a businessman. But when he saw what was going on in Poland, and how the occupiers were treating us, he decided to do something about it. I am quite sure that at first, we were only a source of cheap labor for him. But over the course of the war years, we became human beings he cared for and worried about. Oskar Schindler, the erstwhile profit-oriented businessman, developed into a staunch saver of lives. "It is essential to record," he emphasized in 1956, "that my transformation did not begin on July 20, 1944,[81] long after all fronts had begun to collapse and many people no longer wanted to keep going, but rather four years earlier, when the German *blitzkrieg* was taking everyone's breath away."[82]

Schindler even became a close friend to many of us. When I came to work more closely with him in Brünnlitz, I could see that he very much enjoyed his role as a rescuer. The responsibility he had taken upon himself was enormous; hundreds of eyes were watching him, expecting his help. He composed his farewell address to us on May 8, 1945, the day the Germans capitulated, with great attention to detail. In it, he evoked the bonds of friendship: "I appeal to all of you who have been with me for so many difficult years, fearing never to see this day." He urged us to remain calm and disciplined. I find it difficult to imagine how he himself could still possess such prudence and emotional power at that late date. He was concerned about the postwar period. He hoped to return to Czechoslovakia, and even imagined that some of us would stay with him and help him become the great industrialist his father had yearned to become but was never able to.

Oskar married his wife, Emilie, in Zwittau in 1928. She came to Kraków with him, but soon returned to her native Sudetenland. But when her husband moved his factory and "his Jews" to Brünnlitz, she came to the camp and helped out however she could. She had good contacts with farmers and millers in the surrounding countryside and was tireless in her search for extra rations, because our food supplies were very meager, despite official ration cards. Emilie Schindler also risked long drives farther afield, into the region around Brünnlitz, to obtain medicines and bandages for our improvised camp infirmary.

At first, Schindler had trouble finding a good new location for his factory. People in the villages surrounding Brünnlitz did not want an arms factory nearby, to say nothing of Jews. Later, we heard that it was due to Emilie Schindler and her powers of persuasion that Schindler obtained permission to set up production in an abandoned spinning factory.

Schindler was proud of his plucky wife and spoke of her with great respect. Reflecting on the war, he recalled, "She wasn't afraid to deal with anyone; she even treated some of the SS officers as if they were domestic help." In contrast, he scoffed at his fellow industrialists in Kraków-Zabłocie. "I know some 'quite decent' fellows who probably live better today than I do. But they failed at the critical juncture" and left their Jewish workers to their fate in the last year of the war. "These 'quite decent' fellows now stride through life, heads held high . . . once again manufacturing cables and condensers. . . . I wonder how many of these men's wives would have traveled 200 miles through intense cold, lugging a suitcase full of schnapps too heavy for a man to carry, to exchange it for medicine for emaciated Jews whom German barbarity had almost robbed of their last spark of life? Such magnanimity was a matter of course for my wife. She didn't give a damn about danger if there were people in dire need."[83]

Schindler's concern for us extended even beyond the end of the war. Near the factory in Brünnlitz there was a German navy depot. Schindler bargained with the depot managers for large amounts of blue and mustard-colored cloth. We brought the rolls of material to the camp and our tailors measured out lengths for dark blue suits and yellow pajamas for each of us so that we would all have something to wear after the war. I wore those pajamas for years. But I only found out a few years ago how much this deal had cost Schindler. He wrote, "Before the end of the war, eighteen truckloads of pure worsted yarn, material for suits, coats, and underwear, thousands of spools of thread, shoes, and other supplies" were driven into the camp so that every one of our group

Izak Stern, left, and Oskar Schindler in Paris, 1949.

of a thousand "would have enough material for two suits, a coat, underwear, etc. once we were free."[84] Experts estimate the value of those materials to have been more than $150,000. Schindler later also drew up a list of the construction costs for his satellite camp on Lipowa Street in Kraków-Zabłocie, the cost of having his own SS guards there, the enormous bribes he had to pay them, and the huge costs for food bought on the black market for his Emalia workers. His total costs came to more than 5,250,000 reichsmarks.

Everyone in the camp knew about Schindler's opulent lifestyle, and he was self-critical enough to admit it. "I'm not a saint by any means. I'm a self-indulgent person with more faults than the average man who goes through life minding his own business."[85] Yet his greatest achievement was to invest his entire fortune to save the lives of more than 1,100 people.

In the fall of 1946, we learned that Schindler and his wife were living in southern Germany. He asked us to do everything possible to help him emigrate. At the time, there were still quite a few survivors in Kraków. We contacted various Jewish agencies, and the "Joint," the umbrella organization for Jewish welfare societies, invited the Schindlers to come to Paris, where help would be arranged for them. Schindler said he wanted to set up as a rancher in Argentina and raise nutrias for their fur. I can just imagine the Joint people looking at each other in astonishment when they heard that. Jewish women's organizations in England purchased a bungalow in Argentina so the Schindlers would have a place to live rent free. I was surprised to learn that the ranch failed after only a short time. Although in my opinion Schindler was exceedingly daring, he was a good entrepreneur, capable of calculating his costs. Later, his marriage also foundered and the Schindlers separated for good. In 1957, Schindler returned to Germany, alone and broke, to try to obtain a *Lastenausgleich*, compensation paid by the West German government to those who had suffered losses under the Nazis. I helped him as much as I could. It was the least I could do. It's always been my belief that you can make or lose as much money as you like, but only what you do for others has permanent value. Oskar Schindler lived by this principle and saved lives.

Oskar Schindler outdid himself during the war, but he quickly lost his vigor once the war was over. The six war years were his glory years. Neither before 1939 nor after 1945 did he particularly distinguish himself. He was an extraordinary man, but only in extraordinary times. After the war, in everyday life, he never really got back on his feet again. Nor did Germany ever give him the public recognition he deserved during his lifetime. As his former secretary Elisabeth Tont remarked in 1994, "I'm telling you what I remember for Oskar Schindler's sake, because our compatriots from the Sudetenland have never adequately appreciated what he did. I was always offended by that, because I knew he helped the Jews out of the pure goodness of his heart. I still have a bone to pick with them. They have never given him any recognition."[86]

Schindler was venerated in Israel as one of the "Righteous among the Nations" and was asked to plant his own tree at the Yad Vashem Memorial in 1967. In Germany, he was awarded the *Grosses Bundesverdienstkreuz*—the Great Federal Cross of Merit—the highest award for service to the nation. But there was never widespread appreciation for what he had done. His health deteriorated rapidly in his final years. We always thought he would live to be a hundred, but sick and lonely, Oskar Schindler died in Hildesheim in 1974. When Emilie Schindler died in October 2001, however, condolences poured in from people all over the world, including heads of state. A letter to Schindler's niece from the president of the United States shows that even today, the rescue operation of Oskar and Emilie Schindler is often more appreciated abroad than in Germany.

After the war, I often heard it said that Oskar Schindler helped us mainly from a sense of obligation toward former Jewish class-

Oskar Schindler in the early 1960s.

mates and friends. As I mentioned, I have a different take from my many conversations with him. I believe his motives were mixed and their relative importance shifted during the war. At first, Schindler was nothing but a businessman interested in making a quick buck. But when he saw what a miserable life we were leading in the ghetto, his urge to help us began to grow. By the time we were in the camp, his determination to stand by us was so strong that he ran risks and made sacrifices. And then came his truly great and unique deed: his rescue operation, the list, and the move to Brünnlitz. And he stayed the course until we were liberated in May 1945. In all these things, his behavior bore no relation to the usual image of a Nazi industrialist running a satellite concentration camp.

Although Schindler was not without his faults, in my opinion one should speak only of his good side. When I give talks and people ask me afterward if it's true that Schindler had a lot of women friends and lovers, I always reply, "Here's how it was: we were drowning and we saw a man on the shore who had already taken off his jacket and was about to jump into the water to save us. Do you really think we should have said to that brave man, 'Excuse me please, but are you faithful to your wife? Because if you aren't, you mustn't fish us out of the water.'"

I think we were lucky that Schindler was the way he was: devil-may-care, plucky, gutsy, fearless, and able to hold his liquor. Before and after the war, he had little to show for his life. But during the war, he and his wife mounted an unprecedented rescue operation. Today, counting spouses, children, and grandchildren, more than six thousand people directly or indirectly owe their lives to Schindler. That's what counts. Nothing else matters.

THE UNTOLD STORY OF HOW SCHINDLER'S LIST CAME TO BE

IN RETROSPECT, two things did not turn out as expected. I was wrong to assume that Göth was sure to shoot me sooner or later, and Göth was wrong to think he would remain a camp commandant until the final German victory. For months, I waited like a condemned man for my death sentence to be carried out, without the slightest hope of being able to change my lot. At one point, Schindler even told me that he, too, regretted I would never have a chance to get out of working at the commandant's office. But then something unforeseen happened. While on leave in Vienna, Göth was arrested by SS Examining Magistrate Dr. Konrad Morgen. This was a surprising and positive turn of events for me. My survival is partly due to that magistrate. Morgen was in charge of investigating cases of embezzlement and had already arrested other SS men. Göth had excellent contacts in Kraków, and would surely have deployed them to block his arrest there. But in Vienna, he had no such network. Göth's bad luck was my good fortune.

Göth's arrest on September 13, 1944, seemed to us prisoners as improbable as the arrest of the King of England for stealing silver spoons at a diplomatic reception. He was accused of malfeasance. During the liquidation of the Kraków and Tarnów ghettos, he had unscrupulously appropriated the Jews' valuables for himself, snapping up furniture and objets d'art. In the camp, he had sold foodstuffs on the black market that were intended for us inmates. The final count against him was mistreatment of prisoners. When I was in the German Federal Archives in Berlin in 2000, I saw a 1944 telegram from Himmler's headquarters to Wilhelm Koppe, General Krüger's successor as higher SS and police chief east. "Where is Göth?" it asked, and Koppe answered that he was imprisoned in Kraków, awaiting trial on other charges.

As I testified at Göth's trial for war crimes in the fall of 1946, "It was his subordinates who turned him in. . . . He was well known for his brutality and for taking advantage of both prisoners and subordinates."[87] The egomaniacal commandant had treated even his own SS men very harshly. In return, they envied and feared him. Göth's openly conducted black-market deals were especially maddening to his subordinates, since he would have them hauled before an SS and police court for the slightest offense. On Göth's orders, I wrote up several such indictments. Those convicted would have had to serve their sentences after the war. I remember one of them almost whining, "You'll all be celebrating the end of the war and I'll have to go to jail." One time Göth sent the Jewish mechanic Warenhaupt to town to get some parts for his private BMW, and SS-*Rottenführer* Krupatz—an older, easy-going fellow—was detailed to accompany him. Warenhaupt, an athletic skier from Zakopane, was able to escape. At a building with a front and back entrance, he told Krupatz, "The Pole with the replacement parts lives in here. But he'll only give them to me if I go in alone. Wait here for me." Krupatz was fooled and had to return to camp without Warenhaupt. Predictably, Göth turned in Krupatz for "negligent freeing of a prisoner" and "abetting an escape." Later on, I learned that regulations actually required there always to be two SS men accompanying a prisoner on an errand to town.

This turned out not to have been an isolated incident, and at last the fury of the SS men against Göth reached its boiling point. They got together and composed a complaint that essentially said, "Göth is living like a pasha while our soldiers are dying on the eastern front." This complaint eventually reached the desk of the SS judge Dr. Morgen, the transcripts of whose hearings were later used even by the military tribunal in Nuremberg. Abruptly, Göth's career in the SS was over.

At first, we in the camp knew nothing about these events, not even that we had one less dangerous enemy to fear. We only got wind that something out of the ordinary must have happened when SS attorneys appeared in Płaszów on September 13, 1944, to interrogate the commandant's immediate coworkers. They questioned everyone who had had direct contact with Göth. In particular, they spoke at great length with the Jewish camp physician Dr. Leo Gross, the architect Zygmunt Grünberg, and with me. The inmates working in other offices at headquarters were questioned but soon sent back to their quarters in the camp. But it turned out that the chief of the camp detention center, Lorenz Landstorfer, had told one of the SS investigators that I was a special confidant of Göth's. Landstorfer was an uneducated, simple man, an unskilled laborer. I knew from his personnel file that he came from a village in eastern Bavaria. He looked up to Göth and thought he was doing me a favor by imparting this tip. On the contrary, it put me into a dangerous position. The SS officer ordered me to wait after questioning.

He had set up shop in the spacious living room of Göth's villa. I waited in the room to the left, next to the stairs, the so-called trophy room hung with racks of antlers and framed proverbs. Finally he called me in. "You told me before that you only did insignificant secretarial jobs for Göth. But Landstorfer informs me that you even drew up the secret Alarm and Defense Plan for the camp."

I felt like I'd been struck by lightning. The top-secret plan! I thought I was a dead man for sure. Landstorfer had in fact once seen me working on it. There was no way I could deny it.

I tried to make light of the matter. "I wrote various things. It's possible that one of them was a defense plan. But it had to do with how many watch towers we have. And everybody knows that; you can see them. And then, in case of an alarm, the guard details were supposed to be reinforced. That's nothing new for us inmates, either. But of course, I don't know what sort of official stamp was put on the finished document afterward."

The tone and length of the interrogation indicated to me how dangerous they thought it would be to let me run free, knowing such information, even if it was only within the camp. My attempt to trivialize the issue did nothing to defuse the concern of the examining magistrate. I was not allowed to return to camp. Instead, they put me into solitary confinement, confirming my worst fears. No one was allowed to speak to me. When they brought my food, there was always an SS man present to prevent the possibility of any conversation with the guards. My isolation cell was in the basement of the Gray House. It had only one small, barred window, half below ground level. If I stood on a chair, I could see the legs of the prisoners on their way to work. That was my only contact with the outside world. Everyone knew how quickly and effectively the Nazis could silence me, the lowly Jewish inmate, who was aware of so many classified SS procedures and knew so many disagreeable secrets. Two weeks later, I was interrogated again. They brought me to the commandant's barracks. The magistrate who questioned me this time was an older SS officer, quiet and restrained. A woman stenographer was there to record the lengthy interrogation. Again, they asked me about the work I did for Göth and what secrets I may have learned. I tried to explain to the SS magistrate that many things in the reports I wrote might be regarded as "secret" outside the walls, but for the inhabitants of the camp they were perfectly obvious. The "classified" designation was only important for the normal chain of command. The man listened to my explanation with interest, but was not convinced. He asked me to explain what I meant more precisely. Schindler told me later that the SS usually sent people who they thought possessed classified information to Dachau to be liquidated.

The interrogation took place at the end of September 1944. In the preceding two months, Płaszów had been scaled down and thousands of prisoners transferred to other concentration camps. Some of our barracks were being knocked down and sent off to other locations. The building materials were loaded onto heavy steel lorries at sidings in distant parts of the camp, and then female inmates were hitched to these lorries like horses and had to pull them to the commandant's office. There a standard freight rail siding ran across the yard in front of the commandant's barracks, and pieces of roofing and siding were loaded onto regular railroad cars. From that point on, their transport was supervised by the Economic and Administrative Main Office of the SS, Working Group D. They were sent on to the headquarters of other concentration camps. The official transport invoices, containing the amount and type of building materials, were stamped "classified." During my second interrogation, I used this as an example. I explained to the magistrate, "There are railroad cars waiting here inside the camp. The freight cars are loaded up with pieces of disassembled barracks that are being shipped off. That's obvious to us here in the camp. But the transport reports say 'classified.' So, what everybody on the inside knows, is 'classified' for the outside."

The man thought it over for a moment. "Hmm, that seems obvious," he said. I think he also liked my explanation because I had slipped a few Latin phrases into my argument. I had said it seemed to me a good example of the distinction between being classified *pro foro extero*, but not *ad usum internum*. My explanation seemed to have worked, since now he even betrayed some interest in my person. "How much more time do you have to do in the camp?" he asked, "What was your sentence?"

Was it possible, I thought to myself, that by the end of 1944, there was an SS judge who still didn't know what the camp policies of his country were? Who didn't know that no legal sentence was necessary to send Jews to their death? Then he asked if there was any possibility I would ever be assigned to a work detail outside the camp. Apparently, he was afraid I would be able to carry secrets to the outside. I assured him truthfully that I had

Women pulling a lorry in the Kraków-Płaszów camp.

never been employed outside the camp, which was confirmed by SS-*Hauptscharführer* Schupke.

It was a relief that all the magistrate's remaining questions revolved around Göth's personal machinations and private schemes. Göth had actually toyed with the idea of purchasing a country estate and a banking house. He had once asked me to prepare a list of questions he would need to ask when negotiating such purchases, and had also discussed the matter with his father. After I showed the magistrate the binder with the documents proving Göth's purchase plans, I was finally allowed to return to the camp. It was September 27, 1944, two weeks to the day after Göth's arrest and the eve of Yom Kippur, the end of the Jewish High Holy Days.

For the time being, I probably had nothing more to fear from the SS judiciary, yet the sword of Damocles continued to hang over my head into the spring of 1945, for they interrogated me again in Brünnlitz after we were moved to the new satellite camp. When the camp supervisor Leipold heard the words "SS and Police Court for Special Cases," he told me I could expect to be taken away for good. But once more, I was able to allay the suspicions of the SS jurists, and, fortunately, the war was over soon thereafter.

In September 1944, Schindler was involved in intense negotiations with the relevant authorities, seeking permission to bring with him as many of his Płaszów-Emalia camp workers as possible to Brünnlitz. He was eager to speak with me as soon as I was released from solitary confinement in the Gray House. He was also overjoyed at my release and immediately gave instructions to "add Pemper and his whole family to the list." This was his explicit wish. Neither my parents nor my brother had ever worked in his factory camp on Lipowa Street. But Schindler knew how valuable the classified information I had given him was, and he knew he could count on me. A special bond of trust also connected him to Izak Stern, and so Stern's mother, his brother Natan, and Natan's wife were also put on the list. In the two weeks between my release from solitary and our transport to Brünnlitz via Gross Rosen, I worked in the office of the director of work assignments. At that point in time, there was no more commandant's office as such. In fact, after the large transports to Auschwitz, Mauthausen, and Stutthof in mid-summer 1944, there were only about seven thousand inmates left in the camp. It was clear that the Płaszów concentration camp was in the process of being liquidated.

What became known as Schindler's list originated in the office of the director of work assignments, headed by SS-*Hauptscharführer* Franz Müller. During the filming of Steven Spielberg's film in Kraków in 1993, I spoke with Urs Jenny, the cultural editor of the German news magazine *Der Spiegel*. In the issue of May 24, 1993, he described me as the man "who wrote Schindler's list." But actually, the list was typed by me and several other camp inmates, all working in the same office. Every entry on the list had to be accurate: sequential number, inmate number, first name, family name, date of birth, and profession. Errors could not occur. Quite a few pages had to be reissued and revised several times and I myself retyped some pages of the list.

But the crucial accomplishment was less the typing of the list than the multifarious acts of resistance that, like tiny stones being placed into a mosaic one by one, had made the whole process possible in the first place. Unfortunately, while the list was being assembled, a few hundred of Schindler's Emalia workers not making the grenade parts "crucial for victory" were among the thousands of inmates transported to other camps. Most of those poor tormented people did not survive. Even Schindler was not able to prevent this from happening because the majority of the spaces on his list were limited to those Jewish inmates working in the MU branch of production.

I had already worked closely with Schindler in the Płaszów camp from the spring of 1943 to the fall of 1944. Our collaboration existed through the unique position Amon Göth had forced upon me. Without the information I obtained in the camp commandant's office, many things would have turned out differently. In the headquarters anteroom, I was able to analyze information about SS prison camp policies and pass it on to Schindler in coded form. As the eastern front drew nearer and nearer, the Nazis closed many smaller camps and sent the inhabitants to their deaths. However, through the scope of our very different positions, by the fall of 1943 Schindler and I succeeded in preventing the early closure of the Płaszów camp, and it was able to continue to exist as a concentration camp into the autumn and winter of 1944. This was one of several fortunate circumstances to which I and many others owe our survival. Schindler's list was then the final, crowning result of the lengthy preliminary work of preserving the camp, as well as of many individual acts of courage whose success few would have predicted.

The compilation of Schindler's list did not occur as portrayed in Spielberg's film, where Oskar Schindler dictates people's names to Izak Stern at his typewriter. The list was neither personally dictated by Schindler nor typed by Stern. It must be emphasized that list-keeping of prisoners was part of everyday life in the camp.

When inmates were transferred from one camp to another, lists were required as a sort of bill of lading. But then it was usually just a record of a certain number of people of a given profession. For instance, Dachau would order fifty metalworkers, Buchenwald fifty carpenters or a hundred seamstresses. But with Schindler, it was different. He would always stipulate which workers he wanted, requesting them by name.

For a prisoner transfer—the official term was *Überstellung*—you needed permission from Working Group D. This office alone had the authority to decide whether inmates could be sent from one camp to another. So permission for transfers of prisoners was under no circumstances at the discretion of a given camp commandant. I am not familiar with all the administrative details, but according to what I do know about the jurisdiction of Working Group D in the Economic and Administrative Main Office of the SS, Schindler must have contacted Berlin-Oranienburg directly. He must have sought out the relevant SS officer and persuaded him—perhaps with the help of a few expensive gifts—that he couldn't take just any old Jewish prisoners with him to Brünnlitz when he moved his satellite camp. His contacts from his previous career as a spy were no doubt useful in helping him convince people. In view of the difficult situation on the war front, he probably argued that time was too precious to spend it training new workers, and that his machines were too valuable and, at this point in the war, irreplaceable to allow them to be operated by unqualified workers. Without his own trained people, the production of grenade parts "crucial for victory" would be delayed and perhaps even in jeopardy.

After a long struggle, Schindler's dogged persistence succeeded at last. Oranienburg signed off on a list containing the names of three hundred women and seven hundred men. In the 1950s, Schindler declared,

> No outsider can imagine how much work was involved, from the moment I made the decision to bring my Jews west with

> me to the moment I got them all—over a thousand people—safely to the new location. Chaos and bureaucracy, envy and malevolence stood in my way, making the move seem impossible and bringing me to the brink of despair. Only my adamant determination helped me reach my goal: not to lose my Jews—many of whom had become my friends in the course of six years together—to a crematorium in Auschwitz or elsewhere, after making so many personal sacrifices to keep them out of the clutches of the SS.[88]

As the eastern front approached in August and September 1944, the move westward to Brünnlitz became ever more urgent, and the corrupt SS officials in Berlin and Kraków were aware that with every arbitrarily created delay in their decision to grant the move, the value of the gifts offered by Schindler would increase. In turn, Oskar Schindler had to be careful not to expose himself to charges of bribery. He could easily have relocated his factory—that is, the heavy machinery and valuable inventory—to the Rheinland or near the Semmering Pass, but he would have had to leave "his Jews" in the lurch. Yet to bring them along, Schindler had to attach his newly set-up factory to some other concentration camp. Since Emilie and Oskar Schindler had many good connections in the Sudetenland, Brünnlitz became the final location for Schindler's new factory. The Brünnlitz camp was now one of perhaps a hundred satellite camps of the Gross Rosen concentration camp, about forty miles southwest of Breslau (today, Wrocław).

Some of the most memorable scenes in Steven Spielberg's film show how some deviation from reality is necessary to emphasize certain plot developments for the audience. The film has Oskar Schindler simply showing up at Göth's villa with a suitcase full of cash and paying the commandant to let him take "his people." That of course never happened—never could have happened. Nor was there likely ever a poker game for Helena Hirsch. Even as influential a camp commandant as Amon Göth was, he would

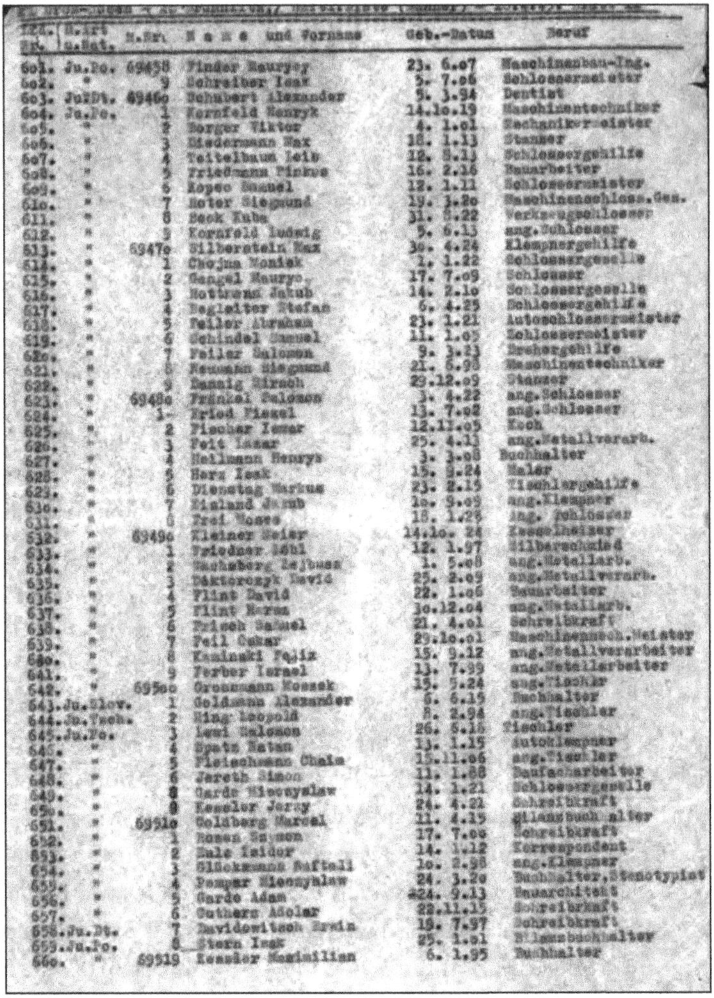

Lfd. Nr.	H.Art u.Nat.	H.Nr.	Name und Vorname	Geb.-Datum	Beruf
601.	Ju.Po.	69458	Pinder Maurycy	23. 6.07	Maschinenbau-Ing.
602.	"	9	Schreiber Izak	5. 7.06	Schlossermeister
603.	Ju.Dt.	69460	Schubert Alexander	5. 3.94	Dentist
604.	Ju.Po.	1	Kornfeld Henryk	14.10.19	Maschinentechniker
605.	"	2	Berger Viktor	4. 1.01	Mechanikermeister
606.	"	3	Biedermann Max	18. 1.13	Stanzer
607.	"	4	Teitelbaum Leib	12. 8.13	Schlossergehilfe
608.	"	5	Friedmann Pinkus	16. 2.16	Bauarbeiter
609.	"	6	Kopec Samuel	12. 1.11	Schlossermeister
610.	"	7	Roter Siegmund	19. 3.20	Maschinenschloss.Ges.
611.	"	8	Beck Kuba	31. 8.22	Werkzeugschlosser
612.	"	9	Kornfeld Ludwig	5. 6.13	ang.Schlosser
613.	"	69470	Silberstein Max	30. 4.24	Klempnergehilfe
614.	"	1	Chojna Moniek	1. 1.22	Schlossergeselle
615.	"	2	Gangel Maurycy	17. 7.09	Schlosser
616.	"	3	Hoffmann Jakub	14. 2.10	Schlossergeselle
617.	"	4	Begleiter Stefan	6. 4.25	Schlossergehilfe
618.	"	5	Feiler Abraham	23. 1.21	Autoschlossermeister
619.	"	6	Schindel Samuel	11. 1.05	Schlossermeister
620.	"	7	Feiler Salomon	9. 3.23	Drehergehilfe
621.	"	8	Neumann Siegmund	21. 5.98	Maschinentechniker
622.	"	9	Dannig Hirsch	29.12.09	Stanzer
623.	"	69480	Fränkel Salomon	3. 4.22	ang.Schlosser
624.	"	1	Fried Fiszel	13. 7.02	ang.Schlosser
625.	"	2	Fischer Ismar	12.11.05	Koch
626.	"	3	Feit Lazar	25. 4.11	ang.Metallverarb.
627.	"	4	Heilmann Henryk	3. 3.08	Buchhalter
628.	"	5	Herz Izak	15. 8.24	Maler
629.	"	6	Dienstag Markus	23. 2.15	Tischlergehilfe
630.	"	7	Eisland Jakub	10. 9.09	ang.Klempner
631.	"	8	Frei Mozes	18. 1.28	ang.Schlosser
632.	"	69490	Kleiner Meier	14.10.28	Kesselheizer
633.	"	1	Friedner [illegible]	12. 1.97	Silberschmied
634.	"	2	Wachsberg Zejbusz	1. 5.08	ang.Metallarb.
635.	"	3	Daktorczyk David	25. 2.09	ang.Metallverarb.
636.	"	4	Flint David	22. 1.06	Bauarbeiter
637.	"	5	Flint Aron	30.12.04	ang.Metallarb.
638.	"	6	Frisch Samuel	21. 4.01	Schreibkraft
639.	"	7	Feil Oskar	29.10.01	Maschinensch.Meister
640.	"	8	Kaminski Feliz	15. 9.12	ang.Metallverarbeiter
641.	"	9	Ferber Israel	13. 7.99	ang.Metallarbeiter
642.	"	69500	Grossmann Moszek	15. 5.24	ang.Tischler
643.	Ju.Slov.	1	Goldmann Alexander	6. 6.19	Buchhalter
644.	Ju.Tsch.	2	Ring Leopold	8. 2.94	ang.Tischler
645.	Ju.Po.	3	Lewi Salomon	26. 6.18	Tischler
646.	"	4	Spatz Natan	13. 1.15	Autoklempner
647.	"	5	Fleischmann Chaim	15.11.06	ang.Tischler
648.	"	6	Jereth Simon	11. 1.88	Baufacharbeiter
649.	"	8	Garde Mieczyslaw	14. 1.21	Schlossergeselle
650.	"	9	Kessler Jerzy	24. 4.21	Schreibkraft
651.	"	69510	Goldberg Marcel	11. 4.15	Bilanzbuchhalter
652.	"	1	Rosen Szymon	17. 7.06	Schreibkraft
653.	"	2	Bale Isidor	14. 1.12	Korrespondent
654.	"	3	Glückmann Naftali	10. 2.98	ang.Klempner
655.	"	4	Pemper Mieczyslaw	24. 3.20	Buchhalter,Stenotypist
656.	"	5	Garde Adam	24. 9.13	Bauarchitekt
657.	"	6	Gutherz Adolar	22.11.15	Schreibkraft
658.	Ju.Dt.	7	Davidowitsch Erwin	19. 7.97	Schreibkraft
659.	Ju.Po.	8	Stern Izak	25. 1.01	Bilanzbuchhalter
660.	"	69519	Kessler Maximilian	6. 1.95	Buchhalter

The page of Schindler's 1944 list that includes Izak Stern's name and mine.

not have been able to simply "transfer" a thousand inmates from his camp to another. On the contrary, the whole procedure went according to regulations, with the written consent of Working Group D. And the documents were almost certainly signed by either SS-*Standartenführer* Gerhard Maurer or by General Richard Glücks himself. The papers also had to be endorsed, again according to official regulations, by the arms inspection agency of the Generalgouvernement, headed by Major General Maximilian Schindler. Without the appropriate formal directives from Berlin-Oranienburg and Kraków, it would have been impossible for a thousand people simply to leave the Płaszów concentration camp and head for Gross Rosen and then on to Brünnlitz. But in the end, this long-winded and persnickety bureaucracy proved to be an advantage. For in November 1944, it enabled Schindler to get three hundred of "his" female workers, who were transferred via Auschwitz, sent on to the Brünnlitz work camp, something he could never have effected just with gifts of diamonds or personal favors.

Thus several people worked on putting together Schindler's list. I'm sure that in a few cases, gifts of money or other valuables were given for a place on the list. This I gather from the accounts of other people who were involved. In such contexts, the name of Marcel Goldberg keeps coming up. He was the so-called inmate clerk of the Director of Work Assignments SS-*Hauptscharführer* Franz Müller. But the final decision was always Schindler's to make. It was on his instructions that "his people," that is, the contingent of Jewish workers in his Emalia factory, were put on the list. They included those who had been reassigned to the MU department to manufacture grenade parts. It was also his decision that married couples would not be split up. If a woman who worked in the Emalia had a husband employed in the main camp, he too would be put on the list. That was often the case for siblings and other immediate family members as well.

Schindler's suitcase, now deposited in the archives of Yad Vashem in Jerusalem, contains among other items a list that since its discovery has been designated as Schindler's list. It is dated April 18, 1945. It is, as far as I know, the latest list of inmates in the Brünnlitz camp. Its sequentially numbered listing of male camp inmates contains a few gaps, and the total number of inmates amounts to about eight hundred. This number includes the inmates from Golleschau (today Goleszów) who joined us in January 1945, as well as a few other Jews from the vicinity of Brünnlitz whom Schindler had later taken in. In the archives of the Auschwitz-Birkenau w Oświęcimiu Museum there is a list of names of male inmates headed "KL Gross Rosen—AL Brünnlitz"[89] and dated October 21, 1944. It contains exactly seven hundred names, including —on the last page, next to the sequential number 668—my own. This document is a list of prisoners drawn up upon our arrival in Gross Rosen, for on it my inmate number is 69514, which was not my Płaszów inmate number. And the new number assigned to me in Gross Rosen is the one I kept until my liberation in May 1945. According to the director of the archive, Dr. Piotr Setkiewiz, the list we typed in Płaszów must be considered lost. At least, he knows of no such list of Płaszów concentration camp prisoners from mid-October 1944. This was the original Schindler's list and would most likely have been headed "KL Płaszów—KL Gross Rosen" to indicate that it was used for our transfer from Płaszów to another concentration camp, namely Gross Rosen.

Comparing the two versions of the list—the one from the fall of 1944 with that of April 1945—two things are obvious. There are no elderly and no very young people, and almost all the inmates are skilled craftsmen. We knew there would be intermediate stops on our transport to Schindler's new factory, but had no idea where they would be. And we wanted to prevent anyone being selected out by a cursory inspection solely on the basis of his age or trade. Since we also knew what the Nazis' criteria for selection were, we arbitrarily assigned a skilled trade to almost everyone on the list, and we made the children and young people somewhat older, and the very old a few years younger than they actually were. We undertook these falsifications to protect people as much as we could. We made my father Jakob Pemper, inmate number 68936, ten years younger, changing his date of birth from 1888 to 1898. We made my brother Stefan, inmate number 68928, two years older.

On the occasion of Emilie Schindler's death in the fall of 2001, a former Schindler Jew told an interviewer that he had been listed as an "employed" mechanic. But the abbreviation *ang.*, which we placed in front of certain trades, didn't stand for *angestellt* (employed) but rather *angelernt* (semi-skilled). If someone was a real craftsman, we didn't use this abbreviation. It got appended only to the trades listed for the intellectuals and academics among us. For if the Nazis had checked their qualifications as fully trained and skilled joiners, painters, metal workers, plumbers, or bricklayers, the deception would have been exposed immediately. However, as merely "semi-skilled" metal workers, such people were better protected. A statement of their real professions—teacher, rabbi, sales representative, or businessman—would have made them highly suspicious for positions in the arms industry. Among those with a university education, we listed only the physicians under their actual profession. Since we were naturally unable to broadcast these falsifications to the world at large, even those listed often did not know what trade they had been assigned. Everything we did was fraught with danger, and even this small contribution to the rescue effort was extremely risky for those of us involved.

The number of inmates authorized by Working Group D—seven hundred men and three hundred women—was somewhat larger than the actual number of Jewish workers left in Schindler's factory by the end of September 1944. That explains why there were still openings on the list. Whoever got added to the list now had some chance of surviving; whoever didn't faced more or less certain death. But there was not much room to maneuver in entering additional names. We could not just arbitrarily add the names of relatives or friends. Regrettably, egoistic considerations still played some role. It was primarily Marcel Goldberg who saw to it that some of his protégés made it onto the list. He is no longer living, and I do not like to speak ill of the dead. But Goldberg had to go into hiding after the war because even the Israeli Secret Service was looking for him. He was accused of putting some people onto the list on the basis of not inconsiderable bribes. This charge alone would be bad enough. But supposedly he made room for these people by deleting others who were already on the list. For the latter, Goldberg's maneuverings often meant a death sentence.

It must have been almost immediately after Amon Göth's arrest that the textile manufacturer Julius Madritsch asked Schindler to include on the list about twenty of his foremen to whom he owed a special debt of gratitude. Schindler agreed. But even after this addition, the contingent of seven hundred men and three hundred women was not yet full. Now inmates from the main camp in Płaszów were added to the list even without previous consultation with Schindler. After the war, my friend Heinz Dressler asked me if I was responsible for getting him and his parents and sister onto Schindler's list. But I can't remember the details any more. I only know that I did something for Heinz. Everything had to be done with great circumspection, because after all, what was officially taking place was the relocation of an important arms factory, not a rescue operation to save Jewish lives. Schindler always had to be very clever in his negotiations with the SS.

I had no authority to make decisions on my own, and always followed Schindler's instructions. Perhaps that was a mistake. I still feel that I didn't do enough for some of my distant relatives. The name Pemper is not obviously either Jewish or Polish. It's rather rare and would have caught the attention of a German, especially because it is short. As I've already said, this list had to make it through several intermediate stops for approval. It was a list of skilled craftsmen in an industry "crucial for victory." If at one of the checkpoints, some SS man or other noticed the frequently repeated name "Pemper," it could have provoked further inquiries and checks. They also might just arbitrarily have deleted some people with the same last name. Thus my cousin, only a few years younger than I, did not survive. On the other hand, I don't know how I could have saved him, for Marcel Goldberg's manipulations were so extensive that I thank my lucky stars every day that he hadn't suddenly deleted my father, my mother, my brother, or me. The treacherous thing about all our decisions in the camp was that you could never predict their consequences with any degree of certainty.

At literally the last possible moment, Oskar Schindler urged Julius Madritsch to save all of his people as well, but Madritsch didn't seem interested. He moved only his machinery to the Lake Constance region, leaving almost eight hundred of his workers, Jewish men and women, to their fate. With the help of Raimund Titsch, the supervisor of the Madritsch factory, Schindler undertook a final rescue effort, putting together an ad hoc group of sixty people whom he simply added to the list as his "company tailors."[90] To Schindler's repeated plea to reconsider rescuing his workers, Julius Madritsch supposedly replied, "Don't waste your breath, *lieber* Oskar. It's a lost cause and I won't invest another penny in it."[91]

On October 15, 1944, a transport of about 4,500 male prisoners left the Płaszów camp. They jammed us into cattle cars without water or sanitary facilities. A day later, we arrived in Gross Rosen. Without Schindler present, we felt abandoned and vulnerable. The fact that we seven hundred "Schindler Jews" were in the first seven freight cars, separate from the other inmates, did nothing to lessen our apprehensions. Who would stick up for us if something didn't go according to plan? Nor was anyone sure that Gross Rosen would not prove to be our final destination after all.

Something unexpected did indeed occur on the way. In the middle of the night, the train suddenly halted somewhere in open country. Some of us thought we weren't far from Gleiwitz, but nobody knew why we had stopped. We waited. Then we heard my name being called out, "Pemper . . . , Pemper . . . !" SS guards were running along the train. "Pemper . . ." My only thought was, it's the SS police court! They're coming to get me after all. I pushed my way to the door of the car and knocked on it to attract their attention. The door opened and I jumped down onto the graveled embankment. A sharp pain shot through my ankle. I picked myself up with difficulty, clenched my teeth, and limped along behind an SS guard, with another one behind me. We reached the compartment of Lorenz Landstorfer, chief of the camp detention center and leader of our transport. I stood there, shivering from cold, fear, and suppressed pain.

Landstorfer, whose admiration for his master Amon Göth knew no bounds, stepped from his compartment and said, "The commandant's birthday is at the beginning of December, isn't it? Do you know what day it is?"

"Yes." I even know the birthdays of his wife and children, I thought to myself. But why is he asking me right at this particular moment? Had he really made a whole train of fifty cars stop there, in the middle of nowhere and the middle of the night, just to ask me that question? I was standing next to the train sweating profusely while one of the guard detail shined a spotlight on me. And then Landstorfer actually asked me to draft a telegram of congratulation to Göth, who was in prison. I was stunned. Suddenly, my fear disappeared and gave way to my sense of humor. "Well, *Herr Hauptscharführer*," I replied, "I really ought to compose two telegrams."

"Why two?" Landstorfer was confused.

"One, in case the *Herr Kommandant* has been released by his birthday. And another, in case he hasn't."

The idea made immediate sense to Landstorfer. "Pemper," he exclaimed enthusiastically, "you're right! *Ja*, draft two telegrams!" And he murmured how smart he was to have called for me. So there I stood, a Jewish inmate somewhere in Silesia, on my way from one concentration camp to another, drafting congratulatory telegram A and congratulatory telegram B to a mass murderer in the beam of a spotlight, under the watchful eye of an SS guard.

After this grotesque incident, I was escorted back to my cattle car and the surgeon Dr. Ferdynand Lewkowicz examined my injured ankle. Diagnosis: sprained, but fortunately not broken. Later he massaged my foot, after warning me not to go to the infirmary in Gross Rosen under any circumstances, because I couldn't be sure of getting out in time to continue on with the transport. After the war, Lewkowicz emigrated to America, where he died in a traffic accident.

Our sojourn in the Gross Rosen concentration camp lasted seven days. Until they allowed us to continue our journey, we were subjected to a harsh regimen which began with being stripped naked. We had to surrender everything we had with us and then stand naked on the parade ground all through the night of October 16 to 17. We stood beneath a large tarpaulin, but there wasn't room for everyone. So we warmed each other by letting the people on the periphery move to the center after a certain amount of time. When dawn broke, they herded us into a disinfection station where Ukrainian trusties shaved all the hair from our bodies, obviously enjoying injuring us with their blunt razors. Many of us suffered for months from the wounds they inflicted on us during this procedure. Not until it was over did we receive the customary striped uniforms. The week that followed demanded all our strength, for although we seven hundred continued to be kept separate from the others, we didn't know until the last minute whether we would be able to remain on the list, or if the list even meant we would survive.

Shortly after we arrived in Gross Rosen, Landstorfer was ordered back to Plaszów. Before he left, he told his SS colleagues the names of two prisoners who should serve as contacts: Marcel Goldberg and me. Whenever the camp SS wanted something from us, we two were always summoned. I had quite limited mobility on account of my sprained ankle, and Goldberg always reported as soon as the SS summoned us both, pushing himself forward. He must have regarded it as his lucky break and reported several times by himself. I later heard that even in Gross Rosen, he was juggling names on and off the list in exchange for jewelry and other items of value. I don't know how he may have justified striking this or that person from the list and adding others. Since the list prepared in Plaszów apparently no longer exists, we don't know how many of the seven hundred men who eventually reached Brünnlitz had replaced others who were deleted. One of those deleted was Roman Polanski's father. I heard his story when we met in Kraków after the war. The physician Dr. Aleksander Biberstein was added on the parade ground in Gross Rosen. His nephew, the engineer Scheck, who suffered from heart disease, had already worked for Schindler and his name was on the list from the beginning, otherwise he certainly would not have survived.

Among other names, Marcel Goldberg deleted that of Noah Stockmann, a former non-com in the Polish army who had been in the Budzyn camp near Lublin. He had been the senior Jewish inmate there, a post to which SS-*Untersturmführer* Josef Leipold, the new camp supervisor in Brünnlitz, would surely have appointed him as well. Goldberg was probably speculating that he could advance to senior Jewish inmate himself if Stockmann did not arrive in Brünnlitz. But Stockmann was precisely the man Leipold asked for upon our arrival. Leipold never forgave Goldberg for his machinations. Noah Stockmann did not survive the war.

While waiting in Gross Rosen, we were sent to the SS dentist's office, where our gold fillings and bridges were painstakingly recorded on index cards. That was a terrible blow. "Do we need any further proof," said some, "that the Nazis are just going to shoot us down? Now they know just how much gold they can count on when they knock our teeth out afterward."

We tried to cheer each other up: "We mustn't despair now. Schindler won't abandon us."

At last, on October 22, we arrived in Brünnlitz, where a closed-down Jewish spinning factory had been remodeled according to

SS specifications, with watchtowers, barbed wire, a kitchen, an infirmary, and separate sleeping quarters for seven hundred men and three hundred women. The heavy machinery from Schindler's factory in Kraków-Zabłocie was already installed on the shop floor, ready to resume production of the MU grenade parts. The guard details consisted mostly of older SS men no longer fit for active duty at the front. They displayed no great eagerness for the job. From the beginning, Oskar Schindler kept them in good spirits with gifts and alcohol.

But where were the women? The transport of female prisoners had left the Płaszów camp on October 22, the day of our arrival in Brünnlitz, and on October 23, it arrived in Auschwitz-Birkenau. When I give lectures, people often ask whether the women from Płaszów were sent to Auschwitz rather than Gross Rosen by accident. No, it wasn't an oversight or a mistake. Since Oskar Schindler's new factory in Brünnlitz was a satellite of the Gross Rosen concentration camp, all inmates from the Płaszów camp had to be officially registered at Gross Rosen. An additional regulation stipulated that when being transferred to a camp within the territory of the German Reich, inmates had to have their entire bodies shaved, including their genitals. Only men could shave the men, and only women the women. But by this time, there was no longer a women's camp in Gross Rosen. So the three hundred female prisoners from Płaszów had to be diverted to the next-closest concentration camp, which was Auschwitz. Only then could they be moved on to Brünnlitz. The women reached us in mid-November 1944, having spent the previous three weeks under wretched conditions in Auschwitz, where the group had been split up and distributed among various barracks. It was very difficult to reassemble exactly the same women from Schindler's list to continue the transport to Brünnlitz. By then, Auschwitz was severely overcrowded and as a result, quite disorganized. But since the list had been officially approved by Working Group D, it was considered binding. Nevertheless, Schindler had to use his contacts to prevent some of "his" women from being inadvertently replaced by others. The female guards in Auschwitz had to sort out the "Schindler women" one by one from the gigantic camp's numerous barracks. Schindler continued to insist that only the women on the list, including the youngest ones, would be accepted in Brünnlitz. The young girls, he said, had slim fingers that could reach into the interior of a grenade part and identify surfaces that needed to be deburred, or filed smooth. For the transport to Brünnlitz, the women were in fact called out by name, which never happened otherwise, for in Auschwitz all that counted was your number.

Stella Müller-Madej recalled in a television interview that "the journey to Schindler's factory took two days." Schindler was there to welcome the women in Brünnlitz. "We stunk to high heaven because we hadn't had so much as a bucket to bathe in. What poor Schindler had to smell must have been abominable. The women who already knew him from the Emalia broke out in hysterics. He gave us a surreptitious smile and when there were no German guards nearby, he managed to whisper that we were safe now. From that moment on, I believed that Oskar Schindler was really determined to rescue us."[92]

While the three hundred women arrived in Brünnlitz, two of them on the Płaszów list were no longer among them: Izak and Natan Stern's mother, Perla Stern, who caught typhus in Auschwitz and died there, and my mother, Regina Pemper. Because of her limp, she was picked out on November 3, 1944. In place of these two women, two others reached Brünnlitz. The November 1944 list of female prisoners was alphabetical, with consecutive inmate numbers from 76201 to 76500. These numbers, too, were not their numbers from Płaszów. There is also no indication on the list that two women who were originally on it had not arrived in Brünnlitz. In contrast to the male prisoners, there were no women in Brünnlitz who had been added later from other camps. So if one compares the list of November 1944 with that of April 18, 1945, one can see that except for Elisabeth Chotiner, Janina Feigenbaum, and Anna Laufer, 297 of the 300 women who arrived in Brünnlitz lived to be liberated.

In Auschwitz, my mother was put into an international barracks for women who were not capable of full-time work. At that time, selections for mass killings had ceased, probably as a "goodwill gesture" of Himmler's toward the Allies in order to strengthen his negotiating position as "Hitler's successor."

On January 27, 1945, Soviet and Polish soldiers liberated Auschwitz I and Auschwitz-Birkenau. A few days later, my mother was taken to Kraków. She told us afterward that not many days before they were liberated, an older man in uniform had appeared in the barracks. My mother couldn't remember whether he was wearing a Wehrmacht or an SS uniform. He was carrying two black cases that looked like doctor's bags and probably contained explosives. They had been hearing detonations from all over the camp, because the Nazis were blowing up parts of the Birkenau camp at the last minute. My mother told me that the man in uniform looked inquiringly around the dimly lit barracks, saw only elderly women, then shook his head and left the building again.

My mother survived and was with us until her death eight years later.

THE LIBERATION OF BRÜNNLITZ

JOSEF LEIPOLD, the Brünnlitz camp supervisor, chose me to be his liaison to the factory supervisor's office. Leipold had briefly served as Göth's adjutant in the summer of 1943, so he had met me when Płaszów was still operating as a forced labor camp. When we arrived in Brünnlitz without Noah Stockmann, I was probably the only person Leipold could recall, but he also chose me because of my linguistic abilities and office skills. He was a Sudeten German and didn't speak a word of Polish. A barber by trade, he was a well-groomed but one-dimensional man who worshiped authority and was a devoted Nazi. After the war he was sentenced to death in Lublin. One of the duties he assigned me in Brünnlitz was to supervise work assignments. In Płaszów, that had been Marcel Goldberg's function, but he was so hated by the other prisoners that Oskar Schindler insisted I take over the position. From then on, Goldberg was constantly dissatisfied and never lost an opportunity to bellyache. He was isolated, for no one wanted anything to do with him.

I was now processing the daily invoices for the compensation Schindler had to pay to the SS for each of his Brünnlitz workers. From time to time, Schindler would also tell me who should be given what job, because someone had been working for him for a long time or because he'd known his father in Kraków. My job was not at all a pleasant one. I had to decide who would work outdoors and who got to be on the warm factory floor. The winter of 1944–45 was terribly cold, and no one wanted to work outdoors voluntarily. So I left such decisions to the physicians. If anyone's health was seriously compromised, I naturally assigned him a job on the factory floor, while the younger, able-bodied inmates worked outside. This arrangement caused me no further troubles from my fellow prisoners. Even after the war, there were no recriminations, because everyone knew that I didn't take bribes. It would have run counter to my sense of justice either to favor or to penalize anyone for no substantial reason.

Late one evening, a few days after our arrival in Brünnlitz, Leipold summoned me and gave me a confidential assignment. At 4 a.m. the following morning, I was to awaken some fathers and their sons. They were slated to be picked up and taken away. Leipold didn't tell me where they were going. Among them were the camp physician Dr. Leo Gross and Zbigniew, the son of his common-law wife; Abraham Ginter and his son Eugeniusz; Leon Ferber and the eleven-year-old Roman (whom we had made two years older on the list); Dawid Horowitz and his little Ryszard; as well as the musician Herman Rosner and his son Aleksander.[93] I was horrified and racked my brain about what to do. Should I wake the fathers up right away and warn them, "Watch out! In six hours you may have to go to Auschwitz"? Should I encourage them to try to escape? Impossible. There was no escape.

It was ten o'clock at night. I let them sleep until 4 a.m. Then I woke them up. I myself was unable to sleep that night. None of them blamed me afterward. Since our women had not yet arrived in Brünnlitz at that point, some of their wives and mothers later said that they indeed had seen their husbands and sons in Auschwitz. The families couldn't greet each other openly, but they managed to wave to each other surreptitiously and exchange a few words through the barbed wire fence. I was overjoyed to hear this news. Luckily, all those fathers and sons, except for Leon Ferber, survived the war.

Early in 1945, Amon Göth suddenly turned up in Brünnlitz. As far as I know, he was incarcerated first in the military prison in

Breslau, and then taken back to Vienna. He had probably been released temporarily because of poor health. What a shock it was to see him again! But Schindler reassured us: "He's no longer the same Göth. He can't hurt you anymore. He's only here to pick up his things." In the meantime, Göth had found out that I had been interrogated by SS lawyers. He wanted to grill me about the details. Schindler put a room at our disposal, and since he had indicated that Göth had no more power over us, I was fairly unconcerned and relaxed during the interview. I even allowed myself a little joke. When Göth pressed me to tell him what they had asked me, I answered, "I'm not allowed to say." Göth was speechless. Although he was fun-loving—at least, I often heard him laugh—he had no sense of humor. At this moment, right at the end of the war, he couldn't believe that a Jewish inmate had the gall to refuse to give him information. I finally did tell him a few things about the interrogation, but without going into much detail. Our conversation was brief. Göth soon left the camp. The next time I saw him was one and a half years later, in the fall of 1946, and he was in the dock.

One day, three or four pious Jews approached me with a request. They had known my grandfather quite well and so they came to me, asking that they be given their soup—the only warm meal of the day—before the pieces of pork were put into it. The pork was of poor quality, but that wasn't their point. Since they were in Schindler's camp now, they wanted to eat kosher again despite their hunger. I was glad to help them out, and without explaining exactly why, I got the kitchen staff to do as they asked.

Since I was in charge of the work assignments, I was able to give my slightly lame father a job where he didn't have to be on his feet all the time. From then on, he handed out tools. The other two who worked with him in the tool storeroom were Abraham Bankier and Rabbi Jacob Levertow. There was an enormous cabinet full of precision tools made of expensive Vidia steel. Workers had to sign them out individually. Throughout the day, the three of them sat there in amicable conversation and probably also prayed together. There wasn't much for them to do. One day—I can't remember why—we received a bonus for working "in the arms industry." We were given coupons we could exchange for cigarettes. I gave the three men at the tool storeroom the smallest number of coupons. Two or three days later, Engineer Schöneborn, the technical director, summoned me to his office and gave me a very stern look. "Pemper, there's been a complaint lodged against you. You did not distribute the bonuses fairly." I hemmed and hawed a bit, then said, "I can imagine that a few individuals might feel unjustly treated, but I really did try to be fair." Schöneborn suddenly burst out laughing. "Just imagine," he said in amusement, "your own father complained about you and said that Rabbi Levertow, Herr Bankier, and he had gotten the smallest bonus. The two other gentlemen reasoned that as his son, you wanted at all costs to avoid giving the impression that you were slipping your father something extra. And so your father was complaining that Levertow and Bankier were being unjustly disadvantaged by your exaggerated sense of justice." Since the three of them had hardly any work to do, they had plenty of time to concoct this argument. When I offered to share some of my own bonus with my father, Engineer Schöneborn put a reassuring hand on my shoulder and said, "I know how fair you are. But I just couldn't resist telling you this story!"

At the end of January 1945, Schindler got a call from the station master in Brüsau. He said there were two sealed cattle cars at his station with a bill of lading saying they contained Jewish workers, and wondered if Schindler knew anything about it. Quick-witted as always, Schindler replied immediately, "At last! Those are the people I requested ages ago. I've been calling Berlin asking where they were. Move the cars onto my factory siding." It turned out that the eighty-six emaciated human beings inside were from Golleschau, a satellite camp of Auschwitz. They'd been loaded into the cars and sent off to die. Himmler had ordered that no concentration camp inmates should fall into the hands of the Allies.

We needed welding torches to thaw out the sliding doors of the cattle cars. According to the bill of lading, these people had been traveling for over a week with no food or water, no blankets, no hope of survival. They were originally from Holland, France, Belgium, Hungary, and Czechoslovakia. Twelve of them were already dead. The men sitting right next to the door had it best, since they were able to break off icicles to suck on for a little fluid. I was present when the seventy-four survivors were brought to our camp, weighed, and interviewed. It was the first time in my life I had seen an adult human being who weighed sixty-five pounds. To this day, I never use the phrase "skin and bones" because it always recalls that sight.

The men from Golleschau were so emaciated that they couldn't keep down our usual camp rations. Our doctors said they would have to be fed semolina porridge. Emilie Schindler had whole tubs of semolina prepared. We wondered how she was able to scare up that much of the precious foodstuff in February and March 1945, but she did it. She had personal ties to the aristocrat who owned the Daubek mill, which is where she got the semolina at a time when it was not to be had even for a generous bribe. It was moving to see how Emilie Schindler looked after the sick and disabled among us. I recall her as a serious, disciplined woman. What she saw every day in the camp and especially in the infirmary must have saddened her greatly, but she never showed it. Dr. Biberstein wrote a report to the Joint in the summer of 1945 in which he said, "Frau Schindler sacrificed all her supplies of semolina, butter, milk, cheese, sausage. Herr Oskar Schindler brought back all sorts of foodstuffs and medicines from Mährisch-Ostrau, packed in ammunition crates."[94]

Four survivors of the cattle cars died despite the best possible medical care. The remaining seventy survived. In the course of the following weeks, other scattered groups of prisoners from liquidated satellite camps ended up in Brünnlitz. Schindler made it possible for the new arrivals to survive as well. By the end of the war, the number of "Schindler Jews" had grown from the original thousand to about twelve hundred.

Very few people died while in Brünnlitz. One who did was a young woman suffering from leukemia. Oskar Schindler reached an agreement with the local Lutheran pastor to make a separate row of graves in his cemetery. There, our dead were buried according to Jewish ritual. The young Rabbi Levertow said the prayers. This alone clearly shows how kind Oskar Schindler was to us. Thanks to his intervention, Brünnlitz was as different from the other remaining camps as it could possibly be.

For Oskar Schindler, the months in Brünnlitz were by far the most difficult of his entire rescue operation. By the end of the war, the immense pressure he had been under since Płaszów doubled. Nevertheless, you would hardly have noticed it from his outward appearance, and to the end, he never flagged in his efforts to rescue us. During the last phase of the war, Emilie and Oskar Schindler lived in a modest flat on the factory grounds. Schindler wrote about it to the Joint in 1945, "Because the safety of my endangered workers was more important to me than my own peace and quiet, and because I had taken an unequivocal stand and knew my life to be bound up with the fate of the people in my factory, the factory became my front line! The outstanding discipline of my people and the great trust they invested in my work made victory possible."[95]

In March, the visit of an inspector from the Armament Ministry in Berlin was announced. Schindler arranged for me to take part in the meeting as a stenographer. He and I worked out the details of how we would proceed. While Schindler was conferring with this important visitor, I would remind him of two machines that had been ordered but hadn't arrived yet. Out of curiosity, I asked Schindler why he didn't have his regular secretary take shorthand at the meeting. Schindler grinned and told me, "You know, if Frau Hoffmann heard all the lies I'm going to tell this man, she could report me to the Gestapo the next day."

The inspector arrived. He was short and slim, with black hair—the image of a Frenchman. I never learned the man's name. Schindler showered him with gifts that were very hard to come by at that point: foie gras, wine, liqueur—only the best. After that, the man raised almost no objections to the report on the factory and its accounts. Schindler was in his element. He talked animatedly about the factory's excess production capacity. As we had agreed, I reminded him of the two machines he was still waiting for and mentioned the percent by which they would increase our production. It all went over beautifully, and the inspector left Brünnlitz firmly convinced that he had inspected the well-functioning arms production plant of a dedicated National Socialist. When he was gone, Schindler clapped me appreciatively on the shoulder and said, "You see, we got rid of him, too."

Another time he said, "Come with me, I want to show you something." He took me to the camp's power plant and showed me the data on our electricity usage. The curve sank rapidly twenty minutes before the end of each shift. Obviously, workers were turning off their machines. Schindler gave me a worried look. "If Leipold should see that, he's going to start talking about 'sabotage.' He'll report it to Berlin and there'll be hell to pay." I promised Schindler I'd fix things. "How did you do it?" he asked in amazement a few days later. "Now the curve hardly falls at all at a shift change." I explained to him that people hadn't been putting a new component into their machines if there were only a few minutes left until end of their shift, because they wouldn't be able to finish working on it. So I'd told them to at least leave their machines running. "But that's a waste of energy," they objected. "You're right, but we can't let Leipold use the falling energy curve to claim you're sabotaging the work. That's the greater danger."

In Brünnlitz, it was my daily task to figure out how to solve such supposedly trifling details. And whenever such problems arose, Schindler directed me to solve them as quickly and quietly as possible.

As camp supervisor, Josef Leipold was a dyed-in-the-wool Nazi. We feared that he could still be dangerous to us if some order came from a higher-up, for he would unquestionably carry it out. For that reason, Schindler seldom left the factory, but sometimes he had to take a trip to purchase supplies and look after his black-market deals. Those were the only times when the guards got aggressive toward us. In a 2003 interview, Stella Müller-Madej testified how apprehensive the inmates were in Schindler's absence, "As soon as Schindler disappeared through the gates, we felt like orphaned children. . . . We always felt if he were gone, even for a minute, something bad could happen to us."[96] On the other hand, if Schindler was present in the camp, the guards didn't dare to mistreat us. Moreover, Schindler continually cautioned Leipold, who was cowed by his authority, that the Reich needed our production and he would therefore not tolerate any brutal treatment of his workers. He mentioned his excellent connections in the armament industry and among the authorities in Berlin. If there were uniformed guards on the shop floor, he said, the workers would start trembling, and then the expensive machines might get damaged. And then—reluctantly, of course—he would have to report the Herr Camp Supervisor to the SS. "After all," he would add, "the important thing is that the workers not escape, right? And for that, all we need are guards at the camp gates." Schindler's combination of explicit threats and reasonable arguments impressed Leipold. Thereafter, the SS men were not allowed into the workshops or onto the factory floor.

In the final phase of the war, sometime at the beginning of 1945, SS-*Sturmbannführer* Johannes Hassebroek, the camp commandant of Gross Rosen, came to inspect Brünnlitz. Leipold was very nervous about this visit. Hassebroek, clad in a black leather coat, had a long conversation with Leipold, apparently about the fact that a thorough inspection of the Brünnlitz factory had not yet taken place, only cursory ones or none at all. We also noticed that on several occasions, Leipold and other SS men left the factory grounds. Only later did I find out the real reason this "high-level visitor" had showed up in Brünnlitz. Hassebroek and Leipold were marking out a few locations in the forest adjacent to the grounds as part of a plan for the evacuation of the camp. On a signal from Oranienburg or some other higher office, camp inmates who were physically capable of a forced march would be drawn up in a column and marched west to escape the advancing Soviet troops. But first, elderly and invalid prisoners would be shot and buried in shallow graves in the forest.

When Schindler asked me if Leipold was likely to carry out an SS order to execute some of the prisoners, I unfortunately had to answer yes. I told Schindler that Leipold was a confirmed Nazi and would have no scruples about carrying out such an order. Whereupon Schindler said we would have to get rid of Leipold somehow. He had an astonishing idea, and it proved effective.

Schindler invited officials from Brünnlitz and the surrounding area to a reception, where he gave, as he later told me, a fiery, patriotic speech to the assembled military and SS dignitaries: "In this hour, Germany needs every man at the front. Germany needs people like you. I will personally chauffeur anyone who volunteers for the front to the recruiting office in my Horch." As he had hoped, Josef Leipold volunteered on the spot. Schindler kept his promise and drove him out the camp gates; Leipold sat beside him in the front seat. Once again, Schindler had succeeded in getting rid of one of our greatest enemies. Stella Müller-Madej described what it was like when Schindler returned from the recruiting office. He came into the factory, sat down on a machine part, and "couldn't stop laughing. He was laughing uncontrollably and finally said that the man hadn't been born who could fool him. He was laughing like a madman."[97]

Nevertheless, we had to be on guard to the very last day of the war. Death threatened us at every turn. One danger was that a retreating SS unit might happen upon our camp and just mow us down with their machine guns. To be on the safe side, we always had two or three men posted outside the factory building, watching traffic come and go on the country road that ran just above the camp compound. Even Schindler was worried. However, when it came to fooling the camp's own SS guards, he had an inexhaustible variety of tricks up his sleeve. His plans were always original, if sometimes risky, and he usually carried them out behind the scenes and rarely, as in the case of Leipold's volunteering, out in the open and before everyone's eyes.

We knew the front was getting closer and closer, but we couldn't predict how the Red Army would behave toward us and especially toward Oskar Schindler. From scattered conversations with local Czechs who had contacts with the partisans, however, we could make a guess: as an industrialist and a Nazi party member, he would be immediately stood up against a wall and shot, and our descriptions of his rescue operation would do nothing to prevent it. We urged him and his wife to flee west before the Russians arrived in Brünnlitz, but Schindler wouldn't hear of it. He had no intention of abandoning us. He probably also thought we would be his best protection, and so it was not easy to persuade him to flee. For our part, we had to be diplomatic because on no account did we wish to give the impression that we wanted to be rid of him. Nor did we—we were all too aware of how precarious our position would become without his presence and authority.

Finally, Schindler decided to leave the camp. His plan was to head west with his wife, accompanied by a few of us who already knew with sad certainty that none of their relatives had survived and had no desire to return to Poland. But before he left, Schindler wanted to celebrate his birthday with us on April 28. A few days before then, a telegram arrived from the company to whom we shipped our half-finished grenade parts for final assembly. It said, "Inspection procedure number such and such was obviously not correctly carried out. It was impossible for us to assemble any of your shipment." In our little group of Schindler's closest associates, we were extremely worried. "If we show this to Schindler, he might suspect us of sabotage." What should we do? We agreed to wait until his birthday to give him the bad news, since he'd be in excellent spirits that day. On April 28, 1945, a few days before the end of the war, we sheepishly handed Schindler the telegram. He skimmed it and then broke into a broad smile, "That's the best birthday present I ever had!"

After the war, I heard that from time to time, Schindler would knowingly miscalibrate the machines that produced the grenade parts. In other words, our "arms production" didn't end up contributing much at all to the continuation of the war.

On April 28, we ceremoniously presented Schindler with a letter of safe-conduct in three languages: Hebrew, English, and Russian.[98] "Mietek Pemper was holding a gigantic sheet of paper, as long as a bath towel," writes Stella Müller-Madej. "Everyone signed it, including me. It made me almost happy."[99]

We didn't know whom Schindler might encounter when he crossed the border into the Reich and weren't sure how the Americans would react if they ran across a former Nazi. Thus, at the end of the war, we whom Schindler had protected for so long became in turn *his* protectors.

With the end near enough to touch and almost no possibility that the SS would still have a chance to kill us off at the last minute, we wanted to convey our gratitude to Schindler with a personal gift. But what could we give him? We had nothing, were almost literally naked. Then Simon Jereth volunteered his gold fillings. Jereth was by then an elderly man. He'd been a lumber dealer with a business in Zabłocie, right next to the Emalia. Some prisoners who had been goldsmiths melted down Jereth's fillings and made a ring out of them in which they engraved a saying from the Talmud: "Whoever saves a life saves the whole world." Schindler couldn't read it, of course, because it was written in Hebrew. Since Hebrew writes only the consonants, but not the vowels, the whole sentence fit around the inside of the ring. We presented this ring to Schindler the night of May 8–9, 1945. Shortly thereafter, his little column left Brünnlitz, heading west.

The day he left, Schindler gave a speech of farewell. All of "his Jews" were there, more than a thousand men and women, and a few children. Schindler once again portrayed in broad strokes his efforts during the last five years. "If it was difficult to defend the few remaining rights of my Polish workers, to keep them in the factory and protect them from being sent to the Reich as forced laborers . . . the difficulties of defending my Jewish workers often seemed insurmountable. You who have worked with me from the beginning, for all these years, know how many times I had to personally intervene after the ghetto was liquidated, how often I petitioned the camp administration to preserve you from being transported to the East and exterminated."[100] Schindler also hinted that he had kept many of his maneuvers from us so as not to endanger the rescue operation as a whole: "I required efforts in production from you that may have seemed senseless to most of you, since you had no access to the bigger picture, but the goal was always to demonstrate humanity and to preserve its sacred principles."

Schindler spoke for about an hour. He was in great form, and what he had to say testified to his profound humanity. I was amazed that a man facing the collapse of his own career could make such a well-considered speech. He didn't read it, but spoke without notes, which lent his words a special dynamic immediacy. Two of us took down what he said in shorthand. Later we discovered a typed draft of his speech, from which one could deduce that Schindler had not only composed this speech, but also typed it up himself, since he had the habit of not pressing the space bar after a comma or period when he typed. So he had prepared the speech with care. In it, he also mentioned the SS guards. He wanted to prevent us from taking out our fury on these "elderly family men" and exhorted us to let them go their way in peace.

They had neither tortured nor struck us—but of course, we couldn't know if they would have behaved so peaceably without the gifts Schindler had dispensed. Schindler entreated us to behave humanely and fairly. "Leave judgment and revenge to those in authority. If you have an accusation to make against someone, make it to the proper authorities. There will be judges in the new Europe, incorruptible judges who will take up your cause." Schindler also appealed to us not to plunder. "Show yourselves worthy of the millions of victims from your ranks. Perform no act of individual revenge or terror."

While he spoke, I kept thinking, how can a person in his situation, here, on this day, give such a wise and balanced speech? Schindler also mentioned the Daubek family who owned the mill. Without their help in obtaining foodstuffs, many of us would have starved. Finally he thanked some of us by name for our help in the rescue operation. "Don't thank me for your survival. Thank your own people who worked day and night to save you from destruction. Thank your fearless Stern and Pemper and the others who sacrificed themselves for you, especially in Kraków, staring death in the eye every moment as they thought of the good of all and looked out for all of you."[101] At the end of the speech, Schindler asked for three minutes of silence in memory of the countless victims from among our ranks.

In the last few years, after I've given one of my lectures, people often ask why Oskar Schindler only mentioned two of us, Izak Stern and me, by name in his farewell address, and why he said the others should thank us. This question is not surprising, since my lectures are usually quite brief and do not go into much detail about how the camp was preserved from liquidation. Izak Stern was in contact with Oskar Schindler from the first months of the war, and a sort of friendship developed between them during their long conversations and discussions. In my case, Schindler was probably thinking of the classified information he had gotten from me, and of my bold stroke with the inflated production tables in the late summer of 1943. As only he and I knew, the pretense that we could mount significant arms production preserved the Płaszów camp, and thus Schindler's satellite camp as well, until the fall of 1944. Without the inflated production tables I had prepared, there would have been no Schindler's list and no Brünnlitz.

Schindler left the camp with his wife and some of our people during the night of May 8–9, 1945. We put him in blue mechanic's coveralls and dressed his wife accordingly. Then the column of cars set off toward the Bavarian border. On May 13, we were officially liberated by the Red Army.

RETURN TO KRAKÓW, A CITY WITHOUT JEWS

MANY OF THE JEWS Oskar Schindler rescued returned to Kraków in the summer of 1945. But it was no longer the Kraków the Germans had occupied in 1939. Of the 56,000 Jews who had lived there before the war, only about 4,000 returned. Almost my entire extended family of seventy-some people had been murdered. Moreover, most of the returnees remained only a short time, waiting for permission to emigrate to Canada, South America, Australia, the United States, or Palestine. They wanted to get as far away from the scene of their sufferings as they could. Today, at the beginning of the twenty-first century, after some six centuries of Jewish history in Kraków, a mere two hundred Jews remain in the city. My family, too, returned to Kraków right after the war. From there, my younger brother Stefan made his way to Germany. He settled in Augsburg and moved to Hamburg a few years later, where he died and was buried in 1978.

For those of us returning to Kraków after the Brünnlitz camp was liberated, it wasn't an easy trip. The Soviet Union, which had conquered and occupied this part of central Europe, had replaced the railroad tracks with the wider-gauge tracks that were standard in Russia. On those tracks, they transported coal from the upper Silesian coalfields in Poland to steel mills in the Ukraine, and so the main axis of the line Katowice-Kraków-Lwow was closed to passenger trains. While we waited impatiently for a chance to return to Kraków, we got a wonderful piece of news. In those first postwar days, there were young fellows who would travel by hitching rides on trucks. They would drive back and forth, carrying messages to and fro between relatives and friends. Through these informal couriers, we learned that my mother was still alive. It was sensational news. After the liberation of Auschwitz, Polish and Russian soldiers had driven her and other invalids to Kraków in a horse-drawn cart. She was waiting for us in a hospital in the city. She never recovered completely and I had to hire a nurse to take care of her in the following years. My father was also quite debilitated by years of privation in the camp.

We were penniless when we got to Kraków and had to start thinking about earning a living. My father tried to renew his old contacts in the grain business. During the worldwide depression at the end of the 1920s, the Polish government had declared a moratorium—I think it was to be for twenty years—on the repayment of all agricultural debts. As a result, my grandfather Arthur Gabriel Pemper lost a large part of his financial assets. Hoping to collect on some of these outstanding debts, my father hired a taxi and drove around to various district courts in and around Kraków to search through their title registries and compile a list of what was owed. But Poland had been destroyed and people had no money to pay. So it fell upon me to support my family. I was willing to take any job available. However, I also resumed my studies in business administration at the Academy of Economics, so it was not possible for me to work full-time. I managed to earn a bit of extra income as an interpreter at various Nazi war crimes trials. The pay was less than modest, but it also enabled me to find out what had happened in other camps. In 1948, I wrote my master's thesis on German accounting theories, primarily on static and dynamic theory. Many years later, I learned that Eugen Schmalenbach, originator of the dynamic accounting theory, had had to give up his professorship in Cologne during the Nazi period because he refused to divorce his Jewish wife. The famous German philosopher Karl Jaspers also remained loyal to his Jewish spouse, and both he and his

My father after the war.

wife survived the war in Germany and later moved to Basel.

Soon after finishing my degree, I became an assistant to a professor of accounting and balance-sheet analysis at the Academy of Economics. For a short time, I held a teaching position and the title of assistant professor. My research focused on certain accounting systems used in modern industrial cost analysis.

In 1945, I had also begun to study sociology at the Jagiellonian University. I hoped to understand better the psychosocial mechanisms that could effect such a profound change in almost an entire nation that men like Amon Göth, Josef Mengele, and many other members of the SS could behave as they did. But after a few semesters, sociology was branded a "bourgeois" field of study and the department summarily shut down on the orders of Andrey A. Zhdanov, the member of the Moscow Politburo in charge of cultural affairs. My professor for business administration then recommended me as head of the Accounting Department for State Enterprises, a division of the Finance Ministry.

During our first months back in Kraków, we were disheartened by riots that occurred in the surrounding rural areas when returning Jews tried to reclaim their property. In July 1945, there was even a kind of pogrom in Kraków, although it wasn't nearly as bad as the one a year later in Kielce, when a few dozen returning Jews were massacred in the spring of 1946.

We were not able to move back into our old apartment on Parkowa Street because Polish tenants were now living there, and they couldn't just be put out onto the street. So we moved in with relatives instead. A cousin on my mother's side and his fiancée had survived the war with false papers that declared them to be "Aryan." They owned a small apartment in the inner city, and my mother, my father, and I moved into one of its rooms, my brother having already moved to Augsburg. As soon as I had earned a bit of money, though, we rented an apartment of our own.

Shortly after the war.

My mother died eight years later and was buried in Kraków. After her death, I worked at obtaining permission for my father and me to emigrate to Germany. As part of the effort to reunite families, we reached Augsburg in 1958. I could have continued on to the United States, but my father was dependent on me and wanted to stay in Europe. I also was suffering from a bout of depression at the time and believed that, like my mother, I would not reach an advanced age. I was already almost forty years old, so I quickly gave up on the idea of trying to start a new life in the United States. My father died in Augsburg in early 1963, almost exactly ten years after my mother.

MURDERERS WITHOUT REMORSE

IN THE WINTER OF 1944–45, even before the official end of the war on May 8, 1945, the Polish government appointed a special commission to investigate Nazi crimes. The commissioners were well-respected judges and prosecutors. One of the leading members of the commission was Dr. Jan Sehn, an examining magistrate before the war. In the 1950s, he was appointed professor of criminal justice at the Jagiellonian University. He was among the first to enter the liberated Auschwitz camp on January 27, 1945, to gather evidence of mass murder.[102] The commission also visited Płaszów. I was present during their inspection and reported on the special situation forced upon me in the commandant's office. On the basis of that testimony, Sehn sent me a letter in the summer of 1945, asking me to write down what I could recall. He was preparing to try Amon Göth and was seeking witnesses and evidence.

Jan Sehn came from a long-established Polish family and spoke perfect German. By chance, we had known each other slightly before the war, since his parents-in-law had been the neighbors of my maternal aunt, who was deported to Bełżec in 1942. By the summer of 1945, Sehn was already in contact with the Allied prosecutors in Nuremberg[103] and had exchanged letters with General Telford Taylor. It was fairly certain that the Americans would honor the agreement of foreign ministers reached at the Third Moscow Conference of 1943, and would extradite Amon Göth to Poland.[104]

The SS trial of Göth, begun in the fall of 1944, had been cut short by the end of the war. By the summer of 1945, Göth was being held in a reception camp for German soldiers on the grounds of the former Dachau concentration camp near Munich, where he told the Americans he was a demobilized Wehrmacht soldier. Despite the simple uniform he was wearing, however, he was identified as a member of the SS and was extradited to Poland together with Rudolf Höss, the former commandant of Auschwitz. The two of them arrived at the main station in Kraków on July 30, 1946.[105] Reportedly, there was quite an unruly crowd gathered, and Göth was roundly cursed by former inmates. He stood out in any crowd because of his enormous size.

Göth was put into pretrial detention, and there Sehn presented him with an indictment based largely on my testimony. Sehn told me later how Göth reacted to the indictment. He didn't begin by reading it closely, but turned immediately to the last pages, where the witnesses for the prosecution were listed. According to Sehn, when he saw how many names there were, his precise words were, "What? So many Jews? And they always told us not a single one of the pricks would be left." I've never forgotten that response, for it suggests how vulgar Göth was, and why his brutality and that of the others was so unrestrained. They acted in the conviction that they would never be brought to justice because no witnesses would survive.

Absurdly enough, in the course of preparations for his trial, Göth asked to have his "friend" Oskar Schindler, the Jewish physician Dr. Aleksander Biberstein, the former Jewish camp physician Dr. Leo Gross, and me summoned as witnesses for the defense. Göth was of completely sound mind, as the subsequent trial proved, but on this count, he seriously miscalculated. He was the last person we few remaining Jews had to thank for our survival. Perhaps his strange request was meant to suggest the opposite to the court. He was informed that Dr. Gross was imprisoned himself, accused of collaboration, while Dr. Biberstein and Mietek Pemper were already witnesses for the prosecution.

Oskar Schindler was somewhere in occupied Germany, inaccessible to the Polish courts. We didn't know then that Schindler was in Regensburg. Later, when Schindler read a newspaper article about Göth's execution in the fall of 1946, he got in touch with me. His letter was addressed "To the witness Mietek Pemper in the trial of Göth, Kraków Court."

At his first interrogation by an American examining magistrate in Dachau, Göth claimed to have been the commandant of a prison camp that produced, among other things, goods for the German army on the eastern front. The words "forced labor camp" or "concentration camp" were not mentioned.[106] But then four former inmates from Płaszów recognized him and exposed him, identifying who he really was and where he had worked. The deceitful house of cards Göth had constructed quickly collapsed. One of these witnesses even made a macabre joke. With American soldiers watching, he clicked his heels together in front of Göth and announced, "Four Jewish swine reporting for duty, *Herr Kommandant*!"[107] During a subsequent preliminary hearing in Kraków, Göth claimed he had only carried out the orders of his superiors.

I explained to the court the organizational structure and chain of command with which I was quite familiar from my work in the former Płaszów headquarters. I was the only witness they were able to summon who could give a complete and exact overview.

Göth's trial was the first large proceeding of its kind in Poland. The investigative and legal procedures used conformed to the statutes of the International Military Tribunal in Nuremberg. Göth had two defense counsels and an interpreter assigned to him by the court, and a medic was on call outside the courtroom. The indictment was available in both Polish and German. During the trial, Göth was permitted to ask questions, rebut testimony, and even cross-examine witnesses.[108] He was allowed to compose a clemency plea, which he did. In it, he asked that the death sentence be converted to a prison sentence. He wanted to prove, he wrote, that he could be a useful member of society.

One of my appearances in the trial of Amon Göth, August–September 1946.

In my opinion, Göth was fairly treated. He was by no means convicted in a summary procedure, as some have claimed.[109] Following extensive preliminary inquiries and careful gathering of evidence, the trial proper lasted a week, from August 27 to September 5, 1946. When the death sentence was announced, the public reaction in Kraków was one of relief. Göth's execution by hanging on September 13, two years to the day since his arrest by the SS in Vienna, was announced on large placards posted on kiosks in the center of town.

The trial was held in the court building on Senacka Street, the largest criminal courtroom in the Polish appellate court system. It was the talk of the day both in Kraków and the rest of Poland, and was followed abroad. The courtroom could seat several hundred, and people fought over admission tickets. If someone only had time to spend an hour listening to the trial, he passed his ticket on to someone else still waiting to get in. The court even ended up broadcasting the proceedings over loudspeakers set up outside. Hundreds of people assembled in the park diagonally across

Amon Göth on the way to his trial under Polish escort, August–September 1946.

from the courthouse to listen. The trial aroused so much attention because Göth was widely known and hated as the merciless torturer and murderer not just of Jews, but of Polish gentiles as well. Many had seen the fake newspaper ad that had circulated as a macabre joke in 1943: "Gold and silver jewelry, cleansed of Jewish blood, available at attractive prices from Amon Göth, Camp Commandant, Płaszów." The presiding judge, Dr. Alfred Eimer, had already been a judge before the war. As his name suggests, he was of German descent, but he was a Polish patriot who had not surrendered his citizenship in 1939 in order to become a *Volksdeutscher*, an ethnic German from outside the Reich. That is why the Germans had not allowed him to remain on the bench, and he had had to pursue other work during the war.

According to the indictment, Göth was responsible for the death of eight thousand people in the Płaszów camp alone, and an accessory to the murder of two thousand more during the liquidation of the Kraków-Podgórze ghetto on March 13–14, 1943. Those numbers did not include the tens of thousands he had sent on to their almost certain death in Auschwitz or Mauthausen, nor the hundreds murdered during the liquidation of the ghettos in Tarnów and Szebnie in the fall of 1943. Göth had embezzled the bulk of items of value—mainly jewelry and diamonds—seized during those operations. The reading of the indictment alone took up almost the entire first morning of the trial.[110] Dr. Eimer asked the defendant how he pleaded. Göth answered with a loud "Not guilty!"

Then Dr. Ludwig Ehrlich, professor of international law at Jagiellonian University, was called as an expert witness. He characterized Göth's actions as "crimes against humanity." This was a new formulation at the time, introduced into international law by the Allies to distinguish the crimes of the Nazis from military actions on the one hand and everyday felonies on the other. In international law, a "crime against humanity" is defined as the attempt to systematically enslave, deport, murder, or exterminate an entire part of a civilian population. Ehrlich's testimony accorded with the statutes of the International Military Tribunal in Nuremberg.[111] On the same grounds, he declared Göth's membership in the Waffen-SS to be criminal. Lastly, Göth was charged with genocide. This was also a newly coined word.[112] Amon Göth then had the opportunity to answer the indictment. He offered what in his opinion were exculpatory arguments and repeatedly insisted that he was only following the orders of his superiors.

Later, it was my turn to testify. While doing so, I assiduously avoided eye contact with Göth. I wanted to remain objective and not get distracted, confused, or unnerved. During a recess, friends of mine in the audience said, "You know, he's sitting there between two policemen, at a considerable distance from us. He can't do us any more harm. And yet we're afraid of him. We're still afraid. We can't understand how you could have spent all those months in the office with him." Our fellow inmate Leopold (Poldek) Pfefferberg used to say, "If you've seen Göth, you've seen death."

Again and again during the trial, I couldn't help reflecting that Göth had two defense attorneys, an interpreter, and medics waiting outside the courtroom in case he needed them, all the services that he would never have provided for his victims. And so, in view of what he did to so many innocent human beings, I regard his trial as an act of justice. For no other reason than that we were members of a Jewish "race" (which doesn't even exist), we were systematically humiliated, persecuted, tortured, and finally murdered—children and adults, the old and the young. As a survivor, I regarded it as my duty to testify at Göth's trial.

I chose my words carefully. My testimony under oath is preserved in the court records. Many inmates had seen Göth torturing or shooting people, but only I was able to describe the entire network of Göth's responsibilities and powers. While I spoke, the room was utterly silent. Many people were hearing for the first time the details of the deportation of their parents, children, spouses, or relatives. My testimony lasted almost two hours. When I was done, Alfred Eimer set the next session for the following day, but first he turned to the accused. "Do you have any questions?"

I can recall Göth's precise words: "Yes, several!" His voice was again loud and hard, and his answer made me very uneasy. What might he have up his sleeve, I thought. How will he try to talk his way out of this tomorrow? I hardly slept at all that night.

The second day of the trial began with some questions from the prosecutor and the judge about details of my testimony. Then came Göth's cross-examination, and he bombarded me with questions for at least an hour and a half. Only one thing seemed to interest him: "How does the witness know all the things he's testified to here in court?" It was an utter mystery to Göth where I had gotten all my information. At first, I held back with my explanations, for I was interested in hearing Göth try again and again to rebut or disprove my allegations. For example: "The witness's mother had a stroke and was not able to walk. Nevertheless, she was not selected for transport but was able to remain in the camp. How does the witness explain that?" I then briefly explained my risky deception of the camp physician, Dr. Blancke.

Göth's questions demonstrated his sharp spatial memory. He

often tried to use it to discredit what other witnesses said on the basis of tiny details and small inaccuracies. As a rule, his objections were usually on the order of, "How could the witness have seen such-and-such, when he worked in a different barracks, from which there was no view of this-or-that part of the camp?" If a witness testified to having seen the defendant torturing another inmate in front of the commandant's office, Göth would ask, "Where in the camp was the witness employed?" And when the answer was "in the furrier's shop" or "in the tailoring shop," Göth would counter with, "Then his testimony cannot be that of an eyewitness, since from that part of the camp, he couldn't even see the headquarters building." Only if the witness then added that he had been sent to headquarters with the daily production report and on the way there had seen the mistreatment going on would Göth back down. He was without a doubt in full possession of his faculties and had a very good memory. Gone were the weariness and lethargy I had so often observed in the camp. He followed the proceedings attentively and took extensive notes.

There was even a bizarre exchange during Göth's cross-examination of the former inmate Wilhelm Kranz that elicited laughter from some people in the audience. Kranz was a decent, cooperative guy. As a member of the *Ordnungsdienst*, the inmate security force, it had been his thankless job to oversee the camp's detention center. After the war, Kranz developed an enormous appetite and by the time of the trial had gained about forty-five pounds. Göth, on the other hand, had become remarkably slim. "I can recall the Jewish *Ordnungsdienst* man you're talking about very well," Göth said, "even though I can't remember his name. But it definitely was not this witness."

When the judge asked Kranz what he had to say, he replied, "It's simple. Back then I was as skinny as Göth is now, and now I'm as fat as Göth was then."

The transcript of the trial was published as a book in 1947. Although I believe that the indictment, Dr. Ehrlich's expert testimony, and the verdict appear exactly as they were presented in court, I think that the testimony of other witnesses, the rebuttals of the accused, and the cross-examinations are often reproduced in abbreviated form, and tend to be more a summary of what was said. At the time, there were few if any tape recorders and not everything got taken down verbatim by the court stenographers. I can recall that during the trial, one or the other of the four judges would dictate something to the stenographers or give them special instructions. The actual testimony of both Göth and the witnesses was much more extensive than what was ultimately printed in the published version.

I was recalled to the witness stand to testify on the details of the "health roll call" of May 1944, and the framing and murder of the senior Jewish inmate Wilhelm (Wilek) Chilowicz. I told how I had tricked Frau Kochmann with the carbon paper. I also explained how I had been able to read the classified correspondence in the headquarters safe thanks to Adjutant Grabow. As I mentioned already, while testifying I avoided eye contact with Göth, so I can only imagine his stunned look, sitting there in the dock, when he heard the words "carbon paper," "safe," and "classified correspondence." He had instituted such a reign of terror in the camp that it would never have occurred to him that anyone—much less a Jewish inmate!—would dare to read classified camp correspondence, telegrams, and official memoranda.

But now, three years later, he suddenly became aware that Mietek Pemper, his most dutiful office slave, had been systematically gathering information and using it to help fellow prisoners. It was surely not the first time he must have regretted not shooting this Pemper fellow, for my testimony was clear and incontrovertible. As an intelligent man, Göth must have now begun to realize what he was in for.

From then on, although he challenged certain details and made a comment here and there, he was no longer able to deny the truth of what I was saying. In fact, I had the impression that he wasn't even trying to do so anymore. He was probably coming around to the reality of his situation: His time was up. The game was lost.

After the trial, I complained half-jokingly to the examining magistrate Sehn, "You sent me into a battle that might have ended up badly for me. If Göth had tried to publicly discredit me or accuse me of some sort of collaboration, I could have had all the Furies after me."

"No, no," Sehn reassured me, "we foresaw that Göth might try to pin something dishonorable on you. We carried out extensive investigations beforehand and knew you had always conducted yourself properly and with integrity. If Göth had tried to accuse you of anything, we would have intervened immediately."

After the Göth trial, the Kraków legal community regarded me with some degree of amazement. They had difficulty imagining how an unimposing young man of twenty-three or twenty-four, had been able to fool a camp commandant—an uninhibited, impulsive murderer—for so long and in such a systematic and cunning way.

On the strength of my bilingual fluency, the Kraków judicial authorities then offered me a job as interpreter in other Nazi trials. They also knew that I was familiar with Nazi terminology and the SS ranks. Most prewar interpreters were completely stymied by words like *Aussiedlung* or *Sonderbehandlung*.[113] One young woman who was an interpreter said to me, "I have no idea what the word *Arbeitseinsatz* means. To me, an *Einsatz*[114] is some embroidered insert on a blouse or a sweater, but what does it have to do with work?" So I was enlisted as an interpreter for the big Auschwitz trial of 1947 in Kraków. I also testified at the trials of the "second tier" of SS men such as Lorenz Landstorfer, about ten other SS men from Płaszów, as well as Arnold Büscher, Göth's successor. In the short time that Büscher was commandant, he didn't do anything particularly culpable, but in order to save his own neck he did boast to the court that he had helped bring Göth down! Some of these defendants were sentenced to death. Later, in Germany, I testified in Nazi trials in Hanover and Kiel.

The trial of Rudolf Höss, the commandant of Auschwitz, was held in Warsaw. Höss had become *the* symbol of the persecution and murder of Jews and Poles. That was why he was tried separately, in the capital. On April 2, 1947, he was sentenced to death, and the execution was carried out on the grounds of the former Auschwitz main concentration camp. Dr. Sehn was in charge of the preliminary investigation for the Höss trial as well. He brought me in as an advisor to help decipher stenographic notes written by Höss as well as by Maria Mandel, the infamous *Lagerführerin*—female head guard—of Auschwitz-Birkenau. Not many people in Poland at the time could read the new German standard shorthand, introduced in 1936, which I had taught myself during the war. I only got one look at Rudolf Höss in Dr. Sehn's Kraków office, and did not further participate in his trial beyond this preliminary work.

I did testify at the trials of some of his subordinates, however, and in others I was an interpreter. In the big Auschwitz trial of 1947, there were forty defendants before the court, among them Artur Liebehenschel, Maria Mandel, Dr. Johann Paul Kremer, Ludwig Plagge, and Dr. Hans Münch. Twenty-two of them were sentenced to death on December 22, 1947, but not all those sentences were carried out. This trial, held in Kraków, was the largest trial of Nazi war criminals in Poland. Once again, Jan Sehn conducted the preliminary investigation.[115] For months, he worked day and night to the point of exhaustion. His was the first systematic account of the horrible crimes committed in Auschwitz. SS-*Obersturmbannführer* Artur Liebehenschel was the highest-ranking defendant. He was named commandant of Auschwitz after Höss was promoted to head of Department D I in Berlin-Oranienburg.

Witnesses at the trial described terrible scenes. Maria Mandel, the notorious head guard of the women's camp at Auschwitz-Birkenau, who had been a postal employee in Austria before the war, would beat the women unmercifully. Other witnesses told of an utterly inconspicuous-looking female guard who used sticks to probe the vaginas of newly arrived women, looking for items of value. The torments of the Jewish women were almost unimaginable. The physician and SS-*Obersturmführer* Dr. Münch was the only defendant to be acquitted and deported to Germany, where he had a practice in Rosshaupten am Forggensee, south of Augsburg, until his retirement. He had worked in the SS Institute of Hygiene in Rajsko, which was attached to the Auschwitz concentration camp. Some women witnesses wept as they related how he had looked after them and slipped them extra food. Münch sometimes warned them that there would be a selection on the following day and would let them spend the night in the institute.

After the trial, I asked the prosecutor why someone like Münch would be tried at all. "Well, you see," he replied, "if his extradition documents state he was an SS-*Obersturmführer* and a camp physician in Auschwitz, then we have to try him. The trial will determine his guilt or innocence. It's part of our job to establish the facts and understand the historical circumstances." That made sense to me.

Today, however, I've concluded that Münch was only acquitted in 1947 because of lack of documentation, for in the 1990s, I read some extremely derogatory, anti-Semitic remarks of his in a German magazine. According to Münch, eastern European Jews were vermin, *Untermenschen*, animals. He also said he was an admirer of Josef Mengele, the Auschwitz camp doctor who had conducted barbarous experiments on both adults and children. So now I wonder whether it was right to acquit him.

I also testified at the trial of SS-*Sturmbannführer* Willi Haase, the chief of staff for Julian Scherner, the SS and police chief of the Kraków district, and thus Göth's immediate superior.[116] In the indictment, some witnesses had given Haase's name as "Wilhelm von Haase." The first question put to me was, "Do you know the accused?"

"Of course. It's Willi Haase."

"But the accused has testified that's not who he is, and other witnesses have said his name is Wilhelm von Haase."

I saw immediately what was going on. I knew Willi Haase from his many visits to the commandant's office in Płaszów. I was also familiar with his signature, and even the identification marks he and his secretary used on dictated letters. By contrast, the other witnesses knew of Willi Haase only from hearsay. They were familiar with his name in reference to the "evacuation operations" in the ghetto in June 1942, that had been commanded "*von* Haase" (*by* Haase) and his subordinates, and evidently thought that the man had the aristocratic name Wilhelm von Haase and that Willi was a nickname.

Haase exploited this confusion to claim that this was a case of mistaken identity and that they were trying the wrong person. His trial had gotten stalled over this issue. I drew facsimiles of the defendant's signature and identification mark for the court. I even wrote down the name "Scherner" with a thick red pencil, for that's how Haase's boss signed his letters. But Haase insisted, "No, there's been some mistake. I'm not the man you're looking for."

So I turned and spoke to him directly. I reminded him of the time Göth had been away from the camp and Haase had shown up at headquarters with his two little daughters, insisting on having their hair cut in Göth's office. I gave an exact description of the blonde five- or six-year-olds while looking Haase square in the eye.

Finally, he lowered his gaze and said, "Yes, that's right."

Willi Haase was condemned to death for the crimes he committed during the liquidation of the Kraków ghetto.

In connection with the major Auschwitz trial, I also helped draft the clemency plea of Dr. Johann Paul Kremer, a doctor from Münster who kept a diary during his time in Auschwitz. Kremer had a Jewish defense attorney, Dr. Berthold Rappaport, a prominent attorney and former in-house lawyer for the largest Polish newspaper publisher in Kraków. In September 1942, Kremer had written that Dante's *Inferno* was nothing compared to Auschwitz. He also quoted the remark of the army doctor SS-*Obersturmführer* Dr. Heinz Tilo, that Auschwitz was the "*anus mundi.*" Kremer had never written anything derogatory about Jews in his diary.

I wrote in the plea for clemency that it should be taken into account that Kremer spent only a few months, against his will, in Auschwitz, and soon tried to get transferred out. The most important thing seemed to me that the extensive entries in Kremer's diary proved that Auschwitz and Birkenau had really existed. I regarded the diary of a German physician and university professor as an especially important and convincing document for posterity. Kremer's diary is a clear proof of the fact that Auschwitz was indeed an extermination camp.[117] At the time, however, I could never have imagined that there would ever be people who would cast doubt on, or even deny, the existence of the industrially organized mass murder in Auschwitz.

But the court found it objectionable that in the same breath, so to speak, Kremer could describe the extraction of fresh liver cells from an inmate and then a delicious lunch he ate in the SS canteen: roast chicken with so and so many grams of butter and wonderful vanilla ice cream. The court considered that an indication of Kremer's brutish nature, while I considered what he did in Auschwitz not on the same level as the crimes of the other defendants.

In 1947, it cost me enormous effort not to fall into the trap of generalizing about people and their behavior. Only when I had freed myself from such blanket condemnation was it possible for me to help Kremer's court-appointed counsel to draft a clemency plea. I didn't do it as a personal favor, but from the sincere belief that it is important to make distinctions. You have to differentiate the deeds of a Göth from those of a Kremer. It's not for nothing that there are gradations in sentencing: five years, ten years, fifteen years, or life. It didn't seem to me right or justified that Kremer should be hanged along with the other murderers.

Over time, I lost track of the "Kremer case." It wasn't until after 1958, when I was already living in Germany, that I learned he was again facing trial in Münster. In 1947, his death sentence had been reduced to ten years in prison on the basis of the clemency plea. Kremer had served his sentence in Bydgoszcz and then was deported to Germany. There, he was sentenced to several years for his activities in concentration camps within the Reich, but since they credited him with the time served in Poland, he left the courtroom a free man.

In 1948, a year after the large Auschwitz trial, I served as court interpreter in the trial of Dr. Josef Bühler. Until 1945, he had been deputy to the *Generalgouverneur* Dr. Hans Frank and as such, administrative head.[118] Before the war he had been a junior partner in Frank's law office. Frank had been the official attorney of the National Socialist German Workers Party in Munich and represented Adolf Hitler and the Nazi Party in over one hundred and fifty cases. On October 1, 1946, the International Military Tribunal in Nuremberg sentenced Frank to death, and he was hanged a few weeks later.

The Bühler trial was especially important to the Poles, since Frank's trial had not taken place in Poland. As Bühler's interpreter, I sat right next to him, separated only by a small wooden barrier. I translated the entire proceedings into German for Bühler and his answers into Polish for the court. He was the only defendant. His defense attorney, Dr. Stefan Kosinski, was an outstanding lawyer. He had been hired by the archiepiscopal curia of Kraków, because Josef Bühler was a Catholic. His brother was a priest in Bavaria, where the Bühler family lived in the church rectory. Most of the witnesses for the defense were Catholic clergy. They emphasized that Bühler had been helpful whenever possible—especially when Catholic interests were involved. That was also stressed by the vicar-general of the Kraków curia, Prelate Mazanek.

About a week into the trial, I was strolling through Planty Park with the prosecutor, Professor Jerzy Sawicki. It was a sunny day in mid-summer and Kraków was at its most beautiful. "How will you argue for the death penalty?" I asked. "I've heard nothing but positive testimony."

"All well and good, up to now," Sawicki replied, "but the most important thing hasn't been mentioned yet. Bühler was present at the Wannsee Conference." I gave him a blank look. At the time, I had not yet heard of the Wannsee Conference. At the invitation of SS-*Obergruppenführer* Reinhard Heydrich, Bühler had taken part in it on January 20, 1942. The minutes, written by Adolf Eichmann, documented that Bühler had proposed to begin the extermination of the Jews in the Generalgouvernement.[119] Sawicki told me that in the spring of 1947, the only copy of the minutes of this conference had been discovered in Berlin. Bühler, as deputy head of the government, must have known that the Nazis had already begun building the Bełżec death camp in November 1941, and "his proposal to begin exterminating two and a half million human beings in the Generalgouvernement," the prosecutor concluded, "is by itself enough to justify the death penalty."

As Josef Bühler's interpreter, I often spoke with him during the recesses. Once we were talking about the foreword he had written for a book about the "connections among Jews, crab lice, and spotted fever." In it, Bühler claimed it was a characteristic of "Jewish blood" to infect other humans with spotted fever without the Jews themselves contracting it. I asked him if he really believed such nonsense. Bühler replied, "We live in an age of specialization, and I could only rely on what a famous immunologist told me. How could I, a lawyer, contradict him?" Another time, I asked him about the proposal he had made in Berlin-Wannsee. Again without a trace of shame or regret, he answered, "There were about two and a half million Jews in the Generalgouvernement, and we had no way to employ them, no work for them, no proper way to house them. There were problems with food distribution, and we were afraid of epidemics. I just wanted to get rid of the Jews, but I didn't know that they were being sent to their death."

As head of the government, Josef Bühler commanded a vast and complex bureaucracy. The court declared that although he was not one of the most immediate perpetrators, he had committed war crimes and crimes against humanity while sitting at his office desk. He was sentenced to death and executed.

"If Frank had been extradited to Poland," Sawicki told me after the trial, "then he would have been executed here instead of in Germany. And Bühler would very probably have gotten off with ten or fifteen years. But Poland needed a symbol for the horrific things done during the occupation."

Many survivors of the concentration camps neither wished nor were able to speak at length about their experiences during the Nazi occupation. For me, it was different. A few months after my father and I returned to Kraków, at the end of 1945 or the beginning of 1946, the examining magistrate got in touch with me and asked me to write down in as much detail as possible everything I had lived through between September 1939 and May 1945. There was great interest in my notes. They contributed to the preparation of a number of trials, especially that of Amon Göth. It was important to me to put at the disposal of the court all I knew about the persecution of the Kraków Jews and the history of the Płaszów camp, and to make sure that the criminals would receive their just punishment. It was also important to document publicly that during the more than 540 days—from March 17, 1943, to September 13, 1944—I spent as Göth's stenographer, I never did anything culpable. That was the other reason I agreed to be the main prosecution witness in the trials of Amon Göth and Gerhard Maurer.

In all of the trials in which I participated as a witness or an interpreter, I never heard any of the defendants utter a single word of regret or display any honest remorse. None of them said, "Now I see how wrong my actions were. I should never have followed criminal orders." None ever used his final words to say anything like, "I was influenced by false propaganda. I didn't know then what I know now. I am surprised that I could have acted in such a way, and I regret it." Nothing of the kind. No avowal of sorrow at the death of all those innocent victims, no apology, no contrition, no remorse.

WHY WE MUST NEVER FORGET

I MOVED TO GERMANY IN 1958. If I mentioned that I had been in a concentration camp when conversing with non-Jewish acquaintances, I was often met with embarrassed silence. People asked hardly any questions and didn't seem interested in what had happened to me. Instead, they often attempted to justify their own behavior, telling me how many Jews they had helped during the war. At first, I was perplexed and disappointed. I thought to myself, there weren't even remotely as many Jews in all of Germany as the number these people are claiming to have helped. To be sure, I don't doubt that, now and then, empathetic civilians would slip a piece of bread or an apple to a Jewish prisoner on some work detail outside the camps. But the number of people who actually risked their lives to protect Jews from the Nazis was small, very small. And those few helpers consider their rescue efforts a matter of course and don't make a big deal of their moral courage.

Many Germans must have had to struggle with their own historic guilt and the traumatic baggage of the war. I was disappointed to see widespread denial of the great contributions Jews had made to European culture. And so after I moved to the Federal Republic of Germany, I seldom spoke of my experiences in the camp. I focused on earning a living for my father and myself. But to this day I always carry an old 200-mark bill around with me. Few people know that the Nobel laureate pictured on it, the great immunologist and founder of chemotherapy Paul Ehrlich, was a German Jew.

When I returned to Kraków right after the war, I joined an association of former camp inmates, where I learned it was possible for us to get psychological counseling. I availed myself of this opportunity, because I was struggling with depression at that time. That's how I met the neurologist and psychiatrist Dr. Eugeniusz Brzezicki, professor at Jagiellonian University. He had had a concentration camp experience of his own: a few weeks after the Nazi occupation of Poland, Kraków University had reopened as usual after the semester break. The occupiers used this "unauthorized act" as an excuse to command all professors and instructors to attend a lecture in the university auditorium at the beginning of October 1939. The lecture was given by a certain SS-*Obersturmbannführer* Müller and was reportedly very short. It ended with the declaration that since it was a well-known fact that Polish academics had always been anti-German, those present would be taken directly to a camp for immediate reeducation. In the meantime, paddy wagons had drawn up in the narrow streets behind the university to pick up the professors. They were all taken to the Sachsenhausen concentration camp, where they were interned for several months and tortured. Many died soon after this ordeal.

When I had described to him my experiences during the past six years, Professor Brzezicki, said, "What you've been through would be too much for even two lifetimes. You can have yourself admitted to a psychiatric hospital and begin therapy right away, but I can't promise you'll ever be cured. But if you have a strong psychic constitution and a bit of luck, you can try to do it without therapy. To ward off depression, however, you must keep busy and distract yourself from brooding about what happened. Go to school, finish your education, get a job, but don't ruminate!" I was very grateful for this advice and adhered to it as much as possible. But my traumatic memories persisted. Although I am outwardly calm and composed and try not to brood too much about the past, to this very day scenes from the ghetto and the camp still remain vivid to my inner eye. When memories are triggered by a certain date or some chance remark, I try to suppress them and distract myself. No matter how long ago they happened, I still can hardly bear to remember, much less describe, their barbaric cruelty. When choosing which incidents to describe in detail in this book, the decisive criterion was whether they helped to substantiate the circumstances of important historical events or reveal a person's character.

At home with my family, of course, I talked about Płaszów. And I've always had contacts with other survivors in Germany, the United States, and Israel. In the 1960s, when I helped Oskar Schindler with his application for a *Lastenausgleich*—compensation from the West German government—we often spoke about Kraków and Brünnlitz. In public, however, I avoided the subject. But that changed when Steven Spielberg invited me to Kraków to watch the shooting of the film *Schindler's List* in April 1993, and ever since, I'm often invited to participate in programs where survivors talk about their experiences.

When I asked Spielberg why there were only two brutal SS men in his film—Amon Göth and Albert Hujer—he replied that you had to focus on a small number of main characters in a film, otherwise the audience is overwhelmed and leaves the theater with fuzzy images. He said that another concession to the audience was the significant toning-down of the SS brutality toward Jews, especially toward the children. In addition, for dramaturgical reasons, he had considerably simplified the way the list came about. In reality, it would have been impossible for Oskar Schindler to dictate the entire list from memory to Izak Stern, sitting at his typewriter. No one could have kept all the names, inmate numbers, birth dates, and professions of a thousand people in his head. And some marketing consultant must have suggested that Spielberg include the "cellar scene" between Amon Göth and Helene Hirsch. During the filming, I tried to convince Spielberg of the historical improbability of this scene, since Göth had completely internalized the Nazi racial laws. The taboo against *Rassenschande*—miscegenation—largely protected Jewish women from sexual assault by either the SS or the other camp guards.

Spielberg also told me that he had always meant to combine Izak Stern and me into one composite figure in the movie. However, the details of Stern's long acquaintance and eventual friendship with Oskar Schindler and the facts of my involved story as Göth's personal stenographer and the creator of the inflated production tables were too complex to be presented in a feature film.

Since the film's release, I began to take part in so-called *Zeitzeugengespräche*—conversations with Holocaust survivors—at the universities of Augsburg, Munich, and Regensburg, at adult education centers, at schools, and on television and radio. I have given lectures for the German–Israeli Society, the Society for Christian and Jewish Cooperation, and other organizations, and I donate all my lecture fees to charities.

It is especially important to me to talk to young people. For one thing, I always find the new generation open-minded. They have no preconceptions and really want to know what it was like back then. For another, the future depends on these young people. It will be they who ensure that the darkest chapter in history is not repeated anywhere in the world.

With students at the Schickhardt Gymnasium (high school) in Herrenberg, Germany, March 22, 2000.

Today's youth can hardly imagine their grandparents living in a time of such barbarity. Again and again, I'm asked, "What can we do to prevent it from happening again?" or "How was it possible?" Another question I hear occasionally shows how sensitive and empathetic many young people are: "How could you stand the psychic pressure of direct contact with Göth for so long?" The more sensation-hungry question, "Did you ever meet Hitler?" shows what's going through the heads of other young people and what they're interested in. Many questions give me a chance to indirectly address unexamined assumptions and even prejudices against Jews and other minorities. One such is the assumption that Jews allowed themselves to be led "like sheep to the slaughter." That's why in my lectures, I always emphasize the fact that we were the victims of a sophisticated campaign of propaganda and lies that had been long in the making. It enabled the murder of millions of people to function so perfectly. As Jews, we were clearly the victims of an asymmetric power relationship vis-à-vis the Nazis. As unarmed civilians, we were at the mercy of the most powerful military machine imaginable.

Despite this explanation, my young listeners often ask, "Why didn't you just kill Göth?" Aside from the fact that Göth was an experienced wrestler, and at 265 pounds more than double my weight and at least a head taller, his murder would have done nothing positive for us prisoners. On the contrary, assassinating Göth would have unleashed an unimaginable bloodbath, and Schindler's rescue operation would never have come to pass. I am always open to questions, and only once did a question upset me, especially since it came from someone who ought to have known better. During the shooting of Spielberg's movie in Kraków in 1993, a journalist from the *New York Times* asked, "Why did you apply for the job in Göth's office when you knew he was a murderer?"

Especially when I lecture in schools, I'm sorry that I don't have time to go into more detail about how I was able to help rescue so many of my fellow inmates. I'm constantly astonished at how intensely and seriously young people listen to what I have to say. When I ask their teachers why this is so, they often tell me that it's probably due to my unprejudiced, precise, and occasionally humorous delivery. In addition, my presence in the classroom suddenly makes history come alive for students. You could say I put a face on the dry statistics of the Holocaust. It also seems to help promote interest and empathy among the students that at my liberation more than sixty years ago, I was only a few years older than they are now. As a young man of barely twenty-three, I had been able to "trick" Göth and the SS on a grand scale and help keep Płaszów from being liquidated. That seems to impress young people and obviously gives them something to think about.

A few years ago, a journalist called Schindler's list and everything that went with it an act of "intelligent resistance." I like that phrase. It expresses what has been important to me all my life. I always try to understand the causes behind contemporary events and human behavior so that if necessary, I can defend myself against discrimination, injustice, and violence. For me, there is not just a right but a duty to resist—nonviolently, of course.

In my lectures, I avoid sweeping generalizations and black-and-white judgments. I always mention the young SS man Dworschak who refused to carry out an inhumane order. His example makes clear to students that they, too, must guard against judging people by how they look, by their nationality, their profession, or their religion. In life, the principle of individual responsibility must not be suspended, even if the price to be paid for it may be unknown and possibly extremely high. Of course, Dworschak's refusal to obey orders did not save the lives of the young woman and her child, but his reaction made a difference nevertheless. It gave me, a prisoner, courage, for it meant at least one person recognized the inhumanity of the order, courageously refused to obey it, and instead suffered the consequences. And it made the other SS man who did carry out the order later the same day uneasy, for afterward, he felt it necessary to justify his action to me, a Jewish inmate. Even in apparently hopeless situations, then, there is frequently the possibility of a choice—however minimal—that one needs to take advantage of, even if one believes it will make no difference to the final outcome. The students always become very quiet when I stress that we must judge others by how they behave in difficult situations, by whether they help others or not. No doubt, students sense that when I speak of political influence, manipulation, or even propaganda, I'm not just referring to the past. Democracy cannot survive without productive dissent, self-determination, critical thinking, empathy, and moral responsibility.

When I'm asked now and again if I hate the Germans, I answer with an unqualified "no." Hate gets us nowhere and doesn't contribute to reconciliation. Between 1939 and 1945, we Jews were treated worse than animals, but even in the midst of that inhumane world, I still encountered decent and empathetic individuals who resisted the pressure to be aggressive, brutal, and violent. The Nazi system was criminal and enticed many people to commit crimes they would probably not have committed under different circumstances. They must answer for these crimes as individuals, because for me there is no "collective guilt." I am unable to condemn any nation, religion, or people as a whole. Nevertheless, I am often overcome with great sorrow. I mourn the loss of the many who were murdered. It fills me with apprehension that it was so easy to manipulate so many people and that so few helped us in our need. For the sake of our future, we must not forget what happened. We cannot escape history. Mankind will only progress when the principle of individual responsibility becomes the golden rule, when refusal to play along becomes a virtue, and blind obedience loses its currency. We are all responsible for creating a better future. That includes accepting the "other," the "foreigner," in our midst.

I think it was in the 1920s that the philosopher and writer Martin Buber observed that the New Testament's commandment to love one's enemies was probably asking too much of mankind. If not, how could one explain such events as witch burnings, the

Crusades, and the Inquisition? Instead, Buber proposed a significantly more realistic ethical imperative: show consideration for those weaker than you and treat your neighbor well. For we humans are just as much in need of help as we are dependent on each other.

More than two hundred years ago, Johann Wolfgang von Goethe defined such an attitude as divine, when he wrote,

Edel sei der Mensch	Let man be noble,
Hilfreich und gut!	helpful, good!
Denn das allein	For only that
Unterscheidet ihn	distinguishes him
Von allen Wesen	from all the beings
Die wir kennen.	that we know.[120]

Much has been neglected in the education of man! We must make up for this neglect of humanity by our good example. Above all, we must resist the temptation to confuse violence and ruthlessness with "healthy" assertiveness, or to mistake emotional coldness for reason. Nor must we ever think that a lack of empathy will help us look out for our own interests and not be "weighed down" by the problems of others.

The twentieth century can rightly be called a *saeculum horribile* in both senses of the Latin *horribilis*: terrible and astonishing. I experienced the dual meaning of this term in the mass-murderer Amon Göth and the protector of human life Oskar Schindler.

On the one hand, the twentieth century managed to considerably increase the life expectancy of many people and significantly lower infant mortality. On the other, only twenty-seven years after the First World War, the Second World War claimed six times as many victims. In 1939, ten years after it had been discovered, penicillin began to be widely used against previously fatal infections. In that same year, a war was begun to first subjugate almost all of

Europe, then to murder—on an industrial basis—millions of human beings because they were supposedly of another race.

Right after the war there was a brief period when I was optimistic, almost euphoric. That was on account of a photograph I saw of Ralph Johnson Bunche. In the late 1940s, he served the cause of peace as an international negotiator, especially between the newly founded state of Israel and its opponents Jordan, Syria, Lebanon, and Egypt. As deputy of the secretary-general of the United Nations, he was known as "Mr. Peacekeeping" and was awarded the Nobel Peace Prize in 1950 for his work. If an African-American, the grandson of a slave, can become the deputy of the secretary-general and win the Nobel Peace Prize, I thought to myself, then—thank God!—we've reached a point where we can live well together. That's all we need. Living together and accepting one another will be enough to prevent the next genocide. From today's perspective, my optimism was perhaps naive, and certainly premature. But that must not discourage us from continuing to raise political and human awareness and to set an example of human solidarity and reconciliation in the midst of an often inhumane world.

Contra spem spero. Against all hope, I hope.

ACKNOWLEDGMENTS

We would like to thank the numerous individuals and institutions who made documents available, provided translations, and made many valuable suggestions, especially the Yad Vashem Archive (Jerusalem), the Archive of the United States Holocaust Memorial Museum (Washington, D.C.), the Simon Wiesenthal Center (New York City), the Jewish Historical Institute (Warsaw), the Institut für Zeitgeschichte (Munich), the Deutsches Bundesarchiv (Koblenz), the Instytut Pamieci Narodowej (Warsaw), and the Państwowe Muzeum Auschwitz-Birkenau in Oświęcim. Special thanks to Mr. Jens Petersen for his crucial role in the success of the publication of this book in Germany, and to Professor Josef Becker (University of Augsburg, Germany) and Professor James J. Sheehan (Stanford University).

Mieczysław (Mietek) Pemper
Viktoria Hertling
Marie Elisabeth Müller

I owe Viktoria Hertling an enormous debt of gratitude for several painstaking and critical readings of the translation. Many thanks also to the editorial team at Other Press for their hard work and constructive suggestions: Corinna Barsan, Yvonne E. Cárdenas, and Mimi Winick.

David Dollenmayer

APPENDIX 1

IZAK STERN'S REPORT
AN EXCURSUS BY VIKTORIA HERTLING

In the Yad Vashem archives in Jerusalem there is a fifty-page typescript written by Izak Stern in 1956 in cooperation with the historian Dr. K. J. Ball-Kaduri. Of particular interest to this text are pages 26 to 28. They bear the title "Conversion of the Plaschów Work Camp into the Plaschów Concentration Camp." Here Stern describes himself as the originator and architect of the preservation of the Plaszów camp and its subsequent transformation into a concentration camp.

At the beginning of this report, Stern describes in vivid detail the activities of various Kraków Zionist organizations with which he was involved in the 1930s, his first meeting with Oskar Schindler in 1939, and the final days of the Brünnlitz camp. Stern spoke German well. When he is not writing about the preservation of the camp, his narrative style is precise and coherent. By comparison, his description of the preservation of the Płaszów camp in the fall of 1943 on pages 26 through 28 is astonishingly vague, inconsistent, and historically inaccurate. Its authenticity is especially suspect in light of the fact that on these three pages, Stern repeatedly crossed out the name "Pemper" and replaced it with a handwritten "I" or "me."

Stern writes,

> One Sunday, there was a telegram from Oranienburg: they needed an immediate list of all our machines. Oranienburg was the main office. Since it was Sunday, none of our German

> bosses were in the camp headquarters. When the secretary [here Stern must have had Mietek Pemper in mind] read the telegram, he brought it straight to me. Then another telegram arrived right on its heels: they also needed an inventory of all inmates right away. Göth didn't return to camp that night, nor did he summon Pemper, who was also working in the office. We decided to suggest to Göth that we write a detailed report instead of just a list of numbers. That would impress them and maybe get us converted into a concentration camp. After Göth had read the telegrams, Pemper said we would write an interesting report on the production of all our workshops. We put in a lot of false statistics, listed many things twice, or the same for both the past and the future. It would be difficult to double-check it. The whole thing was then printed up and beautifully bound in our bindery, with lots of illustrations and statistical tables. Göth read the whole thing.

Stern continues that this report was then sent to "Oranienburg" and the camp was subsequently inspected. Later, even "General Pohl, Himmler's deputy" showed up in Płaszów, although "at the end of 1943 . . . they hadn't decided yet whether to turn the camp into a concentration camp."[121]

It is important to determine the details of the transformation of Płaszów into a concentration camp, because the preservation of the Płaszów camp in the fall of 1943 was a successful act of nonviolent resistance during the Holocaust, a unique event that has yet to be adequately appreciated by historians. The camp was never liquidated. The scheme was carried out without any injuries whatsoever, nor were there any reprisals from the Nazis. Not a single death in Płaszów resulted from this astonishing rescue operation. No inmate was tortured or shot as a result of it. The prisoners themselves were not privy to the plan to preserve the camp. They had no clue what was happening "behind the scenes" in the summer and fall of 1943 or who ultimately saved their camp from being liquidated and thus prolonged their lives. Up to now, even historians of the Holocaust could only conjecture why the Kraków-Płaszów camp was not liquidated. All they could say was that a forced labor camp had been converted to a concentration camp. They could state the fact, but could not explain why. No wonder, then, that in his novel *Schindler's List*, Thomas Keneally mentions the conversion in only a single sentence. Keneally must have been familiar with Stern's report, yet there was no way for him to ascertain from it who really contributed to this unique rescue operation or how it was carried out.

In the camp, Stern did work in the headquarters building, but his workshop accounting office was in a different part of the building than Göth's office. Stern thus had no access to Göth's anteroom except on official business and then only during office hours. In his report, however, he claims to have been especially trusted by the commandant, able to make such suggestions as, "I told Göth we should use the metal cuttings from Schindler's factory for further production within our own workshops. So he sent me to Schindler." According to this claim, Amon Göth colluded with inmates to keep the camp from being liquidated. Moreover, by supposedly sending Izak Stern to Schindler to discuss the further use of the metal cuttings his factory had accumulated, Göth would even have conspired with the owner of the Emalia factory in the plan to preserve the camp.

Of all the inmates, only Mietek Pemper had unrestricted access to Göth's headquarters. As the commandant's personal stenographer and secretary, Pemper was the only inmate who could enter Amon Göth's anteroom on Sundays, in the evening, and even at night without the SS guards sounding the alarm. It was well known that Pemper often worked thirteen or fourteen hours a day in the commandant's office. Nevertheless, the egomaniacal SS officer would never have permitted even Pemper to make suggestions to him, as Stern implies when he writes, "After Göth had read the telegrams, Pemper said we would write an interesting report on the production of all our workshops." In other words, would Göth have agreed to allow Pemper and Stern, on their own, to write an official report for the "main office" in Oranienburg? Or does the pronoun *we* include Amon Göth as a coauthor of the "interesting" report? The latter is a bizarre notion with no relation to the reality of the SS hierarchy.

Beginning on January 10, 1944, the Płaszów concentration camp was subject to the authority of the Economic and Administrative Main Office of the SS, Department D II in Berlin-Oranienburg. In the fall of 1943, however, SS-*Oberführer* Julian Scherner, SS and police chief of the Kraków district, still had jurisdiction over the forced labor camp Kraków-Płaszów. In 1943, only his Kraków office could have sent a telegram demanding a supposed "list of all our machines" or an "inventory of all inmates," not the "main office" in Oranienburg, as Stern claims. Such an overstepping of authority would have caused serious conflict between Kraków and Oranienburg.

Historical inaccuracies, inconsistencies, and nonsensical statements (such as, "We . . . listed many things twice or the same for both the past and the future") cast doubt on Stern's claims that he both knew about as well as participated in the scheme to preserve the camp. Based on the data and details of Izak Stern's report, no accurate picture of the rescue operation can be ascertained. Stern's description of the supposedly "beautifully bound" and profusely illustrated report for Oranienburg is more clear and vivid than the description of his involvement in the rescue effort itself.

Furthermore, it is highly implausible that an SS general such as Oswald Pohl (who was never "Himmler's deputy"), would have paid a visit to a forced labor camp without his usual entourage in order to meet with a common SS-*Untersturmführer*. Nor is there evidence in the published proceedings of the Economic and Administrative Main Office war crimes trial in Nuremberg that General Pohl ever visited Płaszów.[122] What's more, Stern's assertion that Pohl "hadn't decided whether to turn the camp into a concentration camp yet" at the end of 1943 is incorrect. We know the exact date of this decision. Pohl wrote a memorandum about it on September 7, 1943.

Izak Stern did not testify at Amon Göth's trial in 1946, although he would have been available to do so. He lived in Kraków until 1949, when he emigrated to Israel. Unlike other former prisoners, Stern must not have been able to add anything of substance to the general testimony about Göth's atrocities. And he certainly did not refute or support Göth's claim that he helped some inmates. In this respect as well, Stern's assertion that Göth was an accessory to the rescue operation is highly unlikely. For if Amon Göth had really done anything to benefit the Jewish inmates, his two court-appointed attorneys would have used that fact to plead for a mitigation of their client's sentence, and Stern would surely have been called as a witness. There is no reference to such actions in the published proceedings of the trial.

Izak Stern was an early confidant of Oskar Schindler's and one of the key signers of the letter of safe-conduct in May 1945 that smoothed the return to postwar Germany for Oskar and Emilie Schindler. There is no question of Stern's many achievements. But he had nothing to do with the effort to preserve the camp from being liquidated in 1943.

APPENDIX 2

CHRONOLOGY[123]

Entries bearing directly on the history of the Kraków-Płaszów camp and Schindler's list are in italics.

Nov. 9, 1938	*Reichskristallnacht*, the first state-sponsored pogrom against Jews in Germany.
Sept. 1, 1939	German invasion of Poland, beginning of the Second World War.
Sept. 6, 1939	*German troops occupy Kraków.*
Oct. 26, 1939	*Kraków becomes the capital of the* Generalgouvernement *for occupied Poland.*
Dec. 1, 1939	White armbands with a blue Star of David become mandatory for Jews in the *Generalgouvernement.*
End of 1939	*Oskar Schindler arrives in Kraków. Beginning in 1940, Schindler considers buying the enamelware factory in Kraków-Zabłocie; later, he purchases the firm.*
April 30, 1940	Establishment of the Łodz ghetto.
May 1940	*Reduction of the number of Jews allowed to live in Kraków from 60,000 to about 15,000. "Voluntary" relocation of at least 40,000 Jews to other towns in the* Generalgouvernement.
May 10, 1940	Beginning of the German invasion of the Netherlands, Belgium, Luxembourg, and France.
June 1940	Construction of the Auschwitz concentration camp.
Oct. 16, 1940	Establishment of the Warsaw ghetto.

March 6–20, 1941 *Establishment of the Kraków ghetto; 18,000 Jews are forced together into an area of only 13 square meters per person.*

June 22, 1941 German invasion of the Soviet Union ("Operation Barbarossa").

Sept. 23, 1941 First experiments with executions by lethal gas in Auschwitz.

Sept. 28–29, 1941 34,000 Jews are massacred in Kiev (Babi Yar).

Oct. 14, 1941 First deportations of German Jews.

Dec. 11, 1941 The United States enters the war.

Jan. 20, 1942 Wannsee Conference in Berlin. Decision to coordinate the "final solution of the Jewish question" in Europe.

End of January 1942 German Jews are deported to Theresienstadt (Terezín).

March 19, 1942 *Approximately fifty prominent Jewish intellectuals in Kraków are deported to Auschwitz and murdered.*

June 1, 1942 *The Kraków ghetto is sealed off. First transport of about 6,000 Jews to the Bełżec extermination camp. Three hundred Jews are shot to death in the ghetto itself.*

June 8, 1942 *Second extermination transport from the Kraków ghetto to Bełżec.*

June 23, 1942 First selections for the Auschwitz gas chambers.

July 22, 1942 First deportations of some 400,000 Jews from the Warsaw ghetto to extermination camps.

Fall 1942 *Beginning of the transfer of Jews from the Kraków ghetto to help build the Płaszów forced labor camp.*

Oct. 27–28, 1942 *Third extermination operation in the Kraków ghetto; 7,000 Jews are deported to Bełżec and Auschwitz; 600 are shot on the spot (liquidation of the hospital and the orphanage on Josefinska Street). The ghetto is reduced even further in size and divided into two parts, Ghetto A and Ghetto B.*

Nov. 7, 1942 Allied landing in North Africa.

Nov. 22, 1942	Beginning of the Soviet counteroffensive.
Feb. 2, 1943	Surrender of German troops in Stalingrad.
Feb. 11, 1943	*Amon Göth is transferred from Lublin to Kraków.*
March 13, 1943	*End of the Kraków ghetto. Relocation of able-bodied Jews from Ghetto A to the Płaszów forced labor camp.*
March 14, 1943	*About 2,300 Jews are deported from Kraków Ghetto B to Auschwitz and murdered. About 700 are massacred in the ghetto itself.*
April 19, 1943	Beginning of the uprising in the Warsaw ghetto.
May 9, 1943	Capitulation of German troops in North Africa.
Summer 1943	*Transfer of the last "clean-up crew" from the Kraków ghetto to the Płaszów forced labor camp.*
Sept. 6, 1943	Withdrawal of German troops from Kiev.
Jan. 10, 1944	*Conversion of the Płaszów forced labor camp into a concentration camp.*
May 7, 1944	*"Health roll call" in the Płaszów concentration camp to compile lists of inmates incapable of full-time work (i.e., children, seniors, the sick).*
May 14, 1944	*Deportation of about 1,500 inmates—primarily children, seniors, and the sick—from Płaszów to be exterminated in Auschwitz.*
June 6, 1944	Allied landing in Normandy.
July 8, 1944	Deportation of over 400,000 Hungarian Jews to Auschwitz.
July 24, 1944	Soviet troops liberate the Majdanek-Lublin concentration camp.
Summer 1944	*Number of inmates in the Płaszów concentration camp reaches a maximum of about 25,000.*
August 1944	*Deportations from the Płaszów concentration camp to Mauthausen and Stutthof.*
Sept. 13, 1944	*Amon Göth is arrested in Vienna; the SS and police court investigates his black-market activities and currency violations. Arnold Büscher is appointed to replace Göth in Płaszów.*
End of Sept., beginning of Oct. 1944	*Compilation of Schindler's lists.*

Oct. 15, 1944	*Transport of men from Płaszów to the Gross Rosen concentration camp.*
Oct. 22, 1944	*Transport of women from Płaszów to the Auschwitz concentration camp.*
Oct. 22, 1944	*Arrival of 700 men from the Gross Rosen concentration camp in Brünnlitz.*
Second half of November 1944	*Arrival of 300 women from the Auschwitz concentration camp in Brünnlitz.*
Jan. 14, 1945	*Last deportation from the Płaszów concentration camp to Auschwitz. During Amon Göth's command, about 8,000 inmates were murdered in the Płaszów camp.*
Jan. 27, 1945	Auschwitz is liberated by Soviet troops.
May 8, 1945	Germany capitulates.
About May 13, 1945	*Soviet troops liberate the Brünnlitz camp.*

APPENDIX 3

SS RANKS AND THEIR U.S. ARMY EQUIVALENTS

SS	US Army
Schütze	Private
Oberschütze	Private First Class
Sturmmann	Corporal
Rottenführer	Corporal
Unterscharführer	Sergeant
Scharführer	Staff Sergeant
Oberscharführer	Technical Sergeant
Hauptscharführer	Master Sergeant
Sturmscharführer	Sergeant Major
Untersturmführer	Second Lieutenant
Obersturmführer	First Lieutenant
Hauptsturmführer	Captain
Sturmbannführer	Major
Obersturmbannführer	Lt. Colonel
Standartenführer	Colonel
Oberführer	(Senior Colonel—no exact equivalent)
Brigadeführer	Brigadier General
Gruppenführer	Major General
Obergruppenführer	Lt. General
Oberstgruppenführer	General
Reichsführer	General of the Army

NOTES

1. Franz von Papen (1879–1969), German chancellor in 1932.
2. I remember a pastoral letter of February 9, 1937, from the Primate of Poland, Augustus Cardinal Hlond, which contained the following passage: "It is a fact that the Jews are struggling against the Catholic Church, that they are steeped in free thought, that they are the vanguard of godlessness, of the Bolshevik movement, and of subversive action. It is a fact that Jewish influence on morals is deplorable and that their publishing houses spread pornography. It is true that they are cheaters and carry on usury and white slave traffic. . . . Not all the Jews are such as described. There are also faithful, righteous, honest, charitable and well-meaning Jews. . . . It is permissible to prefer one's people; it is wrong to hate anyone. Not even Jews. In commercial relations it is right to favor one's own people, to avoid Jewish shops . . . but it is wrong to plunder Jewish shops, destroy Jewish goods, break windowpanes, throw bombs at their houses." In Saul Friedländer, 1997, p. 216.
3. Ibid., p. 215. Friedländer is actually here quoting the Italian journalist Virginio Gayda, "a semiofficial representative of the fascist regime" who used the phrase specifically with reference to the "Danubian states."
4. Gerhard Paul, http://www.abschiebehaft.de/presse/p73.htm.
5. Ibid.
6. The daily *Folkish Observer*, published in Munich, official organ of the National Socialist Party.
7. Frank 1975, p. 104.

8. Translation: "Decree. Identification badges for the Jews in the District of Kraków. I decree that as of December 1, 1939, all Jews over twelve years old must wear a visible badge of identification when outside their homes. Transient Jews are also subject to this decree for the length of their stay in the District. For the purposes of this decree, a Jew is defined as (1) any member or former member of the Jewish denomination, (2) anyone whose father or mother was a member or former member of the Jewish denomination. The identification badge will be an armband, to be worn on the right upper sleeve on one's clothing as well as on outer wear, showing a blue Star of David on a white background, turned toward the outside. The white background must be at least ten centimeters wide. The Star of David must be large enough so that the tips of opposing points are at least eight centimeters apart. The lines of the Star must be one centimeter wide. Jews who do not obey this decree may expect to be punished severely. The Councils of Elders are responsible for the carrying out of this decree, and particularly for supplying Jews with armbands. Kraków, November 18, 1939. Wächter, Governor."
9. Kraków News.
10. Golczewski 1996, p. 433.
11. In the fifteenth century, the Primate of Poland, Cardinal Zbigniew Oleśnicki, wanted to secure the title of prince for the archdiocese of Kraków so that whoever was the Bishop of Kraków would also have a right to the title of prince. Back then, two small principalities were for sale because both lacked a successor to the throne: the communities of Zator and Auschwitz. Oleśnicki purchased both of them. Ever since, the archbishop of Kraków has also had the title of Prince Archbishop.
12. *Krakauer Zeitung*, March 6, 1941, p. 1.
13. Breitmann 1996, pp. 205–206.
14. Ibid., p. 42.
15. Ibid., p. 29.
16. Schulte, Jan Erik. January 20, 2003, lecture in the House of the Wannsee Conference, Berlin. http://www.ghwk.de/deut/texte/voelkermord.htm.

17. Gestapo is an acronym for *Geheime Staatspolizei* (state secret police).
18. An SS rank between *Standartenführer* and *Brigadeführer* with no equivalent in either the Wehrmacht or the U.S. Army.
19. David Crowe is mistaken when he writes that Pilarzik didn't ask for this correspondence back from me until I was in the forced labor camp, subsequent to March 1943. Crowe 2004, p. 249.
20. Testimony of Aleksander Biberstein. In *Prodces Ludobójcy Amona Goetha* (Trial of Amon Leopold Göth). August 26 to September 5, 1946. Kraków, 1947. This document will be referred to below as *Trial of Amon Leopold Göth* TALG.
21. Testimony of Henryk Mandel, TALG.
22. Menachem Stern, *Berliner Zeitung*, January 24, 2004. Stefan Pemper was actually seventeen years old in 1943.
23. Testimony of Regina Nelken, TALG.
24. Testimony of Dr. Aleksander Biberstein, TALG.
25. Spiegel-TV Themenabend. "Schindlers Liste—eine wahre Geschichte." VOX, December 27, 2002.
26. Göth could still recall this nocturnal exchange three years later, and even cross-examined me about it in his 1946 trial:

    "*Prisoner Göth*: The witness says that the camp food was very inadequate. But for the first five months, you got the same as the soldiers.

    Witness Pemper: From March to September 1943, I received somewhat better food as a clerk. Because you saw me working at night and subsequently wrote a letter approving extra rations for me.

    Prisoner Göth: Did you get them?

    Witness Pemper: Yes, twenty-five grams of sugar, ten to twenty grams of fat, and thirty units of marmalade per week.

    Prisoner Göth: If the food was so inadequate, why didn't you accept an extra bread ration, too?

    Witness Pemper: My father worked in the bakery and was regularly able to send me some extra bread. The bread distributed to the inmates was inedible."

    Cross-examination in TALG.

27. Testimony of Henryk Mandel, TALG.
28. Spiegel-TV Themenabend. "*Schindlers Liste—eine wahre Geschichte.*" VOX, December 27, 2002.
29. Deposition of Oskar Schindler for the *Zentrale Stelle der Landesjustizverwaltungen* [Center for State Judicial Administrations] in Ludwigsburg, February 15, 1967, pp. 5–6. In *Oskar Schindlers Koffer* (hereafter cited as "Schindler's suitcase"), original in Yad Vashem.
30. Breitman 1996, p. 312.
31. A copy of the letter of appointment is in Amon Göth's SS personnel file in the German Federal Archives, Koblenz.
32. Personnel file of Amon Leopold Göth, German Federal Archives, Koblenz.
33. Nelken 1996, p. 334.
34. Testimony of the accused, TALG.
35. Churchil 1974, p. 6220.
36. Hitler 1980, pp. 228–229.
37. Frank 1975, p. 516.
38. Ibid., p. 525.
39. Ibid., p. 682.
40. After the war, a researcher at the Institute for Contemporary History in Munich was skeptical that I could have read these three newspapers on a regular basis. To prove that I had, I told him about an editorial in *Das Reich* entitled, "The World Politics of Constants." When I read this piece in the camp, I thought there must have been a mistake in the title, and indeed, there was a correction the following week. The title should have been "The Constants of World Politics." The researcher wanted to see for himself, so he went to the institute's newspaper archive. When he returned, he said, "You're right. I found the editorial, and the title was corrected."
41. Schindler's suitcase. The document is signed by Göth, but clearly marked "Hu," i.e., dictated by Hujer. The dictation mark "MP" stands for Mietek Pemper.
42. Spiegel-TV Themenabend. "*Schindlers Liste—eine wahre Geschichte.*" VOX, December 27, 2002.

43. Pohl 1998, p. 415.
44. *Frankfurter Rundschau*, January 26, 1994.
45. Oskar Schindler, Yad Vashem, Document "Schindler/40333."
46. In *Frankfurter Rundschau*, January 26, 1994.
47. Letter to Kurt R. Grossmann (1956). This and subsequently cited letters of Oskar Schindler are archived in Yad Vashem and were discovered in the suitcase found in Hildesheim in 1999, twenty-five years after Schindler's death on October 9, 1974.
48. The *Ritterkreuz* was the Third Reich's highest award for valor.
49. Pohl 1998, p. 429.
50. Tont 1994.
51. "(Public) order service."
52. Publisher of dictionaries and standard works on German orthography and grammar.
53. Berenstein and Eisenbach 1957, pp. 254–255. Most important was the ruling that smaller camps "whose production is neither crucial for victory nor important for the war effort" be liquidated as quickly as possible.
54. The letter is from October 22, 1943. Pohl ordered that Working Group D of the Economic and Administrative Main Office of the SS take over the following camps: the camp at the old airport in Lublin, Trawniki, Poniatowa, Radom, Duzyn, Płaszów, D.A.W. in Lublin, and in Lemberg (Janowski camp). Ibid, p. 255. A few dozen inmates from the Budzyn camp were also sent to Płaszów-Kraków because they were supposedly skilled workers in the Heinkel aircraft factory and could be put to work at similar jobs in Kraków.
55. Testimony in the judicial inquiry against Gerhard Maurer, Kraków, February 23, 1950, before the Central Commission for the Investigation of Nazi Crimes in Poland. Magistrate, Dr. Henryk Gawacki. Recorder, Stanisław Malec. The Polish original is in the Instytut Pamieci Narodowej in Warsaw under the call number SWKr 11, sygn. Sadowa K291/51. When Gerhard Maurer was appointed head of the D II department in March 1942, he was also promoted from SS-*Sturmbannführer* to *Obersturmbannführer*, and somewhat later, on April 20, 1944,

to SS-*Standartenführer*. Subsequent quotations from this document will be cited as *Testimony in the Judicial Inquiry Against Gerhard Maurer, February 23, 1950*.

56. According to Gerhard Maurer's personnel file, since March 15, 1942, he had been an SS-*Obersturmbannführer*, the equivalent of an *Oberstleutnant* (lieutenant colonel) in the Wehrmacht. On April 20, 1944, he received preferential promotion to SS-*Standartenführer* (colonel) in recognition of his outstanding service to the "*kriegswichtig* and *siegentscheidend* arms production of the Reich."
57. Tuchel 1994, Document 21.4, p. 122.
58. Ibid., p. 118.
59. My testimony in TALG.
60. My testimony in TALG.
61. Pages 426–430 of the transcript of the Testimony in the Judicial Inquiry Against Gerhard Maurer, February 23, 1950.
62. Kluger 2001, p. 89. Ruth Kluger is herself indirectly quoting Tadeusz Borowski.
63. Of the original two and a half million Jews in the Generalgouvernement, less than 150,000 were still alive in November 1943.
64. In his biography of Oskar Schindler, David Crowe writes that the Jewish prisoners were no longer able to walk from the camp to the Emalia factory "unescorted" and "without an SS guard" (Crowe 2004, p. 280). Crowe seems to have partially misunderstood this important document. It is clear both from the original letter and from the summary of it contained in the report of the two Joint representatives that it was not a question of whether the guard contingent was present or not, but whether it was armed. If it was not, the Jewish workers would no longer be allowed to walk to the Emalia. The letter of March 28, 1943, is also reproduced in the documentation of the *Stuttgarter Zeitung*. Cf. Braun and Keller 1999, where Albert Hujer writes: "I personally carried out an inspection on March 28, 1943, and discovered that the civilians accompanying the Jews were not in possession of weapons," p. 19.
65. Oskar Schindler's letter to the historian K. J. Ball-Kaduri in Schindler's suitcase in Yad Vashem.
66. "The Confessions of Mr. X" in Oskar Schindler's suitcase.

67. "Der Untermensch" in Hofer 1960, p. 280. Originally published by the Reichsführer SS, SS Headquarters (Berlin, 1935).
68. Tuchel 1994, Document 16.6., p. 92 f.
69. Ibid., Document 16.4., p. 89.
70. "Work will make you free." Motto on the gates of the Dachau and Sachsenhausen camps.
71. "To each his own." Motto on the gates of the Buchenwald camp.
72. Testimony of Helena Hirsch, TALG.
73. My deposition of February 23, 1950, during the investigative proceeding against Gerhard Maurer.
74. Ibid.
75. Schulte 2001, p. 403.
76. Translation:

    Corporal Punishment: Number of Strokes* (* enter number: 5, 10, 15, 20, 25). Regulations: Must be preceded by a doctor's examination! Administer brisk, consecutive strokes with a single-stranded leather whip, counting the strokes while doing so. Undressing prisoner to expose certain parts of the body strictly prohibited. The person being punished may not be strapped down, but must lie unfettered on a bench. Only strokes on the buttocks and upper thighs are permitted. The delinquent has already received corporal punishment on _____. Strokes ____.

    MEDICAL OPINION:

    I have given the inmate named on the reverse side a medical examination prior to the administration of corporal punishment; from a medical point of view, I have no objections to the use of corporal punishment.

    As a doctor, I have objections to the use of corporal punishment because ________.

    [stamp and signature]

    SUPERVISOR:

    In view of the infraction and supported by the above medical opinion, the administration of corporal punishment is approved / not approved.

    [stamp and signature]

ADMINISTERED BY:
Corporal punishment was administered by the following [word crossed out and "inmates" typed in].
Date ___________. Time _____________.
[inmate numbers and signatures]
WITNESSES AND SUPERVISION:
The following SS leader and witnesses were present at the punishment:
[signatures]
FILING INSTRUCTIONS:
1. Original to protective custody files.
2. Copy to the master file Punishments.
3. Copy to the Leader SS TB/KL.
[signature of camp commandant]

77. Nelken 1996, p. 335.
78. This and the following quotations are from letters of Oskar Schindler in the Yad Vashem archives, discovered in Schindler's suitcase in 1999.
79. The SS replaced the traditional Wehrmacht ranks with new names, e.g., SS-*Hauptsturmführer* instead of *Hauptmann* (captain).
80. Letter from Schindler's suitcase.
81. The date of the assassination attempt against Hitler led by Claus von Stauffenberg.
82. Oskar Schindler to Dr. K. J. Ball-Kaduri, Yad Vashem, September 9, 1956, in Schindler's suitcase, microfilm, Federal Archives, Koblenz.
83. Ibid.
84. Ibid.
85. Ibid.
86. Tont 1994.
87. My testimony in TALG.
88. Oskar Schindler's report, from Schindler's suitcase.
89. KL = *Konzentrationslager* (concentration camp). AL = *Arbeitslager* (labor camp).
90. In his biography of Schindler, David Crowe advances the thesis that Schindler had "absolutely nothing to do with the creation of his famous transport list" (Crowe 2004, p. 361). He bases this

assertion mainly on the brief statement of Dr. Stanley Robbin (formerly Dr. Samek Rubenstein). In an interview with the journalist Elinor J. Brecher in the early 1990s, Robbin talked about meeting Oskar Schindler after the war. (Unfortunately, we know nothing about the time or circumstances of this meeting.) When Robbin asked Schindler why he and some other workers from the Emalia factory didn't make it onto the list, "He told me he was not responsible for it. He never arranged this, and he apologized" (Brecher 1994, p. 430). David Crowe's theory that Schindler had nothing to do with the list seems to hinge on this brief statement, reported at second hand. But at the end of September 1944, at the time the list was being put together, Dr. Robbin was no longer in the Płaszów camp (as Crowe himself notes on p. 361 of his book), having already been sent to the Mauthausen concentration camp in August 1944 during the gradual liquidation of Płaszów. So although Robbin had until then been employed in Oskar Schindler's Emalia factory, he is technically not a survivor of Schindler's list. Nor does David Crowe go into the negotiations that Schindler himself or one of his representatives carried on with intermediaries from the D II department in Berlin-Oranienburg. For without the official permission of D II in the Economic and Administrative Main Office of the SS, a thousand Jewish prisoners would never have been able to get on a list and then be transported to the Brünnlitz work camp.

91. From Schindler's suitcase.
92. Spiegel-TV documentary, VOX, 2003.
93. The names of these fathers and sons are all crossed out on the list of inmates dated October 21, 1944. Their transport must have occurred immediately after the men arrived at the Brünnlitz forced labor camp and before there had been time to prepare an updated list. Their names are no longer on the list of April 18, 1945. In Gross Rosen, we had been assigned sequential inmate numbers, and the numbers of these fathers and sons transported to Auschwitz were simply dropped from the sequence on the list of April 18, 1945.
94. Alexander Biberstein's report is in Schindler's suitcase.
95. Ibid.
96. Spiegel-TV documentary, VOX, 2003.

97. Müller-Madej 1994, p. 253.
98. On May 8, 1945, six leading representatives of the former Jewish community in Kraków signed another letter of safe-conduct for Oskar Schindler in Polish. Among the signatories were Dr. Chaim Hilfstein, physician and cofounder of the Hebrew High School in Kraków; Natan Stern, lawyer; Izak Stern, chairman of the Palestine Office for Western Galicia and Silesia; and Abraham Bankier, until 1939 co-owner of the Emalia factory, which Schindler later took over. The original letter is now in Yad Vashem.
99. Müller-Madej 1994, p. 248.
100. The original typescript of the speech, now in Yad Vashem.
101. Ibid.
102. Sehn 1957, pp. 5–9.
103. The International Military Tribunal sat in Nuremberg from November 20, 1945 to October 1946.
104. At the Third Moscow Conference, the foreign ministers of Great Britain and the Soviet Union and the American secretary of state agreed *inter alia* to punish German war criminals and to extradite them to the country where they had committed their crimes. *Lexikon der deutschen Geschichte* (Stuttgart: Kröner, 1977), p. 825.
105. Höss 2004, p. 227.
106. I possess a photocopy of Göth's statement after his arrest in Dachau.
107. Josef Kempler, who lives in the United States today, was seventeen years old when he and three other former inmates of Płaszów identified Amon Göth in Dachau. Interview with Viktoria Hertling, Reno, Nevada, September 10, 2004.
108. Articles 16 and 17 of the statutes of the International Military Tribunal of October 6, 1945, stipulated that the indictment must be written in German, that the accused must have enough time to prepare his defense, that he had the right to an attorney or that he could act as his own defense counsel, that he could call witnesses and could cross-examine the witnesses for the prosecution. See the Web site http://www.yale.edu/lawweb/avalon/imt/proc/imtconst.htm.
109. For instance, Segev 1995, writes of a "Blitzverfahren," a "lightning trial," p. 189.

110. The transcript of Amon Göth's trial is one of the few transcripts of trials of Nazi war criminals to appear in book form. Most other trial transcripts are available only as documents in archives. *Proces Ludobójcy Amona Goetha* (trial of Amon Leopold Göth), Kraków, 1947. See also *Law Reports of Trials of War Criminals*, The United Nations War Crimes Commission, Vol. VII (London, 1948). A summary of case number 37—Amon Leopold Göth—can be found on the Internet: http://www.ess.uwe.ac.uk/WCC/goeth.htm.
111. See Article 6c of the statutes of the International Military Tribunal. On December 20, 1945, the *Kontrollrat*, the executive authority of the Allied occupation forces, issued Law No. 10 which also defined "crimes against humanity"as "Atrocities and offenses, including but not limited to murder, extermination, enslavement, deportation, imprisonment, torture, rape, or other inhumane acts committed against any civilian population, or persecutions on political, racial, or religious grounds whether or not in violation of the domestic laws of the country where perpetrated." See http://www.verfassungen.de/de/de45-49/kr-gesetz10.htm.
112. See Lemkin 1944, passim.
113. Two examples of words whose innocuous original meanings were exploited by the Nazis as euphemisms for criminal acts: *Aussiedlung* = "evacuation," (compulsory) resettlement; *Sonderbehandlung* = "special treatment," extermination.
114. *Arbeitseinsatz* = (camp) work assignment; *Einsatz* = "assignment" but also "insert."
115. Sehn 1957, p. 11 ff.
116. I also testified in Kiel at the 1963 trial of Haase's successor, SS-*Sturmbannführer* Martin Fellenz.
117. See http://www-tc.pbs.org/auschwitz/learning/guides/reading2.3.pdf.
118. According to the *Law Report of Trials of War Criminals*, The United Nations War Crimes Commission, Vol. XIV (London: HMSO, 1949), the trial of Josef Bühler took place in Kraków from June 17 to July 10, 1948. Internet address: http://www.ess.uwe.ac.uk/WCC/buhler1.htm.
119. On pp. 14–15, the minutes of the Wannsee Conference declare, "State Secretary Dr. Buehler stated that the General Government

would welcome it if the final solution of this problem could be started in the General Government, since on the one hand transportation does not play such a large role here nor would problems of labor supply hamper this action. Jews must be removed from the territory of the General Government as quickly as possible, since it is especially here that the Jew as an epidemic carrier represents an extreme danger and on the other hand he is causing permanent chaos in the economic structure of the country through continued black market dealings. Moreover, of the approximately 2½ million Jews concerned, the majority is unfit for work. State Secretary Dr. Buehler stated further that the solution to the Jewish question in the General Government is the responsibility of the Chief of the Security Police and the SD and that his efforts would be supported by the officials of the General Government. He had only one request, to solve the Jewish question in this area as quickly as possible." http://www.writing.upenn.edu/~afilreis/Holocaust/wansee-transcript.html. German original at: http://www.ghwk.de/deut/proto.htm.

120. The first stanza of Goethe's poem "Das Göttliche"—the divine.
121. *Stern Report 1956*, pp. 27–28. Yad Vashem Archive No. 01164.
122. Trials of War Criminals Before the Nuremberg Military Tribunal under Control Council Law No. 10. Volume V, Washington DC, 1950, pp. 434–623.
123. Partially based on Müller-Madej 1994.

BIBLIOGRAPHY

1. Books and Articles

Allen, Michael Thad. *The Business of Genocide: The SS, Slave Labor, and the Concentration Camps.* Chapel Hill: University of North Carolina Press, 2005.

Améry, Jean. *At the Mind's Limits: Contemplations by a Survivor on Auschwitz and Its Realities.* Translated by Sidney and Stella P. Rosenfeld. Bloomington: Indiana University Press, 1980.

Arad, Yitzhak. *Bełżec, Sobibor, Treblinka: The Operation Reinhard Death Camps.* Bloomington: University of Indiana Press, 1999.

Arad, Yitzhak, Israel Gutman, and Abraham Margaliot, eds. *Documents on the Holocaust.* Translated by Lea Ben Dor. Lincoln: University of Nebraska Press, 1999.

Bastian, Till. *Furchtbare Ärzte: Medizinische Verbrechen im Dritten Reich* [Terrible doctors: Medical crimes in the Third Reich]. Munich: Beck, 2001.

Bauer, Yehuda. *American Jewry and the Holocaust: The American Jewish Joint Distribution Committee, 1939–1945.* Detroit: Wayne State University Press, 1981.

Berenstein, Tatiana and Artur Eisenbach. *Eksterminacja żydów na ziemiach polskich w okresie okupacji hitlerowskiej* [Extermination of the Jews in Polish areas during the Nazi occupation]. Warsaw: Żydowski Instytut Historyczny, 1957.

Biberstein, Aleksander. *Zagłada Żydów w Krakowie* [Destruction of the Jews in Kraków]. Kraków: Wydawn Literackie, 2001.

Braun, Stefan and Claudia Keller, eds. *Schindlers Koffer: Berichte aus dem Leben eines Lebensretters* [Schindler's suitcase: Reports from the life of a saver of lives]. A collection of articles published by the *Stuttgarter Zeitung.* Stuttgart: Turmhaus Druck, 1999.

Brecher, Elinor J. *Schindler's Legacy: True Stories of the List Survivors*. New York: Penguin Books, 1994.

Breitman, Richard. *Der Architekt der "Endlösung." Himmler und die Vernichtung der europäischen Juden*. Paderborn: Schöningh, 1996. Available in English as *The Architect of Genocide: Himmler and the Final Solution*. New York: Knopf, 1991.

Breitman, Richard. *Official Secrets: What the Nazis Planned, What the British and the Americans Knew*. New York: Hill and Wang, 1998.

Browning, Christopher R. *Nazi Policy, Jewish Workers, German Killers*. New York: Cambridge University Press, 2000.

Browning, Christopher R. *Ordinary Men: Reserve Police Battalion 101 and the Final Solution in Poland*. New York: Harper Collins, 1992.

Churchill, Winston S. *His Complete Speeches, 1897–1963*. Ed. by Robert Rhodes James. Volume VI (1935–1942). New York and London: Chelsea House, 1974.

Crowe, David M. *Oskar Schindler: The Untold Account of his Life, Wartime Activities, and the True Story Behind the List*. Cambridge, MA: Westview Press, 2004.

Duda, Eugeniusz. *Jewish Cracow: A Guide to the Jewish Historical Buildings and Monuments of Cracow*. Kraków: VIS-A-VIS/Etiuda, 2003.

Frank, Hans. *Das Diensttagebuch des deutschen Generalgouverneurs in Polen, 1939–1945*. [The Official Diary of the German Governor General in Poland] Ed. by Werner Präg and Wolfgang Jacobmeyer. Stuttgart: Deutsche Verlags-Anstalt,1975.

Frei, Norbert. *Adenauer's Germany and the Nazi Past*. Translated by Joel Golb. New York: Columbia University Press, 2002.

Friedländer, Saul. *Nazi Germany and the Jews: Volume I, The Years of Persecution, 1933–1939*. New York: HarperCollins, 1997.

Golczewski, Frank. "Die Ghettoisierung" [Ghettoization]. In *Dimension des Völkermords: Die Zahl der jüdischen Opfer des Nationalsozialismus* [Dimensions of genocide: The number of Jewish victims of National Socialism]. Ed. by Wolfgang Benz. Munich: dtv, 1996.

Göth, Amon Leopold. NSDAP membership card and personal files. German Federal Archives, Koblenz.

Graf, Malvina. *The Kraków Ghetto and the Płaszów Camp Remembered.* Tallahassee: University Press of Florida, 1989.

Grossmann, Kurt R. *Die unbesungenen Helden: Menschen in Deutschlands dunklen Tagen* [Unsung heroes: Human beings in Germany's dark days]. Berlin Grunewald: Arani, 1957.

Grossmann, Kurt R. "Kein jüdischer Widerstand im Dritten Reich?" [No Jewish resistance in the Third Reich?]. *Rheinischer Merkur*, July 19, 1963.

Gudisch, Rebecca. "Zur rechten Zeit nach links" [Toward the Left at the right time]. *Süddeutsche Zeitung*, June 25, 2004.

Gutman, Israel, ed. *Encyclopedia of the Holocaust.* Four volumes. New York: Macmillan Reference Books, 1995.

Heinsohn, Gunnar. *Lexikon der Völkermorde* [Lexicon of Genocide]. Reinbek bei Hamburg: Rowohlt, 1998.

Heinsohn, Gunnar. *Warum Auschwitz? Hitlers Plan und die Ratlosigkeit der Nachwelt.* [Why Auschwitz? Hitler's plan and the perplexity of posterity] Reinbek bei Hamburg: Rowohlt, 1995.

Herbert, Ulrich, Karin Orth, and Christoph Dieckmann, eds. *Die nationalsozialistischen Konzentrationslager: Entwicklung und Struktur* [Development and structure of the National Socialist concentration camps]. Two volumes. Göttingen: Wallstein, 1998.

Hertling, Viktoria, ed. *Mit den Augen eines Kindes. Children in the Holocaust. Children in Exile. Children under Fascism.* Amsterdam: Edition Rodopi, 1998.

Hilberg, Raul. *The Destruction of the European Jews.* Third Edition. New Haven: Yale, 2003.

Hitler, Adolf. *Monologe im Führer-Hauptquartier 1941–1944* [Monologues in the Führer's headquarters]. Ed. by Werner Jochmann. Hamburg: A. Knaus, 1980.

Hofer, Walther, ed. *Der Nationalsozialismus in Dokumenten, 1933–1945* [The documents of National Socialism, 1933–1945]. Frankfurt am Main: Fischer Bücherei, 1959.

Höss, Rudolf. *Kommandant in Auschwitz: Autobiographische Aufzeichnungen.* 19th edition. Munich: dtv, 2004. Available in English as *Commandant of Auschwitz: The Autobiography of Rudolf Hoess* (London: Phoenix Press, 2000).

Hürter, Johannes. "Auf dem Weg zur Militäropposition. Tresckow, Gersdorff, der Vernichtungskrieg und der Judenmord. Neue Dokumente über das Verhältnis der Heeresgruppe Mitte zur Einsatzgruppe B im Jahr 1941" [The path to military opposition: Treschkow, Gersdorff, the war of extermination, and the murder of the Jews. New documents on the relationship of the Army Group Middle to Task Force B in 1941]. *Vierteljahreshefte für Zeitgeschichte* (2004/3), pp. 527–562.

Jenny, Urs. "Holocaust mit Happy-End?" [Holocaust with a Happy End?]. *Der Spiegel*, May 24, 1993.

Jostmann, Christian. "Kriegsbedingte Erschießungen. Was wussten die Männer des 20. Juli vom Mord an den Juden, bevor sie rebellierten?" [Executions necessitated by war. What did the men of July 20th know about the murder of the Jews before they rebelled?]. *Süddeutsche Zeitung*, July 10, 2004.

Kaienburg, Hermann. *Die Wirtschaft der SS* [The SS economy]. Berlin: Metropol, 2003.

Keneally, Thomas. *Schindler's List*. New York: Simon & Schuster, 1982.

Kluger, Ruth. *Still Alive: A Holocaust Childhood Remembered*. New York: The Feminist Press, 2001.

Kogon, Eugen. *The Theory and Practice of Hell: The German Concentration Camps and the System Behind Them*. New York: Farrar, Straus and Giroux, 2006.

Kremer, Johann Paul. "Diary of Johann Paul Kremer." Translated by Krystyna Michalik. In *KL Auschwitz Seen by the SS*, by Rudolf Höss, Pery Broad, and Johann Paul Kremer, 161–165. Oświęcim, Poland: The Auschwitz-Birkenau State Museum, 1995.

Lemkin, Rafael. *Axis Rule in Occupied Europe*. Washington: Carnegie Endowment for International Peace, 1944.

Levi, Primo. *The Drowned and the Saved*. New York: Vintage, 1989.

Ligocka, Roma. *The Girl in the Red Coat: A Memoir*. New York: St. Martin's Press, 2002.

Longerich, Peter, ed. *Die Ermordung der europäischen Juden. Eine umfassende Dokumentation des Holocaust 1941–1945* [The murder of the European Jews: A comprehensive documentation of the Holocaust, 1941–1945]. Munich: Piper, 1989.

Madritsch, Julius. *Menschen in Not! Meine Erlebnisse in den Jahren 1940 bis 1944 als Unternehmer im damaligen Gouvernement* [People in need! My experiences as a businessman in the Generalgouvernement from 1940 to 1944]. Vienna: 1962.

Müller-Madej, Stella. *Das Mädchen von der Schindler-Liste. Aufzeichnungen einer KZ-Überlebenden.* Augsburg: Ölbaum Verlag, 1994. Available in English as *A Girl from Schindler's List* (London: Polish Cultural Foundation, 1997).

Nelken, Halina. *Freiheit will ich noch erleben: Krakauer Tagebuch.* Gerlingen: Bleicher, 1996. Available in English as *And Yet, I Am Here!* (Amherst: University of Massachusetts Press, 1999).

Oster, Angelina. "Im Schatten von Auschwitz. Das KZ Krakau-Płaszów. Geschichte und Erinnerung" [In the shadow of Auschwitz. The Kraków-Płaszów concentration camp: History and recollection]. *Dachauer Hefte* 19 (2003): 170–179.

Pankiewicz, Tadeusz. *The Cracow Ghetto Pharmacy.* New York: Holocaust Library, 1987.

Pemper, Mietek. "Mut zum Widerstand" [The courage to resist]. *Impressum.* Alumni Augsburg International, May 2003, pp. 16–19.

Pemper, Mietek. Testimony during the preliminary investigation against Gerhard Maurer in Kraków, February 23, 1950, before the Chief Commission for the Investigation of Nazi Crimes in Poland. Judge: Dr. Henryk Gawacki; Court Recorder: Stanisław Malec. German translation by Mietek Pemper, September 2004. The Polish original is located in the Instytut Pamięci Narodowej, Warsaw, call number SWKr 11, sygn. Sadowa K291/51.

Pohl, Dieter. "Die großen Zwangsarbeitslager der SS- und Polizeiführer der Juden im Generalgouvernement 1942–1945" [The large forced labor camps of the SS and police leaders of the Jews in the Generalgouvernement, 1942–1945]. *Die nationalsozialistischen Konzentrationslager*, ed. by Ulrich Herbert, Karin Orth, and Christoph Dieckmann. Göttingen: Wallstein, 1998.

Polanski, Roman. *Roman by Polanski.* New York: Ballantine Books, 1985.

Proces Ludobójcy Amona Goetha [Trial of Amon Leopold Göth]. Kraków, 1947. Partial translation into German by Katharina Karpinska and Eleanora Blazńiak, manuscript, July 2004.

Reder, Rudolf. *Bełżec*. Kraków: Fundacja Judaica, 1999.

Reitlinger, Gerald. *The Final Solution: The Attempt to Exterminate the Jews of Europe 1939–1945*. Second Edition. South Brunswick, New Jersey: Thomas Yoseloff Publisher, 1968.

Ritter, Rüdiger. Review of three books about the "Sonderaktion Krakau." *Zeitschrift für Ostmitteleuropa-Forschung*, volume 48, no. 3, 1999, pp. 439–441.

Rosenberg, Erika, ed. *Ich, Oskar Schindler: Die persönlichen Aufzeichnungen, Briefe und Dokumente* [My name is Oskar Schindler: The personal diaries, letters, and documents]. Munich: Herbig, 2000.

Schindler, Emilie. *Where Light and Shadows Meet. A Memoir*. Translated by Dolores M. Koch. New York: Norton, 1997.

Schindler, Oskar. *Oskar Schindlers Koffer* [Oscar Schindler's suitcase]: two microfilms with handwritten and typed documents, photographs, and newspaper clippings contained in the suitcase in the Yad Vashem archives, Jerusalem. Federal Archives, Koblenz.

Schulte, Jan Erik. *Zwangsarbeit und Vernichtung: Das Wirtschaftsimperium der SS. Oswald Pohl und das SS-Wirtschafts-Verwaltungshauptamt 1933–1945* [Forced labor and extermination: The economic empire of the SS. Oswald Pohl and the economic and administrative office of the SS, 1933–1945]. Paderborn, Germany: F. Schoningh, 2001.

Segev, Tom. *Die Soldaten des Bösen*. Reinbek bei Hamburg: Rowohlt, 1995. Available in English as *Soldiers of Evil* (New York: McGraw Hill, 1987).

Sehn, Jan. *Concentration Camp Oświęcim–Brzezinka (Auschwitz–Birkenau)*. The Chief Commission for the Investigation of Nazi Crimes in Poland, Warsaw, 1957.

Sereny, Gitta. *Into That Darkness*. New York: Vintage Books, 1983.

Smelser, Ronald. *The Nazi Elite*. New York: NYU Press, 1993.

Stein, Jehuda L. *Die Steins. Jüdische Familiengeschichte aus Krakau 1830–1999* [The Steins: History of a Jewish Family from Kraków, 1830–1999]. Ed. by Erhard Roy Wiehn. Konstanz: Hartung-Gorre, 1999.

Stern, Izak. *Stern Report 1956*. Yad Vashem Archive Nr. 01164.

Stern, Menachim. "Mein Holocaust. Ein Kind überlebt das große Morden. Ein Mann erinnert sich an das Kind, das er war. Und erzählt seine Geschichte" [My Holocaust. A child survives the mass murder. A man remembers the child he was. And tells his story]. *Berliner Zeitung*, January 24, 2004.

Taylor, Telford. *The Anatomy of the Nuremberg Trials: A Personal Memoir*. New York: Knopf, 1992.

Tont, Elisabeth. "Es ist mir bis heute unerklärlich, woher er den Mut genommen hat" [I still can't understand how he had the courage to do it]. *Frankfurter Rundschau*, January 26, 1994.

Trials of War Criminals before the Nuremberg Tribunal, volume V. Washington, DC, 1950.

Tuchel, Johannes. *Die Inspektion der Konzentrationslager. Das System des Terrors 1938–1945* [Inspection of the concentration camps: The system of terror, 1938–1945]. Berlin: Hentrich, 1994.

Wegmann, Günter, ed. *Der deutsche Wehrmachtbericht—"Das Oberkommandeo der Wehrmacht gibt bekannt . . . ," Vollständige Ausgabe der 1939–1945 durch Presse und Rundfunk veröffentlichten Texte* [German army dispatches—"The Supreme Command of the Wehrmacht announces . . ." Complete edition of the texts published and broadcast from 1939 to 1945]. Osnabrück: Biblio-Verlag, 1982.

Wildt, Michael. *Generation des Unbedingten. Das Führungskorps des Reichssicherheitshauptamtes* [The unconditional generation: The leadership of the Reich Security Main Office]. Hamburg: Hamburger Edition, 2002.

Wistrich, Gunnar. *Who's Who in Nazi Germany*. Third edition. New York: Routledge, 2001.

2. Texts on the Internet

http://www.ghwk.de/deut/texte/dokument-des-terrors.htm

Axel Frohn and Klaus Wiegrefe, "Das Dokument des Terrors" (article in German on the Wannsee Conference).

http://www.ghwk.de/deut/texte/voelkermord.htm

Jan Erik Schulte, ". . . sollen nun im Zuge der Endlösung die Juden . . . zum Arbeitseinsatz kommen" Die Wannsee-Konferenz im Kontext von SS- Arbeitskräfteplanung und Völkermord 1941/42 (lecture in German on the Wannsee Conference)

http://www.ghwk.de/deut/proto.htm
Facsimiles of the minutes of the Wannsee Conference in German. Also available in English.

http://www1.yadvashem.org/righteous/index_righteous.html
Homepage for the Yad Vashem project "The Righteous Among The Nations." Follow links to "Statistics and Stories" and then to "Germany" for pages on Oskar and Emilie Schindler, Georg Ferdinand Duckwitz, Bertolt Beitz, and others.

http://www.bundespraesident.de/Reden-und-Interviews/Reden-Johannes-Rau-,11070.91701/Grusswort-von-Bundespraesident.htm?global.back=/Reden-und-Interviews/-%2c11070%2c17/Reden-Johannes-Rau.htm%3flink%3dbpr_liste#top
German Federal President Johannes Rau's speech of welcome at the conference "Hilfe für Verfolgte in der NS-Zeit" (aid for the victims of the Nazi regime), March 13, 2003.

http://www.ess.uwe.ac.uk/WCC/goeth.htm
A summary in English of the 1946 trial of Amon Göth.

http://www.ess.uwe.ac.uk/WCC/buhler1.htm
A summary in English of the 1948 trial of Josef Bühler.

http://www.yale.edu/lawweb/avalon/imt/proc/imtconst.htm
The charter of the International Military Tribunal.

http://www.deathcamps.org/occupation/erntefest.html
Information on "Aktion Erntefest" (operation harvest festival), the November 1943 program to murder all Jews remaining in work camps in the Lublin district.

http://www.schoah.org/pogrom/polenaktion.htm
Excerpt in German from a book by Jerzy Tomaszewski on the expulsion of Polish Jews from Germany in 1938.

http://www.abschiebehaft.de/presse/p73.htm
Article in German by Gerhard Paul on the 1938 expulsion.

3. Audio-Visual Media

Alfred Biolek, *Boulevard Bio*, Westdeutscher Rundfunk, February 12, 2002.

Johannes B. Kerner, Zweites Deutsches Fernsehen, December 3, 2002.

Schindler, documentary film by Jon Blair, 1981.

Schindler's List, film by Steven Spielberg, 1993.

Schindlers Liste—eine wahre Geschichte, Spiegel TV Themenabend, VOX, December 27, 2002.

PICTURE CREDITS

Private: [pages 2, 7, 170, 171, 175]

Hermann Sautter, Förderverein "Freunde des Schickhardt-Gymnasiums Herrenberg": [page 192]

Herbert Steinhouse: [page 128]

Johannes Tuchel, *Die Inspektion der Konzentrationslager 1938–1945*, Schriftenreihe der Stiftung Brandenburgische Gedenkstätten, Nr. 1 (Berlin: Edition Henrich, 1994): [page 117]

United States Holocaust Memorial Museum: [pages 4, 15, 19, 21, 25, 26, 32, 39, 53, 64, 90, 137, 176]

USHMM by permission of the Bildarchiv Preußischer Kulturbesitz: [page 31]

USHMM by permission of the Yad Vashem Archive: [pages 79, 105, 130]

Yad Vashem Archive: [page 142]

INDEX

Printed in the United States
By Bookmasters